the new
chatelaine
cookbook

the new chatelaine cookbook

Monda Rosenberg

A LORRAINE GREEY BOOK

chatelaine

Published by
Chatelaine
Rogers Media
777 Bay Street
Toronto, Ontario
Canada M5W 1A7

Produced by
Lorraine Greey Publications Limited
Suite 303
56 The Esplanade
Toronto, Ontario
Canada M5E 1A7

Design and art direction by Andrew Smith
Layout and page composition by Annabelle Stanley
Illustrations by Jeff Jackson / Reactor

Colour photographs by John Reeves (back cover), Edward O'Neil (opposite page 64) and Michael Mahovlich (all others, including front cover)

Food styling by Kate Bush
Props by Miriam Gee

Colour separations by Colour Technologies

Printed in Canada by Friesen Printers

7 8 9 10 FP 06 05 04 03

FRONT COVER: Life-of-the-Party Fajitas (see recipe on page 96).

HALF-TITLE PAGE: Four Seasons Pizza (see recipe on page 212).

OPPOSITE THE TITLE PAGE: Jalapeno "Macaroni" and Cheese with Fresh Salsa Topper (see recipe on page 176).

ACKNOWLEDGEMENTS

Among the many people who helped produce this book, I would especially like to thank:

Lucie Richard, my associate food editor, for her constant hard work, sterling professionalism and extraordinary common sense in keeping the test kitchen running superbly and smoothly.

Jim Warrillow who said "do it." And Lucie Cousineau, a gifted and caring organizer.

Lee Simpson for her enthusiastic encouragement and ability to make you feel special.

Mildred Istona for providing world-class guidance from the conception through all the stages of this book, and for accepting nothing but the best.

Kate Bush, Miriam Gee and Michael Mahovlich, the picture team that makes us look so good.

Lori McDougall and Lynne Simons McCrindell in the *Chatelaine* Copy Department; Judy Allen, Jacques Pilon and Susan Black in the Art Department for their three-star guidance and assistance; Kirsten MacDonell for her good-natured support.

Cheryl Frayn for turning illegible scribbling into understandable type, Gail Copeland for her excellent copyediting and Liz Primeau for her superb editing.

Andrew Smith for turning type into design and always being a pleasure to work with.

Lorraine Greey for her constant support and expert guidance and for maintaining that balance between directing and being a caring friend, and for always being diplomatic, professional and a consummate lady.

Alicia Peres for always being thorough and nice. And my friends who were always there for me — Alasdair and Debbie, Anita and Bill, Elizabeth, Desmond, Rose and Anne.

A.D. Peaches, who made this book sing, and Sonny, my blessing in life.

Dedicated to Trudy Patterson,
a friend and colleague extraordinaire.

With appreciation for her 15 years'
assistance in the *Chatelaine* Test Kitchen,

for her steady encouragement
when all the cakes seem to be turning to puddings,

for her constant willingness
to taste or try any combination
despite what she may be thinking of it,

and for her unflagging hard work,
personal loyalty and incredible kindness
to everyone at *Chatelaine*.

CONTENTS

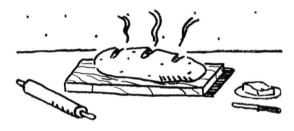

A WORD FROM THE AUTHOR

This is the perfect time to be writing *The New Chatelaine Cookbook*. I'm overwhelmed by the new enthusiasm and passion for cooking.

After the excesses of the 80's we seem to be shifting our priorities. For many reasons — more stress, an uncertain work future, a desire to create a supportive family structure — we're spending more time at home. We're cooking more often during the week, taking pride in family meals and entertaining friends at home in place of rendezvousing at restaurants.

While I've always found the kitchen a cozy escape and most nights I want to sit down to a calm dinner at home, the reality is I'm sometimes feeling too tired to peel a carrot. At times like these, settling down with a bag of microwave popcorn can seem awfully attractive to some. My answer is a microwave baked potato with cheese, or spaghetti tossed with a can of tuna and whatever vegetables are handy.

I love to entertain — one of my greatest delights is to have my friends gathered around my big dining-room table — but I rarely have a lot of time to prepare, and even if I did I no longer want to spend days getting ready for a dinner party as I used to do. Today I want to be able to make the complete meal the evening before the dinner party or on a Saturday afternoon. This is what we kept in mind in planning this book.

In the *Chatelaine* Test Kitchen we probably take our greatest pleasure from creating terrific recipes using food staples we know most of you have on hand — some that take only 10 minutes or less. That's because during the week what we want most is healthy, light, fast-fix foods. So this book is jam-packed with surefire, no-fuss recipes and quick substantial meal ideas — some even begin with a can of salmon or tuna, or a package of macaroni and cheese.

There are lots of laid-back weekend cooking ideas — big-batch pasta sauces and hearty soups for storing in the freezer, and easy one-dish entrées for the cottage or chalet. For therapeutic afternoons of baking, we've included yeast breads from country wholegrain to trendy focaccia, plus no-fail zucchini cakes, butter-tart squares and cookies easy enough for kids to make.

We've also brought back the all-Canadian classics — macaroni and cheese, chicken pot pies, pudding cakes and fruit crisps — but we've given them new taste appeal with spicy tomato salsa, speeded them up with easy phyllo crusts and made them more nutritious with the addition of fresh vegetables and high-fiber grains.

When you're cooking for friends or big-time parties, our choices range from five-minute canapés to such sophisticated presentations as a Dijon-crusted rack of lamb, an intriguing bouillabaisse pasta, baked royal sesame salmon or crisp phyllo tarts brimming with fresh berries and drizzled with crème fraîche.

While we have exacting standards, we don't cook in an ivory tower. We pride ourselves on being realistic. Our recipes do not depend on precious techniques to produce great results. We use T-Fal not copper pots. We buy groceries from local supermarkets instead of expensive gourmet shops.

You know you can count on *Chatelaine* recipes because we test them at least three times. Our mandate is to produce a recipe that tastes great, with fool-proof directions, sound nutrition, convenience and ease of preparation, and we keep testing until we are convinced the recipe cannot be improved upon.

We're confident that *The New Chatelaine Cookbook* will soon become your kitchen life-saver, whether it's for quick fixes with convenience foods, nutritious family meals in minutes, make-ahead party dishes or deceptively simple entertaining extravaganzas. Our best hope is that this book will add an extra pleasurable dimension to your cooking. Bon Appetit!

Monda Rosenberg

NEW BEGINNINGS

First impressions are important. But our philosophy is that you don't have to work for hours to create fabulous appetizers, starter soups or first courses. We've taken a lot of the fiddling and fussing out of making attractive canapés by starting with store-bought ingredients like salsa, colorful pepper jelly and pesto. The local deli provides the basics for Smoked Salmon Pinwheels and Fresh Fruit Wraps. Pumpernickel or cocktail rye bread, spread with creamy chèvre and hot pepper relish, is a five-minute lifesaver. Lots of recipes can be made ahead in big batches then frozen for use later — Golden Ruffled Phyllo Rolls with two sensational fillings or Leek Soup with Dill, for example. First courses are meant to entice and tempt the taste buds, never to overpower or overfill. Something as simple as a sliced pear with a dab of warm cambozola cheese is the perfect light starter for anything from a crown roast of pork to a festive roast duck. Simple and sensational. That's how to begin.

NEW BEGINNINGS · TRIPLE TESTED

CHIC CANAPÉS

Whether you're throwing a cocktail party with fashionable fizz or serving a plate of nibbles with drinks before dinner, the first bite should make a knockout impression without knocking you out before the fun begins. We've selected the best of our finger foods. Some you can make ahead and tuck in the freezer ready for the oven or microwave, others need just a quick stir before the big event. But none involve itsy bitsy pieces or a lot of fussing because we have better things to do with our time. All, however, deliver big-time taste with every tiny bite.

INCREDIBLY EASY SMOKED SALMON BLENDER PÂTÉ

Serve in a white porcelain pâté dish, sprinkled with freshly snipped chives, chopped fresh dill and thick twists of lemon zest. In summer pack the pâté into a hollowed-out baguette, chill and thinly slice. It's also wonderful spread on mini bagels for brunch.

Preparation time: 5 minutes / Makes: about 2 cups

¼ lb (125 g) smoked salmon
7¾-oz (220-g) can red salmon, drained
¼ cup unsalted butter, at room temperature
4-oz (125-g) pkg cream cheese
2 to 3 drops liquid smoke flavoring (optional)
2 chopped whole green onions, fresh dill or chives

1. Combine all the ingredients, except the onions, in blender or food processor fitted with a metal blade. Whirl until smooth. Then, stir in the chopped green onions. Pack in a serving dish.

2. Cover and refrigerate until ready to serve. Keeps well refrigerated at least 2 days. Garnish with thinly sliced green onions, or sprigs of fresh dill and surround with dark bread and thin slices of a small crusty loaf.

PER TABLESPOON: *39 calories, 2.3 g protein, 0.1 g carbohydrates, 3.4 g fat, 17.5 mg calcium, 0.1 mg iron, 0.01 g fiber.*

STILTON BERRY TARTS

Place small pieces of Stilton cheese in mini frozen tart shells. Bake and top with cranberry sauce, hot pepper jelly or chopped parsley.

KNOCKOUT GARLIC DIP

Not only a dynamite dip for veggies, this is also great smeared on grilled steaks, baked potatoes, swirled in fish soup and tossed with salad greens as a dressing. Keep it stocked in your refrigerator all summer long.

Preparation time: 5 minutes / Refrigeration time: 1 hour

Makes: 1½ cups

4 crushed garlic cloves
1 egg
1 egg yolk
1 tbsp freshly squeezed lemon juice
2 whole green onions, chopped
¼ tsp salt
1 cup vegetable oil

1. Place all the ingredients, except the oil, in a blender or a food processor fitted with a metal blade. Whirl until well mixed. Continuing to whirl, add the oil, drop by drop at first, then increasingly in a slow steady stream until all the oil is added. Whirl until light and creamy.

2. Cover and refrigerate for at least an hour to blend the flavors. The dip will keep well for several days. Serve in a bowl surrounded by lots of colorful vegetable crudités.

PER TABLESPOON: 86 calories, 0.4 g protein, 0.3 g carbohydrates, 9.5 g fat, 3.3 mg calcium, 0.07 mg iron, 0.01 g fiber.

ZIPPY DIPS

• Stir pesto into sour cream and serve with sliced vegetables.

• Add chopped avocado to bottled salsa and serve with nacho chips.

• Stir finely chopped crystallized ginger and liquid honey into whipped cream cheese. Dip with apple and pear wedges.

• Stir ½ a package of leek soup mix and ¼ cup chopped smoked salmon into 2 cups sour cream. Let sit overnight in the refrigerator. Serve with French bread. It looks wonderful in a hollowed-out crusty loaf of bread.

QUICK 'N' SNAZZY SEAFOOD APPETIZERS

Seafood is the most sought-after star at stand-up parties. Here are a few glamorous numbers you can whip up in minutes.

Smoked Salmon Pinwheels
Thinly spread whipped cream cheese with chives over a slice of smoked salmon. Sprinkle with freshly ground black pepper. Roll up, jelly-roll fashion. Chill until firm, at least 1 hour. Slice into ⅓-inch pinwheels.

Tangy Clam Dip
Mix ¼ cup sour cream with 2 teaspoons Worcestershire sauce, 1 teaspoon lemon juice and a dash of Tabasco sauce. Stir in a 5-oz (142-g) can of well-drained clams. Serve in a bowl with crackers. Makes ⅔ cup.

Ginger Crab Spread
Mix a 5-oz (142-g) can of well-drained crab meat with 4 oz (125 g) whipped cream cheese and 1 teaspoon finely chopped candied or crystallized ginger. Spread on whole wheat crackers and bread squares. Makes ½ cup.

Southern Shrimp Dip
Purée a 4-oz (113-g) can of well-drained and rinsed shrimp with ¼ cup cream cheese, 1 teaspoon lime juice and ½ teaspoon chopped jalapeno peppers. Serve with breadsticks or crackers. Makes ½ cup.

Luscious Lobster Bites
Mix a 5-oz (142-g) can of well-drained and rinsed lobster with 2 tablespoons mayonnaise, 2 chopped whole green onions and ½ teaspoon dried tarragon. Spoon into store-bought baked canapé cups. Makes 1½ cups.

FRESH TOMATO SALSA

This summertime salsa simply bursts with flavor and can be used in more ways than any other sauce we know. It's great as a dip with tacos. Spoon over toasted garlic bread rounds, sprinkle with Parmesan and broil. Toss with hot or cold pasta, mix with hot green beans or lavishly spread over burgers, steak, chicken or fish.

Preparation time: 15 minutes / Standing time: 1 hour

Makes: 3½ cups

4 large ripe tomatoes
3 whole green onions, thinly sliced
¼ cup finely chopped Italian parsley or coriander
3 crushed garlic cloves
2 tbsp each of olive oil and freshly squeezed lemon or lime juice
1 tbsp finely chopped hot pepper (optional)
½ tsp each of salt and freshly ground black pepper

1. Slice tomatoes in half and remove seeds. Finely chop. (They should measure about 3 cups.) Place in a bowl. Stir in remaining ingredients. Let stand 1 hour. Salsa can be refrigerated overnight, but it will lose texture.

PER ¼ CUP: *33 calories, 0.6 g protein, 3.6 g carbohydrates, 2.2 g fat, 7.3 mg calcium, 0.4 mg iron, 0.9 g fiber.*

CARAMEL CORN TOSS

For the kids at your party, stir 3 tablespoons melted butter with ¼ cup brown sugar, ½ teaspoon cinnamon and ½ teaspoon allspice. Toss with 8 cups popped popcorn. Spread on a baking sheet and bake at 350F for 5 minutes. Stir. Makes 8 cups.

WARM 'N' WONDERFUL WAYS WITH BRIE

A wedge of Brie is always a welcome but ordinary appetizer. Crown it with chopped, sun-dried tomatoes or chopped Mediterranean olives, then warm, and instantly it enters the elegant realm.

Brie Fondue
Carefully slice the top rind from a round of Brie. Place the Brie on a flat baking sheet and broil just until the cheese starts to melt. Carefully slide the cheese onto a heatproof platter and surround with crisp breadsticks, sliced sweet peppers, apples and pears for dipping.

Warm Brie Crowned with Sun-Dried Tomatoes
Soak ¼ cup sun-dried tomatoes in warm water for 45 minutes. Drain and whirl in a food processor with 2 garlic cloves, 2 tablespoons chopped parsley or fresh basil and freshly ground black pepper, until coarsely ground.

Spread on a cold 4-inch round of Brie. Bake in a preheated 350F oven for 10 minutes or microwave on medium for 1½ minutes. Serve immediately with crisp crackers for dipping or crusty bread for spreading. Serves 8.

Sugar and Spice Brie
Slice a round of Brie in half horizontally. Sprinkle the bottom layer lightly with brown sugar, dust with cinnamon, and scatter with thin slivers of dried apricots and chopped pecans. Add the top layer and heat in a 350F oven for 5 to 7 minutes. Or microwave on low until just warm to the touch. Garnish with whole pecans.

Baked Mediterranean Brie
Mix 2 tablespoons each of finely chopped black olives and parsley with 1 large crushed garlic clove. Spread on the top of a 4-inch round of Brie. Bake on a baking sheet at 350F for 10 minutes. Let stand for 5 minutes. Serve warm with crackers or spears of sweet pepper. Serves 8.

GOLDEN RUFFLED PHYLLO ROLLS

Make these cocktail-size phyllo rolls with two sophisticated fillings — Smoked Salmon, and Blue Cheese with Apple — months before the party season. Stir fillings together, roll them in phyllo and pinch the ends into big ruffles. Freeze without baking. When you want hot, classy hors d'oeuvre, pop frozen rolls into the oven and they'll be golden in ten minutes.

Preparation time: 30 minutes / Baking time: 10 minutes

Makes: 36 rolls

Smoked Salmon, and Blue Cheese with Apple Fillings
1-lb (500-g) pkg phyllo pastry, thawed
Melted butter

1. Prepare both fillings and set aside. Unroll the phyllo. Carefully remove 2 sheets. Reroll remaining pastry in its wrapping. Cover with a damp (not wet) cloth. Place 1 phyllo sheet on a clean surface. Lightly brush the sheet with melted butter. Place the second sheet over the first, matching all corners. Brush with butter. Turn the sheets over and brush butter over the other side. Make 2 cuts lengthwise and 3 cuts crosswise to form twelve 4½-inch squares.

2. Place 1 tablespoon of filling in the centre of each square. Bring up the 4 corners of each square. Using your thumb and index finger, squeeze together tightly just above the filling so the pastry flares out into ruffles at the top. Repeat until the filling is used up.

3. Bake right away or spread out on a baking sheet and freeze until firm. Box, then wrap in foil. Do not thaw before baking. Bake room-temperature or frozen bundles on an ungreased baking sheet in a preheated 375F oven for 10 to 12 minutes, until golden.

SMOKED SALMON FILLING

Using a fork, mash ½ cup room-temperature cream cheese with ¼ cup coarsely chopped smoked salmon. Stir in ¼ cup chopped raw spinach and freshly ground black pepper. The filling can be made a day ahead and refrigerated. Makes filling for 24 Phyllo Rolls.

PER TABLESPOON: 24 calories, 1 g protein, 2.2 g carbohydrates, 1.4 g fat, 2.8 mg calcium, 0.2 mg iron, 0.02 g fiber.

BLUE CHEESE WITH APPLE FILLING

Peel, core and grate 1 medium-size apple. Squeeze out the juice. Mash ¼ cup room-temperature cream cheese with 2 tablespoons crumbled blue cheese. Stir in the apple. The filling can be made a day ahead and refrigerated. Makes filling for 12 Phyllo Rolls.

PER TABLESPOON: 45 calories, 1.3 g protein, 4.1 g carbohydrates, 2.8 g fat, 16.9 mg calcium, 0.2 mg iron, 0.2 g fiber.

TORTILLA PARTY PINWHEELS

For a rapid roll appetizer, spread soft tortillas with one of the following combos, roll up and refrigerate. When chilled, slice into 1-inch pinwheels.

• Finely chopped smoked salmon mixed with whipped cream cheese and chopped fresh dill

• Smoked turkey or tuna, puréed with cream cheese, curry powder, fresh coriander and chutney to taste

• Shrimp puréed with cream cheese and a touch of salsa or pesto

PINWHEELS

MINI PIZZAS

This is one of the most popular appetizers sold by Fitz-Henri Fine Foods in Toronto. For a big party, or to have on hand, make up a batch or two in advance, bake and freeze. Reheat, still frozen, in a 350F oven or microwave.

Preparation time: 20 minutes / Standing time: 15 minutes
Baking time: 10 minutes / Makes: 36 mini pizzas

CRUSTS
$\frac{3}{4}$ cup lukewarm water
1 tsp granulated sugar
1 pkg (1 tbsp) dry yeast
2 cups all-purpose flour
$\frac{1}{4}$ tsp salt
2 tbsp vegetable oil

TOPPING
$7\frac{1}{2}$-oz (213-mL) can tomato sauce
1 tsp dried leaf oregano
1 tsp dried basil
1 cup grated Monterey Jack or Swiss cheese, about 3 oz (85 g)
$\frac{1}{3}$ cup freshly grated Parmesan cheese
4-oz (125-g) piece pepperoni

1. To prepare the crust, pour the lukewarm water (110F) into a medium-size bowl. Stir in the sugar until dissolved. Sprinkle the yeast over top. Do not stir. Let stand at room temperature until the yeast is foamy, about 10 minutes.

2. Meanwhile, place the flour and salt in a food processor fitted with a metal blade. Whirl until blended. Set the flour mixture aside in the processor bowl.

3. When the yeast is foamy, add the oil. Then, stir with a fork until evenly blended. With the food processor running, slowly add the yeast mixture to the flour mixture just until the dough starts to form a ball. Don't worry if you don't use all the yeast mixture.

4. Remove the dough and place it on a lightly floured surface. Knead for 5 to 8 minutes, until the dough feels satiny. Place the dough in a greased bowl. Cover with waxed paper and a damp cloth. Let the dough stand for 15 minutes.

5. Then, preheat oven to 400F. Place the dough on a lightly floured surface and roll it out with a heavy rolling pin until it's about $\frac{1}{4}$ inch thick. Cut out rounds with a 2-inch cookie cutter. Place the rounds on a lightly greased baking sheet. Roll out remaining scraps of dough and cut into rounds.

6. To prepare the topping, stir the tomato sauce with the herbs until evenly blended. Spread 1 teaspoon sauce onto each round. Sprinkle each with about 1 teaspoon grated Monterey Jack cheese, followed by ½ teaspoon freshly grated Parmesan cheese.

7. Bake in the centre of the preheated oven for 8 to 10 minutes or until golden.

8. While the pizzas are baking, thinly slice the pepperoni. As soon as the hot pizzas are removed from the oven, press a slice of the pepperoni into the top of each pizza. (If the pepperoni is cooked on these small pizzas, they will become greasy.) Serve immediately. Or cover and refrigerate or freeze and reheat in a 350F oven for 8 to 10 minutes or in a microwave.

PER PIZZA: 65 calories, 2.7 g protein, 5.7 g carbohydrates, 3.5 g fat, 40.9 mg calcium, 0.5 mg iron, 0.3 g fiber.

POSH CAVIAR OPENER

When you want a showstopper appetizer you can make in an instant — this is it. Set in a silver dish or a gold-rimmed plate.

Preparation time: 20 minutes / Makes: 20 servings

8-oz (250-g) pkg cream cheese
½ cup sour cream
2 hard-cooked eggs, chopped
3 whole green onions, finely chopped
1½-oz (50-g) container golden whitefish caviar
1½-oz (50-g) container black lumpfish caviar
1½-oz (50-g) container red roe lumpfish caviar

1. Combine the cream cheese and sour cream in a food processor fitted with a metal blade. Whirl, using an on-and-off motion, until smooth and no lumps of cream cheese remain. Or place in a large mixing bowl and beat with an electric mixer until smooth.

2. Turn half the mixture into a 7-inch round quiche pan or shallow glass serving dish. Smooth it out into an even layer. Scatter the chopped eggs and green onions over top. Then, gently spread with remaining cream cheese mixture to cover completely.

3. Score the surface of cheese mixture into equal wedges. Top each wedge with colored caviar to create a pretty pattern. Cover with plastic wrap and refrigerate until ready to serve. This spread is best made only a few hours before serving. It waters out a little upon standing. Serve with thin rounds of melba toast or bread for spreading.

PER SERVING: 83 calories, 3.6 g protein, 1 g carbohydrates, 7.5 g fat, 40.8 mg calcium, 1.1 mg iron, 0.03 g fiber.

SKINNY SUMMER DIPS

Refreshing Fresh Fruit
Stir 1 cup whipped cream cheese with 1 teaspoon granulated sugar, finely grated peel of 1 orange, 3 tablespoons orange juice and ½ teaspoon vanilla. A delicious dip for sliced pears and apples.

Creamy Low-Cal Salsa
Stir equal amounts of light sour cream and bottled salsa together. Add sliced green onion. Dip with sliced veggies.

Feta and Red Pepper Dip
In food processor, purée 1 cup crumbled feta cheese with ¼ cup chopped red pepper and 2 to 3 tablespoons sour cream or vegetable oil. Serve with fresh vegetable sticks.

CHIC QUICHETTES

This is a big-batch recipe for bite-size quiches. In a single session one Saturday afternoon, you can bake dozens of appetizers to see you through the festive season.

Preparation time: 30 minutes / Baking time: 20 minutes per batch

Makes: 36 quichettes

Bacon and Pepper, Smoked Salmon and Dill, and Hot Pepper and Cheddar Fillings (see below)
36 small store-bought frozen tart shells, big enough to hold 3 tbsp filling
6 eggs
3 cups table cream
½ tsp salt
Generous pinch of ground white pepper

1. Preheat oven to 375F. Prepare each of the fillings to the point that they are ready to be placed in the tart shells. Set aside. (Since each filling is sufficient for 12 tart shells, you can either prepare 1 batch of each or triple one of the fillings.) Place 12 tart shells, still in their foil cups, on each of 3 baking sheets. Whisk the eggs, cream, salt and pepper together and set aside.

2. Sprinkle the desired filling in the shells at this point. If only 1 baking sheet will fit on the bottom rack of your oven, pour the egg mixture into the shells on 1 baking sheet only. Fill the shells to the rims. Bake on the bottom rack of the preheated oven for 18 to 20 minutes or until the filling sets.

3. Repeat with remaining shells. Serve right away or leave in the foil cups and cool. Wrap well and freeze for up to 1 month. Reheat frozen quichettes on a baking sheet in a preheated 350F oven for 15 to 20 minutes.

BACON AND PEPPER FILLING

Cook ¼ lb (125 g) bacon in a frying pan until crisp. Crumble and distribute evenly among 12 tart shells. Pour all but 1 teaspoon of fat from the pan. Add ¼ cup finely chopped red or green pepper and sauté for 2 minutes. Sprinkle 1 teaspoon of the sautéed pepper into each shell. Grate enough Swiss or cheddar cheese to measure ¾ cup. Add 1 tablespoon cheese to each shell. Then, pour in the egg mixture.

PER QUICHE: 156 calories, 5.2 g protein, 6.1 g carbohydrates, 12.3 g fat, 93.1 mg calcium, 0.5 mg iron, 0.2 g fiber.

MARVELOUS MUSHROOMS

Incredibly low in calories, mushrooms are handy packages for fillings and much healthier than pastry tarts.

Italian Melt

Fill mushroom caps with grated cheddar cheese or mozzarella and sprinkle with finely chopped pepperettes and red peppers or use hot peppers, if you like. Top with sliced green onion. Place on a baking sheet about 6 inches from a preheated broiler until cheese melts. Serve immediately.

Walnut and Brie

Whirl 6 oz (165 g) cubed Brie and ½ cup coarsely chopped walnuts in a food processor, until fairly smooth. Spoon into large mushroom caps. Place on a baking sheet in a preheated 375F oven for 5 minutes, just until hot. Makes 1 cup filling.

SMOKED SALMON AND DILL FILLING

Distribute ¼ lb (125 g) chopped smoked salmon and ¼ cup chopped fresh dill among 12 tart shells. Grate enough Swiss cheese to measure ¾ cup. Sprinkle 1 tablespoon cheese into each shell. Then, pour in the egg mixture.

PER QUICHE: 148 calories, 6.2 g protein, 6.1 g carbohydrates, 11 g fat, 98.3 mg calcium, 0.7 mg iron, 0.2 g fiber.

HOT PEPPER AND CHEDDAR FILLING

Grate enough medium cheddar cheese to measure ¾ cup. Place 1 tablespoon cheese in each of 12 tart shells. Distribute ¼ cup chopped jalapeno peppers or 1 teaspoon crushed dried chilies among the shells. Then, pour in the egg mixture.

PER QUICHE: 138 calories, 4 g protein, 5.9 g carbohydrates, 10.9 g fat, 76.4 mg calcium, 0.6 mg iron, 0.2 g fiber.

BRANDIED ROQUEFORT-NUT PÂTÉ

Serve this full-flavored Roquefort blend, spiked with brandy, in a small bowl surrounded with slices of ripe pear, red-skinned apples, walnut halves and thin wedges of Hovis bread.

Preparation time: 10 minutes / Makes: 1 cup

4-oz (125-g) pkg cream cheese, at room temperature
4-oz (125-g) Roquefort cheese, at room temperature
1 tbsp brandy or cognac
¼ cup finely chopped walnuts or pecans
2 chopped whole green onions, or 2 tbsp chopped fresh dill or chives
2 tbsp chopped parsley

1. Cut the cream cheese into cubes. Place the cream cheese in a medium-size bowl or food processor. Crumble the Roquefort cheese over the cream cheese. Add 1 tablespoon brandy. Beat with an electric mixer or whirl in a food processor fitted with a metal blade until the mixture is evenly blended and smooth.

2. Stir in the nuts, green onions and parsley. Then, press the mixture into a small pâté dish or form it into a ball. Serve right away or seal in plastic wrap and refrigerate for up to a week. Do not freeze.

3. Before serving, bring the pâté to room temperature. Serve with crackers, spread on cucumber slices or bake in tiny tart shells at 375F for about 12 to 15 minutes.

PER TABLESPOON: 53 calories, 2.1 g protein, 0.4 g carbohydrates, 4.9 g fat, 54 mg calcium, 0.2 mg iron, 0.02 g fiber.

DRESS-UP TIPS FROM A PRO

Kate Bush is the talented food stylist who translates Chatelaine's recipes into our mouth-watering pictures each month. Here are a few of her presentation tips.

Pâté Platter

Surround a thick slice of peppercorn pâté with sprigs of fresh herbs. Accompany with sun-dried tomatoes in oil, tiny cornichons, mixed olives and a hot red-pepper jelly served in white bowls with slices of crusty bread.

Smoked Salmon Canapés

Roll thin strips of smoked salmon into rosettes and place them on top of pumpernickel squares spread with herbed cream cheese. Fill the centre of each with black caviar and garnish with chives.

Christmas Wreath

Cover the rim of a round white plate with a "wreath" of fresh rosemary and scatter with red grapes or fresh cranberries. Set a quiche, a whole cheese wheel or a tourtière inside.

NEW BEGINNINGS · TRIPLE TESTED

SOUPS TO START

Whether seductive, soothing, spicy or refreshing, today's first-course soups have new first-class beginnings. Unlike the flour and butter bases of many of yesterday's classics, our gloriously fresh-tasting versions start with rich vegetable or cool fruit purées and intensely flavored broths. They always deliver satisfying taste while leaving room for more.

IMPERIAL CURRIED FRUIT SOUP

A mélange of fruits paired with curry and cumin creates an exceptional cold soup. Serve with peppered poppadams.

Preparation time: 15 minutes / Cooking time: 15 minutes
Refrigeration time: 1 hour / Makes: 4 cups

1 onion, finely chopped
1 tbsp butter
1 tsp each of curry powder and ground cumin
2 ripe pears or 4 canned pear halves
2 cooking apples
2 cups chicken bouillon
1 tsp freshly squeezed lemon juice
$\frac{1}{2}$ cup light sour cream (optional)
Chopped coriander

1. Chop the onion. Melt the butter in a large saucepan. Add the onion and sprinkle with the curry powder and cumin. Sauté until the onion is soft, about 5 minutes. Meanwhile, peel and coarsely chop the fresh pears. If using canned pears, simply drain. Peel and coarsely chop the apples.

2. Add the fruit to the onion mixture along with the chicken bouillon and lemon juice and bring to a boil. Taste and add more curry powder and cumin, if needed. Cover, reduce heat and simmer for 10 minutes or until the fruit is tender.

3. Then, drain the liquid from the fruit into a large bowl. Place fruit mixture in a food processor and purée until fairly smooth. Turn purée into the liquid from the fruit and whisk together. Taste and whisk in sour cream, if you like. Refrigerate, covered, at least until chilled but preferably overnight to give flavors a chance to blend. Serve sprinkled with fresh coriander.

PER $\frac{1}{2}$ CUP: 71 calories, 1.7 g protein, 12.6 g carbohydrates, 2.2 g fat, 16.8 mg calcium, 0.7 mg iron, 1.9 g fiber.

ICED BORSCHT WITH FRESH DILL

Borscht brimming with grated beets is a beautiful-looking soup to begin a grilled fish dinner. Its rich pink color is set off by white bowls and a generous sprinkling of coarsely chopped fresh dill. Accompany with small squares of thinly sliced pumpernickel spread with curry butter. Don't hesitate to use canned beets instead of bothering with fresh — we find the flavor just as good and always full bodied.

Preparation time: 10 minutes / Refrigeration time: 1 hour

Makes: 4 servings

2 (14-oz/398-mL) cans whole beets, drained, or
    12 medium-size cooked beets
10-oz (284-mL) can consommé
1 cup (250-mL container) light sour cream
¼ cup chopped fresh dill or 1 tsp dried dillweed
¼ cup coarsely chopped onion
1 tbsp freshly squeezed lemon juice
2 crushed garlic cloves
Pinch each of granulated sugar and freshly ground
    white or black pepper

1. Peel and coarsely grate the beets into a large bowl. Whirl remaining ingredients together in a blender or food processor fitted with a metal blade until fairly smooth. Add to the beets and gently stir together. Taste and add more lemon juice or seasonings, if needed. Refrigerate at least until cold. The borscht will keep well for several days. Serve ice-cold with a dollop of sour cream and a sprig of fresh dill.

PER SERVING: 155 calories, 8.9 g protein, 22.7 g carbohydrates, 4.2 g fat, 111 mg calcium, 1.9 mg iron, 1.5 g fiber.

SOUPS TOO SALTY?
If your soup is too salty, a cut potato added to the simmering broth will absorb some of the salt. After 5 minutes remove and discard it. A pinch of sugar or squeeze of lemon juice also helps cut salt.

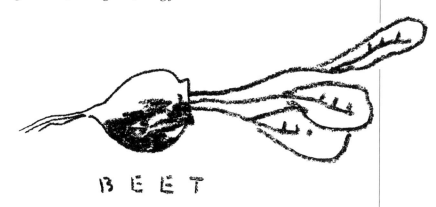

BEET

HONEYDEW-LIME SOUP

This is a wonderfully light way to begin a dinner party. It's so refreshing and low in calories you may want to keep a container in the refrigerator for sipping when you get home from work.

Preparation time: 10 minutes / Refrigeration time: 2 hours

Makes: 6 to 8 servings

1 large ripe honeydew melon
1 lime
¼ to ½ cup regular or light sour cream (optional)
Fresh mint leaves or julienne strips of lime peel

1. Cut melon in half, peel and remove seeds. Cut pulp into chunks and place half the fruit in a food processor. Whirl, using an on-and-off motion, until smooth. Pour into a bowl. Repeat with remaining melon. Stir in half the juice from the lime. Taste and add more lime juice and sour cream, if you like.

2. Refrigerate until chilled or ready to serve, up to 2 days. Just before serving, add a squeeze of lime juice. Garnish with a swirl of sour cream, mint or lime peel.

PER SERVING: *28 calories, 0.7 g protein, 6.9 g carbohydrates, 0.2 g fat, 9 mg calcium, 0.2 mg iron, 0.6 g fiber.*

CREAM OF MANGO SOUP

The tropical flavor of mango makes this soup a superb starter for a curried dinner or fancy barbecue.

Preparation time: 5 minutes / Refrigeration time: 3 hours

Makes: 6 to 8 servings

2 large ripe mangoes
½ to 1 cup half-and-half cream
½ tsp vanilla
Pinch of ground ginger or 1 tsp chopped preserved ginger
    in syrup (optional)

1. Peel the mangoes and remove the pulp from the stones. Place the pulp in a food processor fitted with a metal blade or in a blender, along with about ½ cup cream, the vanilla and ginger, if using. Whirl, using an on-and-off motion, until the mixture is smooth. If the mangoes are not ripe, you may have to strain the soup to get an absolutely smooth consistency.

THE PERFECT MANGO

A ripe mango is smooth-skinned and unblemished yet yields to gentle pressure. The peel should be bright yellow with orange and red highlights. Avoid fruit with black spots or a fermented aroma. Since a good portion of the mango is the stone, a large one is your best buy.

Unripe mangoes have a greenish peel. Ripen by storing at room temperature in a paper bag with holes pierced in it. Refrigerate once the fruit is fully ripened.

2. Turn the soup into a bowl and stir in remaining cream, if needed. (Or the soup can be thinned with some orange juice, milk or water.) Refrigerate until chilled or overnight. Soup may thicken upon sitting. Thin, if necessary, and adjust seasonings — a pinch of cumin or curry is a nice touch. Covered and refrigerated, the soup will keep well for several days.

PER SERVING: *73 calories, 1 g protein, 12.8 g carbohydrates, 2.6 g fat, 29.3 mg calcium, 0.1 mg iron, 1.6 g fiber.*

FAST 'N' FLAVORFUL SQUASH SOUP

This is proof that a soup doesn't have to be made from scratch to be great.

Preparation time: 5 minutes / Cooking time: 5 minutes

Makes: 4 cups

10-oz (283-g) pkg frozen puréed squash
2 cups chicken bouillon
1 tsp ground cumin
4 whole green onions, thinly sliced
$\frac{1}{4}$ cup crumbled creamy goat cheese, Stilton or
    Parmesan cheese

1. Combine the squash, bouillon and cumin in a medium-size saucepan. Cover and place over medium heat. Cook, stirring often, until the squash is completely melted. Meanwhile, stir in the green onions. Sprinkle about 1 tablespoon crumbled cheese over each bowl of hot soup.

PER $\frac{1}{2}$ CUP: *35 calories, 2.9 g protein, 2.9 g carbohydrates, 1.6 g fat, 27.9 mg calcium, 0.7 mg iron, 0.7 g fiber.*

SQUASH

FAST 'N' FIERY SOUPS

For those winter nights when you crave a warming soup with extra punch, but want to spend your time in front of the fireplace instead of the range, try one of these quick, feisty recipes.

Tomato-Basil
Heat a 10-oz (284-mL) can of tomato soup with 1 soup-can of water, 1 teaspoon dried basil and $\frac{1}{4}$ teaspoon Tabasco sauce.

Hot Lentil
Purée a 19-oz (540-mL) can of lentils including liquid with 1 large crushed garlic clove and $\frac{1}{4}$ teaspoon cayenne pepper. Heat with 1 cup chicken bouillon.

Jalapeno Chicken
Drain, seed and finely chop 1 canned jalapeno pepper. Add it to a 10-oz (284-mL) can of cream of chicken soup and 1 cup water. Heat, stirring often.

Green Pea
Heat a 10-oz (284-mL) can of green-pea soup with 1 soup-can of water, 1 cup frozen green peas, 1 teaspoon curry powder and $\frac{1}{4}$ teaspoon cayenne pepper.

CIOPPINO SOUP

A nutritionally rich, wine-laced seafood stew that satisfies the heartiest of appetites, yet light enough to begin a special dinner and make a big impression. See photo opposite page 33.

Preparation time: 15 minutes

Cooking time: 30 minutes *or* Microwave time: 25 minutes

Makes: 8 cups

CIOPPINO
SOUP

$\frac{1}{4}$ cup olive oil
1 large onion, finely chopped
1 red pepper, seeded and finely chopped
3 crushed garlic cloves
$7\frac{1}{2}$-oz (213-mL) can tomato sauce
8-oz (237-mL) bottle clam juice
1 cup dry red wine
2 cups chicken broth or bouillon
1 tsp dried basil
$\frac{1}{2}$ tsp dried leaf oregano
$\frac{1}{4}$ tsp freshly ground black pepper
Dash of Tabasco sauce
2 lbs (1 kg) mussels, scrubbed
$\frac{1}{2}$ lb (250 g) large shrimp, shelled

1. In a large wide saucepan, heat the oil over medium heat. Add the onion, red pepper and garlic and sauté for about 5 minutes or until the onion is soft.

2. Add the tomato sauce, clam juice, wine, chicken broth, basil, oregano, black pepper and Tabasco sauce. Do not add salt. Bring the

QUICK 'N' COMFY SOUPS

Bright new ways to jazz up a can of soup.

Double Cheddar
Heat a 10-oz (284-mL) can of cheddar cheese soup with 1 soup-can of milk and 1 teaspoon Dijon mustard. Add $\frac{1}{2}$ cup tiny cubes of cheddar cheese. Stir until melted.

Potato Parmesan
Heat a 10-oz (284-mL) can of cream of potato soup with 1 soup-can of milk, 1 crushed garlic clove and $\frac{1}{2}$ cup sliced celery. Serve with lots of freshly grated Parmesan cheese sprinkled over top.

Seafood Leek
Heat a $2\frac{1}{2}$-oz (77-g)package of dry leek soup mix with 4 cups water, 1 sliced leek, $\frac{1}{2}$ teaspoon dried basil and a $6\frac{1}{2}$-oz (184-g) can of drained tuna. Simmer, covered, for 10 minutes.

Gourmet Green Pea
Heat a 10-oz (284-mL) can of green-pea soup with 1 soup-can of milk. Add 1 cup frozen peas, 1 teaspoon dried basil and $\frac{1}{4}$ cup julienne strips pepperoni. Simmer, covered, for 5 minutes.

mixture to a boil. Then, cover, reduce heat and simmer gently for 20 minutes to develop the flavors. Stir occasionally.

3. Stir in the mussels and simmer, covered, for 2 to 3 minutes. Then, stir in the shrimp and simmer, uncovered, for 2 to 3 more minutes or until the shrimp turn pink. Taste and add salt and more pepper, if necessary. Discard any mussels that do not open. Serve the soup along with a warm flat bread.

4. To microwave, arrange the mussels in a single layer in a large shallow microwave-safe dish. Microwave, covered, on high for 2½ to 3 minutes or until the shells open. Discard any mussels that do not open. Repeat with remaining mussels. Set aside. Place the oil, onion, red pepper and garlic in a 16-cup (4-L) microwave-safe casserole dish. Microwave, covered, on high for 2 minutes or until the onion is soft. Stir partway through cooking. Stir in remaining ingredients (except seafood). Microwave, covered, on high for 12 to 15 minutes, until the soup boils vigorously. Stir partway through cooking. Stir in the shrimp. Cover and continue cooking on high for 3 to 4 minutes, until the shrimp are bright pink. Stir in the mussels.

PER CUP: 197 calories, 15.7 g protein, 8.1 g carbohydrates, 9 g fat, 42.7 mg calcium, 3.8 mg iron, 0.8 g fiber.

> **CROUTONS WITH CRUNCH**
> Make your own croutons from leftover bread such as pumpernickel, rye, wholewheat or a crusty loaf. Brush the bread with olive oil or melted butter and slice into small cubes. Spread on a baking sheet. Toast in a 400F oven, stirring often, until golden, for 4 to 6 minutes. For more flavor, toss hot croutons with freshly grated Parmesan cheese or fresh herbs.

HOT 'N' HEALTHY MEXICAN TOMATO SOUP

Pass piping hot mugs of this south-of-the-border version of fresh tomato soup when you're gathered around the fireplace. Try it chilled, too, in summertime by the pool.

Preparation time: 30 minutes / Cooking time: 25 minutes

Makes: 8 cups

4 onions
2 hot peppers
3 lbs (1.5 kg) very ripe tomatoes, about 10, or
    28-oz (796-mL) can tomatoes, drained
1 tbsp vegetable or olive oil
3 crushed garlic cloves
1 tsp ground cumin
½ tsp freshly ground black pepper
5 cups vegetable cocktail juice
Pinch each of salt and granulated sugar (optional)
Nacho chips and fresh coriander (optional)

Soups with Spirit

A soupçon or two of wine or liquor can turn ordinary soup into a symphony. Add a little brandy to French onion soup to bring out the meaty flavor of the broth. Sherry simmered with a cream soup adds a depth of flavor. White wine, licorice-flavored liqueur or vodka are luxurious touches for seafood soups and chowders.

1. If using fresh tomatoes, bring a large pot of water to a full rolling boil. Finely chop the onions. Remove the seeds from the hot peppers, then finely chop the peppers.

2. Plunge the tomatoes into the boiling water and blanch for 1 minute. Drain the tomatoes and quickly immerse them in ice-cold water to stop the cooking. Peel off the skins. Cut the fresh tomatoes or drained canned tomatoes in half, crosswise, and squeeze out the seeds. Coarsely chop the remaining pulp.

3. Heat the oil in a large saucepan set over medium-low heat. When hot, add the onions, hot peppers and garlic. Cook, stirring occasionally, until softened, about 10 minutes. Stir in the seasonings, then add the tomatoes and vegetable juice.

4. Bring the soup to a boil. Then, reduce heat and simmer, uncovered, to blend the flavors, about 15 minutes. Taste and add a pinch of salt or sugar, if needed. Serve the soup hot or cold, garnished with broken nacho chips and fresh coriander.

PER ½ CUP: 51 calories, 1.6 g protein, 1 g carbohydrates, 1.3 g fat, 21 mg calcium, 1 mg iron, 2.4 g fiber.

Leek Soup with Dill

A signature of Fenton's, one of Toronto's most popular restaurants in the late '70s. It always came with a crumbling of Stilton cheese. We've discovered it also works well with Parmesan or chèvre.

Preparation time: 20 minutes / Cooking time: 30 minutes

Makes: 9 cups

3 small leeks
2 large onions
⅓ cup butter
1 tbsp Dijon mustard
4 cups chicken broth or bouillon
Freshly grated nutmeg
Generous pinches of white pepper
½ tsp dried dillweed
4 to 6 potatoes
1 cup (250-mL container) half-and-half cream (optional)
¼ cup chopped fresh dill
Freshly grated nutmeg (optional)
Crumbled Stilton or freshly grated Parmesan cheese (optional)

1. Clean leeks by cutting them in half lengthwise. Cut off all tough parts of the green leaves and discard. Separate the remaining leaves and wash under cold running water. Then, slice the leeks into ½-inch pieces. Coarsely chop the onions.

2. Melt the butter in a large heavy-bottomed saucepan. Add the leeks and onions and cook until soft, about 10 minutes. Blend the Dijon into the butter until well mixed. Add the broth and seasonings and bring to a boil. Meanwhile, peel the potatoes and cut them into small cubes. Measure out 4 cups and add to the broth. Cover, reduce heat and simmer for 30 minutes or until the potatoes are soft.

3. Then, strain the vegetables in a large sieve, reserving the broth. Purée the vegetables in 2 batches in a food processor fitted with a metal blade or in a blender until smooth. Add the purée to the reserved broth and whisk together until blended. Stir in the cream, if using, and the fresh dill and heat until piping hot. Taste and add more nutmeg, if you like. To serve, spoon soup into bowls and crumble the Stilton or sprinkle the Parmesan over top.

4. Soup can be refrigerated up to 2 days or frozen. To reheat, simply turn the frozen soup into a large saucepan containing ¼ cup water. Heat gently at first, stirring often, until the soup is thawed. Then, taste and add fresh dill and freshly grated nutmeg, if needed. Cover and heat until piping hot, then spoon into bowls and sprinkle with crumbled Stilton or grated Parmesan.

PER ½ CUP: *88 calories, 2.3 g protein, 11.5 g carbohydrates, 3.9 g fat, 25.1 mg calcium, 0.8 mg iron, 0.7 g fiber.*

LEEK
SOUP

ALL-STAR HERBS

Smart cooks appreciate the flavor punch that freshly snipped herbs add to any dish — a pinch of lemon thyme in breakfast biscuits, a toss of tarragon in scrambled eggs, snipped chive blossoms on a summer salad, or fresh mint sprigs in a fruit mix. And don't forget, herbs are a smart alternative to salt. Here's a sprinkling of fresh new ways.

• Just before serving, scatter a mix of coarsely chopped herbs over soups or stews for an aromatic flavor perk.

• Add whole basil, thyme or dill leaves to mussels and clams when steaming them.

• Chop and toss oregano, coriander, basil or dill into pasta or rice salads.

• Finely chop and stir tarragon, chives and coriander into Dijon mustard. Spread on sandwiches, hot dogs or sausages.

• Finely chop and stir parsley, chives or dill into room-temperature butter and dab on cooked fish.

• Place whole sprigs of thyme, rosemary, summer or winter savory in bottles of vegetable or olive oil. Keep covered at room temperature. Use in salads, as barbecue bastes or sprinkle over hot vegetables.

• Chop and stir basil, oregano, thyme or rosemary into tomato sauces and salads. Sprinkle over grilled tomatoes or tomato-and-cheese sandwiches.

• Use whole leaves of basil, dill, sage or thyme as a stuffing for fish, chicken or pork.

• Blend a variety of chopped herbs into ground meat before forming into patties.

• Add a handful of coarsely chopped chives, lemon thyme, mint or rosemary into baking powder biscuits, bread doughs, scalloped potatoes, even macaroni and cheese.

NEW BEGINNINGS · TRIPLE TESTED

IMPRESSIVE FIRST COURSES

This is your opportunity to present each guest with a special creation, a little plate to set the stage for the rest of the evening, be it an elegant anniversary celebration or a neighborhood barbecue. By including a first course in your menu your guests enjoy a wide repertoire of tastes and more time to chat. Today's starters go well beyond shrimp cocktail and consommé. Consider a Warm Mushroom and Spinach Salad, Saffron Risotto with Shrimp or Chic Spaghettini with Caviar. Take your pick.

FRENCH LEEKS VINAIGRETTE

For a lusty appetizer before a bistro dinner or companion for a winter roast, place 8 small trimmed leeks in a microwave-safe dish with 2 tablespoons water. Cook covered on high for 5 minutes. Drain and place in a plastic bag with ½ cup vegetable oil whisked with ¼ cup white vinegar, 2 teaspoons each of Dijon mustard and dried tarragon, 1 teaspoon granulated sugar and ½ teaspoon salt. Marinate in the refrigerator overnight. Serve sprinkled with sliced whole green onions.

WARM CAMBOZOLA AND PEARS

So simple yet so elegant, the heavenly marriage of fleshy pears and a creamy blue. The ingredients are a perfect union of flavor and texture. Garnish with a bit of fresh mint.

Preparation time: 15 minutes / Broiling time: 1 minute

Makes: 8 servings

4 pears, unpeeled
8 oz (250 g) cambozola, Gorgonzola or Camembert cheese
Freshly ground black pepper

1. Preheat broiler. Cut the pears in half lengthwise and remove the cores. To slice the pears so they can be fanned, make several thin slices lengthwise, starting at the small end but not cutting through the large end. This will hold the pear together but will enable you to separate the slices enough to create a fanned appearance.

2. Place the fanned pear halves on a baking sheet. Cut the cheese into ¼-inch thick slices. Place 1 slice horizontally atop each pear half. Sprinkle liberally with pepper.

3. Broil the pears until the cheese is just melted, about 1 minute.

PER SERVING: *159 calories, 7 g protein, 13.3 g carbohydrates, 9.3 g fat, 174 mg calcium, 0.3 mg iron, 2.2 g fiber.*

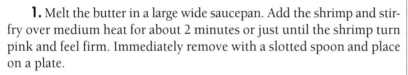

SAFFRON RISOTTO WITH SHRIMP

An incredibly creamy risotto lightened with white wine, perfumed with golden threads of precious saffron and tender shrimp.

Preparation time: 20 minutes / Cooking time: 30 minutes

Makes: 4 servings

¼ cup butter
12-oz (360-g) pkg frozen shrimp, thawed, or
    fresh deveined shrimp
1 large onion, preferably Spanish, finely chopped
1½ cups Arborio rice
½ cup dry white wine
¼ tsp saffron threads
10-oz (284-mL) can undiluted chicken broth
2 cups water
¼ cup freshly grated Parmesan cheese
Salt and freshly ground black pepper

1. Melt the butter in a large wide saucepan. Add the shrimp and stir-fry over medium heat for about 2 minutes or just until the shrimp turn pink and feel firm. Immediately remove with a slotted spoon and place on a plate.

2. Add the onion to the butter remaining in the pan and reduce heat to low. Sauté, stirring often, until the onion is soft, about 5 minutes. Then, add the rice and increase heat to medium. Stir the mixture until all rice grains are coated with butter.

3. Immediately add the wine while constantly stirring the rice mixture. Add the saffron and stir gently until the rice absorbs the wine.

4. Then, add the chicken broth and water, about ¼ cup at a time. Stir constantly and wait until liquid is absorbed before adding the next ¼ cup. (This process is necessary in order to achieve the proper texture.) Continue additions until all the liquid is absorbed and the rice is cooked, about 20 to 25 minutes. When cooked, the rice should be tender but not soft.

5. Stir in the Parmesan cheese until evenly distributed. Then, stir in the shrimp. Taste and add salt and pepper as needed. Serve immediately with more freshly grated Parmesan, if you wish.

PER SERVING: *506 calories, 25.5 g protein, 60 g carbohydrates, 15.2 g fat, 126 mg calcium, 5.6 mg iron, 1.3 g fiber.*

CREAMY COMFORTING RISOTTO

Short-grain Italian Arborio rice and a half-hour marathon of stirring are essential to producing a creamy risotto. The rice is first sautéed in butter, then hot stock is added a half-cup at a time and the mixture is stirred constantly until all the liquid is absorbed before more stock is added. Seafood, mushrooms, peppers, asparagus, etc., can be added, and a good Parmesan is stirred in just before serving.

ELEGANT BOUILLABAISSE SALAD

A dramatic interpretation of Southern France's classic fish stew and an elegant way to begin a special dinner or "want-to-impress" luncheon.

Preparation time: 20 minutes / Cooking time: 20 minutes
Refrigeration time: 30 minutes / Makes: 4 to 6 servings

1 orange
3 tbsp finely chopped shallots
¾ cup dry white wine
Freshly ground white pepper
1 lb (500 g) medium-size shrimp, shelled and deveined
½ lb (250 g) scallops, preferably bay scallops
1 tsp saffron threads
½ cup mayonnaise, preferably homemade
1 tbsp chopped pimento or 2 ripe tomatoes, seeded and
    finely chopped
2 whole green onions, thinly sliced
Pinch of cayenne pepper (optional)
¼ lb (125 g) snow peas (optional)
Bibb lettuce

1. Finely grate the peel of the orange and set aside. Squeeze the orange and place the juice (but not the peel) in a medium-size saucepan. Add the shallots, wine and a generous grinding of white pepper.

2. Bring the mixture to a boil. Add the shrimp. Cover and simmer. Stir after 1 minute and continue to cook, just until the shrimp turn pink and are firm to the touch, no more than 2 minutes. Remove to a bowl with a slotted spoon.

3. If the scallops are large, slice them into ½-inch rounds. Add them to the boiling wine mixture. Cover and simmer just until opaque, about 3 minutes. Remove with a slotted spoon and add to the shrimp. Refrigerate the shrimp and scallops immediately, uncovered, until chilled, about 30 minutes.

4. Strain the hot wine mixture and return it to the saucepan. Add the grated orange peel and saffron. Turn heat to medium-high and boil, uncovered, to develop the flavors and reduce the liquid. Continue boiling until the liquid is reduced to about ⅓ cup, about 10 minutes. Stir frequently near the end of cooking. Using a sieve, strain the mixture into a bowl. Using the back of a spoon, gently press the peel mixture in the sieve to extract all the juices. Discard the peel. Place the liquid in the freezer to chill quickly.

THREADS OF GOLD

Fortunately a little saffron goes a long way, because gram for gram it's more expensive than gold. Saffron threads, the dried stigmas of crocuses, are what give the yellowy-gold color and distinctive fragrance to such classics as bouillabaisse, paella and risotto Milanese. Threads, though pricier than ground saffron, are the smartest buy because they stay fresh longer and can't be adulterated with filler additives. Store in an airtight container in a cool, dark place and use within 6 months. To release maximum flavor, gently crush the threads and steep them in a hot liquid before using.

5. Then, place the mayonnaise in a medium-size bowl. Whisk in the chilled wine-saffron mixture. Stir in the pimento and green onions. Taste and add a pinch of cayenne pepper, if you wish.

6. Stir in the chilled seafood, patting it dry with paper towels, if necessary. Refrigerate, covered, until ready to serve. The flavor will improve with at least 3 or 4 hours' refrigeration, but the salad should be served the same day it is made.

7. When ready to serve, cook the snow peas, if using, in boiling water for 1 minute. Immediately rinse them under cold water. Then, slice them diagonally into 1-inch pieces.

8. Cover salad plates with the Bibb lettuce. Spoon the seafood mixture on the lettuce and sprinkle with the snow peas.

PER SERVING: 316 calories, 18.7 g protein, 4.9 g carbohydrates, 15.7 g fat, 75.1 mg calcium, 3.3 mg iron, 0.3 g fiber.

WARM MUSHROOM AND SPINACH SALAD

Everyone loves this spinach-mushroom combo warmed with a tarragon vinaigrette. For added panache, crumble goat cheese over the top.

Preparation time: 15 minutes / Cooking time: 3 minutes

Makes: 6 servings

1 large bunch spinach
½ lb (250 g) fresh mushrooms
3 whole green onions
¼ cup olive oil
2 tbsp red wine vinegar
2 tsp dried tarragon
¼ tsp Dijon mustard
Generous pinches each of salt and freshly ground
    black pepper

1. Tear the spinach into large bite-size pieces and place in a large bowl. Slice the mushrooms and green onions. Heat 2 tablespoons oil in a large frying pan set over medium-high heat. Add the mushrooms. Cook, stirring often, until lightly browned, about 3 minutes. Meanwhile, whisk 3 tablespoons oil and remaining ingredients together. As soon as the mushrooms are cooked, remove the pan from the heat. Add the entire dressing to the mushrooms in pan. Stir and immediately pour over the spinach. Toss well and serve.

PER SERVING: 112 calories, 3.6 g protein, 5.8 g carbohydrates, 9.5 g fat, 101 mg calcium, 3.3 mg iron, 3 g fiber.

PEPPER

PRESTO PESTO SHRIMP

Lightly coat cooked jumbo shrimp with pesto. Sprinkle with freshly grated Parmesan cheese. Chill and serve on a glass plate garnished with sprigs of fresh coriander.

WARM HAZELNUT-CHÈVRE SALAD

Chèvre with a light dusting of hazelnuts served on a bed of greens makes a sophisticated starter.

Preparation time: 15 minutes / Baking time: 3 minutes

Makes: 8 servings

10-oz (300-g) chèvre log
1 egg (optional)
3½-oz (100-g) pkg unblanched hazelnuts or almonds, coarsely chopped
8 large lettuce leaves or mix of greens
Balsamic or red wine vinegar
Freshly ground black pepper

1. Preheat the oven to 425F. Slice the chèvre into ⅓-inch-thick rounds. Cut in half. Lightly beat the egg in a small bowl. (The egg helps the nuts stick to the cheese, but is not absolutely necessary.) Dip the cheese halves in the egg. Then, press the nuts over the cheese. Place the cheese on a baking sheet.

2. Cover individual salad plates with a lettuce leaf or mix of greens. Drizzle with the vinegar and sprinkle with pepper. Bake the cheese just until softened, about 3 minutes. Immediately place some cheese in the centre of each plate and serve with crackers or crisp bread on the side.

PER SERVING: *182 calories, 8.8 g protein, 2.6 g carbohydrates, 15.8 g fat, 80.2 mg calcium, 1.2 mg iron, 1.3 g fiber.*

CHIC SPAGHETTINI WITH CAVIAR

For an impressive starter pasta, toss ¼ lb (250 g) cooked spaghettini with 3 tablespoons butter, ¼ cup grated Parmesan and 4 sliced whole green onions. Top each serving with about 3 tablespoons of red caviar. Serves 2 to 4.

OYSTERS AND CHAMPAGNE

Oysters and champagne spell celebration. As a matter of fact, our favorite Boxing Day Party menu is simple and superb — oysters, champagne and roast beef. Fortunately, the festive season is a peak period for oysters and Canadian oysters are among the world's finest. Check that they are tightly closed or close quickly when tapped. If oysters fail to close, discard. The shells should be heavy with juices or "liquor" as it's known.

Storing
The fresher the oysters, the better the flavor, so in the best of all worlds you should buy and eat them right away. But if you have to keep oysters, never store them in an airtight container, or in water. Oysters have to breathe. So arrange them in a shallow dish, cover with a damp kitchen cloth and refrigerate. Moisten the cloth as needed and don't count on storing for more than a week.

Shucking
Scrub oysters with a brush under cold running water. You will need an oyster knife with a thick blade for prying apart the shells. Don an oven mitt and place the oyster cup-side down in your palm. Working over a bowl to catch any liquor, insert the blade into the hinged end, rocking it back and forth until it's in at least ¼ inch. Continue the inward pressure while levering the blade up and down to separate the shells. When the hinge gives, run the blade between the shell and the oyster, top and bottom. Lift off and discard the top shell. Nestle the oysters on a bed of crushed ice. Pour any juices from the bowl back over the oysters.

EASYGOING SALADS

Salads should be fun. You don't have to measure ingredients precisely and you can be as innovative as you want. Salads are no longer just a green side dish. They're colorful, crunchy and unpredictable. Take, for example, our pizza toss with all the traditional fixings in an untraditional spunky salad. Or consider a tropical chicken and mango combination for a balmy summer evening. How about Harvest Coleslaw with Apples and Pears as a sidekick with country pork chops? For a unique smoky flavor, lightly barbecue veggies, then toss with a tangy vinaigrette and leafy greens. We still do potato salad but with a lighter lemony dill or robust Italian dressing. Grains and beans play a significant role in our Mean Bean Toss and our Terrific Tabbouleh with Mint. Remember, there are no strict rules — so toss our ideas around and relax.

EASYGOING SALADS • TRIPLE TESTED

SUPPERTIME SALADS

It's silly to subject yourself to a hot kitchen on a sweltering summer night when you can quickly and coolly toss a refreshing, satisfying dinner together. Here is a medley of significant supper salads to assemble with a minimum of effort. Don't expect to find "old-hat" combinations. While we do the best of the classics — Greek and chicken, for example — we've updated them all with flavor bursts like hot peppers and pita croutons. New combos to add to your repertoire include an Italian pasta salad brimming with pizza topping tastes and a new take on a garlicky chicken-Caesar combo.

MOIST MICROWAVE CHICKEN SALAD

The fastest route to moist chicken for tossing in a salad or sandwich-making is to "poach" it in a microwave. Arrange the thick meaty portion of the chicken pieces toward the outside of a microwave-safe dish. Cook, uncovered, for 7 to 8 minutes per pound, regardless of the number of pieces. Turn halfway through cooking. Cover and let stand for 15 minutes. Skin and cut into bite-size pieces.

PHOTO: Tropical Chicken-Mango Salad, see recipe at right.

TROPICAL CHICKEN-MANGO SALAD

Mangoes and a ginger-orange dressing give a tropical twist to this Caribbean sunset salad.

Preparation time: 15 minutes / Makes: 4 servings

DRESSING
¼ cup vegetable oil
2 tbsp preserved ginger, finely chopped
1 tbsp orange juice concentrate
Finely grated peel of 1 orange

SALAD
4 cooked chicken breasts, skinned and boned
½ small English cucumber, coarsely chopped
1 red pepper, coarsely chopped
1 mango, peeled
½ head leaf lettuce
2 tbsp toasted pine nuts or roasted peanuts

1. In a small bowl, whisk the dressing ingredients together until well blended. Cut the chicken into 1-inch cubes and place in a salad bowl with cucumber and red pepper. Cut mango into 1-inch pieces and add to the salad. Toss with dressing. Taste and add more chopped ginger, salt or pepper, if needed. Spoon the chicken mixture onto a lettuce-lined platter. Then, sprinkle with pine nuts.

PER SERVING: *289 calories, 17.5 g protein, 19.6 g carbohydrates, 16.4 g fat, 50.2 mg calcium, 1.4 mg iron, 2.4 g fiber.*

PIZZA SUMMER TOSS

All the best tastes and fixings of a traditional pizza are in this untraditional salad. On hot days, toss it up instead of ordering in.

Preparation time: 20 minutes / Makes: 4 to 6 servings

DRESSING
$\frac{1}{2}$ cup vegetable oil
3 tbsp red wine vinegar
2 crushed garlic cloves
$\frac{1}{2}$ tsp dried leaf oregano
$\frac{1}{4}$ tsp dried basil
$\frac{1}{2}$ tsp granulated sugar
$\frac{1}{2}$ tsp salt
Freshly ground black pepper

SALAD
1 head romaine or iceberg lettuce
$\frac{1}{4}$ lb (125 g) pepperoni or bacon
$\frac{1}{4}$ lb (125 g) fresh mushrooms, sliced
1 cup cherry tomatoes, halved
1 red or Italian onion, thinly sliced
$\frac{1}{2}$ green pepper, finely chopped
$\frac{1}{2}$ cup freshly grated Parmesan cheese

1. Blend or whisk the dressing ingredients together. Set aside. Trim the lettuce and separate the leaves. Wash and dry. Tear the lettuce into bite-size pieces and place it in a large salad bowl.

2. Thinly slice the pepperoni or cook the bacon until crisp and crumble it. Add to the lettuce along with remaining vegetables. Whisk the dressing again and pour it over top of the vegetables. Sprinkle with the cheese. Toss and serve.

PER SERVING: 363 calories, 11.1 g protein, 8.7 g carbohydrates, 26.3 g fat, 139 mg calcium, 1.9 mg iron, 2.3 g fiber.

NEW SALAD SPRINKLERS

Perk up the taste of any green salad by sprinkling with

• Finely chopped fresh coriander, arugula or lemon basil

• Tiny croutons made from pumpernickel, wholegrain, cheese bread or pitas

• Coarsely grated Asiago, smoked cheese, semi-hard goat cheese, Monterey Jack or cheddar cheese with hot peppers

• Crumbled Gorgonzola, goat cheese or Stilton

• Grated fresh fennel, celeriac or finely chopped hot peppers

• Toasted pine nuts, coarsely chopped toasted hazelnuts or cashews

• Finely grated lime peel, chopped blood oranges, clementines or tangerines.

PHOTO: *Cioppino Soup, see recipe on page 22.*

SUN-DRIED TOMATOES AND ASIAGO SALAD

A fashionable combination of tastes. The sun-dried tomatoes are full flavored and chewy, the Italian Asiago cheese, rich. Terrific hot or cold.

Preparation time: 15 minutes / Cooking time: 5 minutes

Makes: 6 servings

1 lb or 450-g pkg capellini or spaghettini
¼ cup olive oil
3 tbsp oil from sun-dried tomatoes
½ cup julienne-sliced sun-dried tomatoes
1 cup pine nuts, toasted
½ lb (250 g) Asiago cheese, coarsely grated or crumbled
¼ tsp salt
¼ tsp freshly ground black pepper

1. Cook the pasta in a large pot of salted boiling water until al dente, about 2 to 3 minutes for capellini. Drain in a colander, then rinse under cold water. Drain very well and place in a large bowl.

2. Add the olive oil and the oil from the sun-dried tomatoes to the pasta and toss well to coat.

3. Then, add remaining ingredients and toss. Make sure to evenly distribute the tomatoes and pine nuts, as they tend to fall to the bottom of the bowl.

PER SERVING: *786 calories, 34.8 g protein, 77.9 g carbohydrates, 41 g fat, 404 mg calcium, 6.3 mg iron, 1.2 g fiber.*

SASSY SUN-DRIED TOMATOES

• Sun-dried tomatoes packed in cellophane bags or in jars with oil or another liquid provide an intensely rich tomato taste and chewy texture.

• Dry-packed are the best buy. Simply soak them in hot water or oil before using. Use the oil for salad dressing, sautéeing or barbecuing.

• Sprinkle finely chopped sun-dried tomatoes over salads, soups, pizza, focaccia and grilled cheese sandwiches or stir them into creamy goat cheese spreads, burger mixtures and pasta sauces.

CLASSY CHICKEN CAESAR

This main-event low-calorie interpretation is guaranteed to satisfy those urges we sometimes get for a garlicky Caesar salad. The hot peppers are a spicy surprise. Instead of croutons, serve with warm focaccia spread with pesto.

Preparation time: 15 minutes / Makes: 6 servings

DRESSING
½ cup good-quality olive oil
2 tbsp freshly squeezed lemon juice
2 large crushed garlic cloves
1 tsp dried tarragon
1 tsp anchovy paste

$\frac{1}{2}$ tsp Worcestershire sauce
$\frac{1}{2}$ tsp freshly ground black pepper
$\frac{1}{4}$ tsp each of granulated sugar, dry mustard and salt
$\frac{1}{4}$ cup freshly grated Parmesan cheese

SALAD

3 cups cubed cooked chicken or 4 chicken breasts
$\frac{1}{4}$ lb (125 g) fresh mushrooms
1 large sweet red pepper
1 hot banana pepper (optional)
2 small heads romaine lettuce

1. Both the dressing and the salad can be prepared a day before serving, if you wish. Prepare the dressing by combining all dressing ingredients, including the Parmesan cheese, in a bowl. Whisk until well blended. For best flavor, prepare the dressing at least several hours before using. Refrigerate if making a day ahead.

2. If cooking the chicken, roast the breasts, uncovered, in a preheated 375F oven for 45 to 50 minutes or until the chicken feels springy. Or place the chicken breasts with thin ends toward centre in a microwave-safe pie plate. Cover with clear wrap and microwave on high for 13 to 15 minutes. Rearrange and turn halfway through cooking. Let stand, covered, for 3 minutes.

3. Cut the cooked chicken into small $\frac{1}{2}$-inch pieces. (It should measure about $2\frac{1}{2}$ cups.) Set aside. Thinly slice the mushrooms. Seed the sweet red pepper and cut it into thin julienne strips about $1\frac{1}{2}$ inches long. Seed the hot pepper, if using, and finely chop. If making the salad ahead, combine the chicken and vegetables in a large bowl. Cover and refrigerate until ready to use.

4. When ready to serve, tear the lettuce into bite-size pieces and place it in a large salad bowl. Add the chicken and vegetables. Whisk the dressing. Drizzle $\frac{1}{2}$ cup dressing over top and toss until evenly coated. Add remaining dressing, if necessary. Toss until evenly coated.

PER SERVING: *351 calories, 26.1 g protein, 5.3 g carbohydrates, 25.2 g fat, 94.1 mg calcium, 2.5 mg iron, 2.1 g fiber.*

GLAMOUR OILS

Premium or flavored oils can take your everyday cooking into new taste territories.

Extra Virgin Olive Oil
This thick, gold extract from the first cold pressing of olives is costly, but devotees swear by it.
• Add a squirt of vinegar (about 2 tablespoons balsamic) to $\frac{1}{2}$ cup oil and toss with strong-flavored greens, such as endive.
• Toss with hot pasta and finely chopped herbs.

Hazelnut Oil
• Drizzle over hot green beans and toss.
• Mix with an equal amount of butter to sauté chicken.

Walnut Oil
• Mix with lemon juice ($\frac{1}{4}$ cup oil to 1 teaspoon juice) for Waldorf salad dressing.
• Toss with pasta, sliced turkey and a sprinkling of dried leaf thyme and dried sage.

OUTSTANDING GREEK SALAD

Crispy pita croutons, briny black olives, fresh mint and tomatoes marinated for extra flavor make this the absolute best Greek salad we have ever tasted — worth the extra effort.

Preparation time: 15 minutes / Marinating time: 1 hour
Broiling time: 3 minutes / Makes: 6 servings

MARINATED TOMATOES
1/4 cup olive oil
2 tbsp red wine vinegar
1 crushed garlic clove
1/2 tsp granulated or brown sugar
1 tsp dried leaf oregano
4 large ripe tomatoes

DRESSING
1 garlic clove, coarsely chopped
1 tbsp red wine vinegar
1/4 tsp salt
1/4 tsp freshly ground black pepper
Pinch of cayenne pepper
1/4 cup olive oil
2 chopped anchovy fillets or 1 tsp anchovy paste

PITA CROUTONS
2 pitas
3 tbsp melted butter
2 tbsp finely chopped parsley

SALAD
6 cups bite-size pieces mixed salad greens, such as leaf lettuce, romaine and escarole
2 whole green onions, thinly sliced
1 small red onion, thinly sliced
1/3 cup small Mediterranean-style black olives
1/4 cup fresh mint leaves (optional)
1 green pepper
1 cup crumbled feta cheese

1. To marinate the tomatoes, measure the oil, vinegar, garlic, sugar and oregano into a medium-size bowl. Whisk until blended.

2. Cut the tomatoes into halves or quarters, depending on their size. Squeeze out all the seeds and juice. Chop the tomatoes into bite-size pieces. Whisk the oil mixture. Stir in the tomatoes and let the mixture sit at room temperature for at least 1 hour, or preferably several hours, to allow the tomatoes to soak up the marinade flavors.

3. To make the dressing, place the garlic, vinegar, salt, black pepper and cayenne in a blender or food processor fitted with a metal blade. Whirl until blended.

4. Continuing to whirl, gradually add the oil, drop by drop at first, then in a thin steady stream. The dressing will thicken. Continuing to whirl, add the anchovies or anchovy paste. Taste and add more salt, if needed. The dressing can be used right away or covered and left at room temperature. If making the dressing more than 1 day ahead, cover and refrigerate.

5. To make the pita croutons, preheat broiler. Cut each pita into 12 triangles. Place the pita triangles on a baking sheet.

6. Stir the melted butter and parsley together in a small bowl. Brush the triangles with the melted butter mixture. Place the baking sheet with the triangles under the broiler for about 2 to 3 minutes or until golden. Cool before tossing with the salad.

7. Prepare the salad by combining the salad greens, onions, olives and mint, if using, in a large bowl. Core and seed the pepper, then cut it into julienne strips. Add to the salad.

8. Add the entire marinated tomato mixture to the salad. Sprinkle the feta cheese over top. Toss until the marinade is evenly mixed with the greens.

9. Drizzle the dressing over the salad. Add the toasted pita croutons and toss lightly.

PER SERVING: 334 calories, 6.1 g protein, 14.3 g carbohydrates, 29.6 g fat, 156 mg calcium, 1.8 mg iron, 2.2 g fiber.

LETTUCE REVIVAL
Crisp up tired, wilted lettuce by plunging it into a sink filled with cold water. Spin dry. Refrigerate in an airtight plastic bag.

ROMAINE

EASYGOING SALADS • TRIPLE TESTED

SIDE SALAD STANDOUTS

We feel no meal is complete without a refreshing bit of salad, either as a palate-teasing intro, a compatible sidekick or an after-the-main-course digestive. Pear and Gorgonzola, Moroccan Party, Barbecued Vegetable with chèvre, Hot 'n' Fiery Slaw — here's a special little star for every occasion.

PEAR AND GORGONZOLA FANFARE

A more luxurious marriage of fruit and cheese you will not find — creamy Gorgonzola and ripe pears on a bed of romaine lettuce.

Preparation time: 15 minutes / Makes: 6 servings

¼ cup olive oil
1 tbsp red wine vinegar
Freshly ground black pepper
½ cup crumbled Gorgonzola cheese
1 head romaine lettuce
2 to 3 ripe pears

1. To prepare the dressing, pour the oil and vinegar into a medium-size bowl. Add a generous grinding of black pepper.

2. Crumble enough cheese to measure ¼ cup. Add the cheese to the oil-and-vinegar mixture. Use a fork to mash the cheese against the side of the bowl. Then, whisk the ingredients together. If making ahead, cover and refrigerate until ready to serve. The dressing will keep well for 1 to 2 days.

3. Before serving, wash and dry the lettuce. Break it into bite-size pieces and place it in a large salad bowl. Chop one pear and add it to the lettuce. Drizzle with the dressing and toss until the lettuce is evenly coated. Arrange the salad on individual plates. Thinly slice remaining pears and place several slices in a fan pattern on top of each plate of salad. Crumble remaining cheese over top.

PER SERVING: *176 calories, 3.4 g protein, 2.4 g carbohydrates, 11.9 g fat, 80.5 mg calcium, 1 mg iron, 1.4 g fiber.*

PEARS

THE GREAT CAESAR

Nothing beats a classic Caesar salad, but for a fresh twist consider using pita, multigrain or cheese bread for croutons. Finish with Asiago or Stilton instead of Parmesan. Terrific with grilled steaks.

Preparation time: 20 minutes / Baking time: 15 minutes
Cooking time: 10 minutes / Makes: 4 servings

CROUTONS
$\frac{1}{2}$ loaf thin French bread
Melted butter
1 garlic clove

DRESSING
$\frac{1}{2}$ cup vegetable oil
2 tbsp freshly squeezed lemon juice
2 crushed garlic cloves
$1\frac{1}{2}$ tsp Dijon mustard
1 to $1\frac{1}{2}$ tsp anchovy paste or 6 anchovy fillets, finely chopped
$\frac{1}{4}$ tsp granulated sugar
$\frac{1}{8}$ tsp cayenne pepper

SALAD
6 slices bacon, cooked
1 head romaine lettuce
1 egg (optional)
$\frac{1}{2}$ cup freshly grated Parmesan cheese
$\frac{1}{4}$ cup crumbled blue cheese (optional)

1. To make the croutons, preheat oven to 350F. Slice the bread into $\frac{1}{2}$-inch slices. Brush both sides with melted butter. Spread the slices out on a baking sheet. Bake for 7 minutes, then turn and bake for another 7 minutes or until the bread is golden. Remove from the oven. Cut the garlic clove in half. Immediately rub the slices of bread with the garlic. While still warm, cut the toast into croutons.

2. Prepare the dressing by measuring the oil, lemon juice, garlic, Dijon, anchovy paste, sugar and cayenne pepper into a bowl. Whisk together. If not using right away, cover and refrigerate. The dressing keeps well for a couple of days in the refrigerator.

3. To prepare the salad, crumble bacon. Tear lettuce into bite-size pieces. Whisk dressing ingredients with egg, if using. Drizzle over the lettuce in a large salad bowl. Toss until the lettuce is coated. Sprinkle with Parmesan, blue cheese and bacon. Toss and sprinkle with croutons.

PER SERVING: *619 calories, 19.5 g protein, 34.2 g carbohydrates, 45.6 g fat, 255 mg calcium, 3.8 mg iron, 3.5 g fiber.*

BACON BIT BONANZA
Too much bacon for breakfast? Put it back in the frying pan and cook until crisp. Drain and pat dry on paper towels. Crumble into small pieces. Refrigerate or freeze. Use over salads, green beans, spinach, baked potatoes or jambalaya.

Hot 'n' Fiery Slaw

Bursting with flavor, this coleslaw is a snazzy partner for any grilled meat and a good companion to other salads on a buffet spread.

Preparation time: 15 minutes / Makes: 10 servings (about 8 cups)

1 cup mayonnaise
½ cup sour cream
2 crushed garlic cloves
2 tsp ground cumin
½ tsp ground coriander (optional)
½ tsp chili powder
½ tsp dried crushed chilies
¼ tsp cayenne pepper
½ tsp salt
1 small head green cabbage
3 red peppers
3 whole green onions, thinly sliced

1. In a large bowl, whisk together the mayonnaise, sour cream, garlic and seasonings, crushing the dried chilies well before adding. Thinly slice the cabbage. Thinly slice the red peppers and cut into bite-size pieces. Stir the cabbage, peppers and onions into the dressing. Serve right away or cover and refrigerate.

PER SERVING: *205 calories, 1.7 g protein, 5.8 g carbohydrates, 20.4 g fat, 51 mg calcium, 1.2 mg iron, 1.4 g fiber.*

SALADS THAT SAVE CENTS

In winter, bypass costly romaine and leaf lettuce for iceberg lettuce and cabbage, then shred them into chunky coleslaws. Instead of pricey red pepper, use julienned canned beets, a few shreds of red cabbage or radish for color.

Harvest Coleslaw with Apples and Pears

When food consultant Heather Trim worked with us, she created this beautiful autumn slaw. The crunch of the cabbage and the aromatic ripe pears give it a satisfying harvest flavor.

Preparation time: 20 minutes / Makes: 8 servings

DRESSING
¼ cup vegetable oil
2 tbsp cider vinegar
1 crushed garlic clove
1 tsp brown sugar
¼ tsp each of dry mustard and celery seed
Salt and freshly ground black pepper

SALAD

½ white cabbage
1 green-skinned apple, unpeeled
1 red-skinned apple, unpeeled
1 ripe pear
1 tsp lemon juice (optional)
1 red pepper
2 carrots, shredded
2 whole green onions, thinly sliced

1. In a small bowl, whisk the dressing ingredients together. Taste and add more salt or freshly ground pepper, if needed. Covered and refrigerated, the dressing will keep well for several weeks.

2. Core and shred the cabbage and set aside in a large bowl. Core the apples and pear and cut them into ½-inch pieces. If making the salad ahead, sprinkle the apples and pear with about 1 teaspoon lemon juice and toss to prevent the fruit from turning brown. Core and seed the red pepper and cut it into julienne strips. Add the apples, pear, red pepper, carrots and green onions to the cabbage and toss.

3. Pour the dressing over the salad and toss again, making sure all the ingredients are evenly coated with the dressing. The salad can be served immediately or refrigerated, covered, for 3 to 4 hours before serving. If refrigerated, bring to room temperature before serving. Then, taste and adjust seasonings, if necessary.

PER SERVING: *118 calories, 1.1 g protein, 14.5 g carbohydrates, 7.2 g fat, 39.3 mg calcium, 0.7 mg iron, 3 g fiber.*

BEYOND ICEBERG LETTUCE

All greens were not created equal, so don't limit your choices. Mix them up for interesting effect.

• Loose-leafed romaine is crisp and mildly sharp in flavor.

• Coarsely textured spinach imparts a slightly musky taste.

• Boston or Bibb is delicate and mildly sweet.

• Red-tipped leaf lettuce is sweet and frilly.

• For sharper accents, consider curly or broad-leafed endive, arugula, dandelion greens, watercress and radicchio.

TERRIFIC TOMATO TOSSES

At the peak of tomato season try these cool new tosses.

Tomato Tuna Niçoise
Slice 2 tomatoes into small wedges. Toss with a 6½-oz (184-g) can of tuna, ¼ cup sliced stuffed olives, 2 chopped whole green onions, 2 tablespoons lemon juice, 2 tablespoons sour cream, salt and pepper. Serves 2.

Tomato Salsa
Toss 3 large seeded, chopped tomatoes with a 4-oz (114-mL) can diced green chilies, 1 tablespoon freshly squeezed lime juice, salt and pepper. Serve with burgers or chops. Makes 1½ cups.

Curried Chick-Pea
Stir 3 seeded, chopped ripe tomatoes with a 19-oz (540-mL) can of drained chick-peas, 1 tablespoon olive oil, 1 teaspoon curry powder and 2 chopped whole green onions. Serves 4.

Caesar Pasta
Toss 4 seeded, chopped tomatoes with 2 cups cooked pasta shells, ½ cup bottled Caesar salad dressing, 1 teaspoon dried basil and ¼ cup grated Parmesan cheese. Serves 4.

Roast Beef Salad
Slice 8 oz (250 g) cooked roast beef into bite-size strips. Toss with 3 chopped tomatoes, ⅓ cup bottled Italian salad dressing and 2 chopped whole green onions. Serves 2 to 3.

BEET AND APPLE AUTUMN SALAD

A robust, colorful salad to enjoy when the nip of fall is in the air. Particularly good with roast pork either as a side dish or a separate mini course.

Preparation time: 10 minutes / Makes: 4 servings

DRESSING
¼ cup olive oil
2 tbsp freshly squeezed lemon juice
1 tbsp chopped fresh dill
1 tsp Dijon mustard
¼ tsp salt
Freshly ground black pepper

SALAD
1 small head romaine lettuce
1 green-skinned apple
½ lb (250 g) cooked beets or 14-oz (398-mL) can beets, drained

1. Whisk the dressing ingredients together. Tear the lettuce into bite-size pieces and place it in a large shallow bowl. Toss with half the dressing. Dice the apple. Toss with half the remaining dressing. Scatter over the lettuce. Peel the beets and dice them. Toss with the remaining dressing and place in the centre of the salad.

PER SERVING: 176 calories, 2.2 g protein, 12.4 g carbohydrates, 13.9 g fat, 45.7 mg calcium, 1.6 mg iron, 3.5 g fiber.

ZESTY LEMON

For a refreshing zip, substitute lemon juice for part or all of the vinegar called for in homemade salad dressings or marinades. Give bottled dressing extra zing by adding about 2 tablespoons lemon juice to 1 cup dressing.

OLIVE OIL

DIJON MUSTARD

DOUBLE TOMATO AND BOCCONCINI SALAD

This dressed-up version of the classic sliced tomato and bocconcini salad calls for marinating the cheese with chilies, shallots and fresh basil. Thin slivers of intensely flavored sun-dried tomatoes provide double-tomato impact. Serve it as a first course or a side dish with fish or beef.

Preparation time: 10 minutes / Marinating time: overnight

Makes: 4 to 8 servings

½ lb (250 g) cheese, such as bocconcini or unsliced mozzarella
½ cup olive or vegetable oil
½ tsp dried chilies
¼ cup coarsely chopped fresh basil or 1 tsp dried basil
2 finely chopped shallots or 1 large crushed garlic clove
½ tsp coarsely ground black pepper
4 ripe tomatoes
2 sun-dried tomatoes, packed in oil, thinly slivered (optional)
1 bunch spinach or watercress (optional)

1. If using bocconcini, simply slice it in half or in ¼-inch-thick slices. If using mozzarella, cut it into slices at least ¼ inch thick, then into pieces or wedges about the size of the tomatoes.

2. In a small bowl, whisk the oil with the chilies, basil, shallots and pepper.

3. Place the cheese in a heavy plastic bag. Whisk the dressing again and pour it over the cheese. Seal the bag.

4. Refrigerate overnight or for several days if you wish. Shake the cheese in the bag several times during marinating to ensure it is evenly coated.

5. When ready to serve, slice the tomatoes. Overlap the cheese slices in the centre of a large tray. Surround the cheese with a circle of slightly overlapped tomato slices and scatter the sun-dried tomatoes, if using, over top. Or overlap the tomato slices, then julienne the cheese and scatter it over top along with the sun-dried tomatoes. Then, add a border of spinach leaves or watercress, if you wish, tucking the ends under the tomatoes.

PER SERVING: *213 calories, 8.1 g protein, 4.1 g carbohydrates, 18.7 g fat, 207 mg calcium, 0.4 mg iron, 0.8 g fiber.*

SMART TOMATO STORING AND SLICING

• Never ripen tomatoes on a windowsill. The direct sunlight will cause them to ripen unevenly. Instead, put underripe tomatoes in a brown paper bag with an apple or pear. The fruit gives off natural ethylene gas that speeds up the ripening process.

• Store ripe tomatoes at room temperature. If it's extremely hot, the butter compartment of the refrigerator is ideal.

• Most people slice tomatoes horizontally, but if sliced vertically — from stem end to bottom — they'll retain more juice.

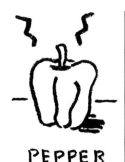

PEPPER

ROASTING PEPPERS

Roasted peppers take on a slightly smoky, sweet flavor. Char over a gas flame, on the barbecue or in the oven until the skins blister and scorch. Then, to make them easier to peel, place the peppers in a paper or plastic bag and seal. After 10 minutes, peel, then store in olive oil in the refrigerator. They're wonderful in salads, great with grilled steak or atop a grilled cheese sandwich.

MOROCCAN PARTY SALAD

A fragrant mix of Moroccan spices makes this one of our favorite party salads. Not only is it best made ahead so the flavors have a chance to mingle, but it's such a complete mix of veggies you need cook no more at the last minute to round out the meal.

Preparation time: 30 minutes / Refrigeration time: 1 to 2 days
Cooking time: 5 minutes / Baking time: 20 minutes
Makes: 6 servings

5 small carrots or 3 cups baby carrots
$\frac{1}{2}$ cup vegetable oil
$\frac{1}{4}$ cup white vinegar
2 tbsp each of paprika and chopped parsley
1 tbsp ground coriander
1 tsp each of ground cumin and chili powder
2 crushed garlic cloves
4 medium green sweet peppers
3 tbsp vegetable oil
1 tbsp white vinegar
1 tsp ground cumin
$\frac{1}{4}$ tsp salt
3 tomatoes, chopped
1 small onion, finely chopped
Lettuce leaves

1. Slice small carrots into $\frac{1}{3}$-inch-thick rounds. Leave baby carrots whole. Cook in boiling water, about 3 minutes for sliced carrots or 5 minutes for baby carrots. Do not overcook. Drain and rinse with cold water. Blend together $\frac{1}{2}$ cup vegetable oil, $\frac{1}{4}$ cup white vinegar, paprika, parsley, coriander, 1 teaspoon cumin, chili powder and garlic. Stir in drained carrots. Cover and refrigerate for 1 to 2 days.

2. At least an hour before serving preheat oven to 375F. Place the whole peppers on a baking sheet. Bake in the preheated oven for 20 minutes or until the skin is scorched and blistered, turning at least once. Remove peppers to a bag and seal for 10 minutes. Then, peel off the scorched and blistered skin. Cut the peppers into bite-size pieces.

3. Blend 3 tablespoons oil, 1 tablespoon vinegar, 1 teaspoon cumin and salt together. Toss with the peppers, tomatoes and onion. Then, drain the carrots, discarding the marinade, and add them to the oil mixture. Leave the vegetables in this mixture until ready to serve. Kept refrigerated, the salad will last for 2 to 3 days. Drain and serve on lettuce leaves.

PER SERVING: *228 calories, 2.3 g protein, 15.4 g carbohydrates, 19.3 g fat, 52.9 mg calcium, 2.3 mg iron, 1.9 g fiber.*

WARM BARBECUED VEGETABLE SALAD

Grill veggies over hot coals to give them an appealing smoky taste, then toss with a balsamic vinaigrette. This is the only side dish you need at a backyard barbecue.

Preparation time: 20 minutes / Barbecuing time: 12 minutes

Makes: 6 servings

SALAD
1 large head lettuce, preferably romaine or curly endive
1 zucchini
2 sweet peppers, preferably 1 red and 1 yellow
1 red onion
Olive or vegetable oil

DRESSING
3 tbsp balsamic or red wine vinegar
1 tsp dried tarragon
2 small crushed garlic cloves
3 tbsp olive or vegetable oil
Pinch of salt
Generous grinding of black pepper
$\frac{1}{4}$ cup creamy goat cheese or feta (optional)

1. Preheat barbecue to medium and grease the grill. Tear the lettuce into bite-size pieces and set aside. To make the vegetables easy to handle on the grill, slice the zucchini lengthwise into $\frac{1}{4}$-inch-thick slices. Seed and core the sweet peppers and cut them into quarters. Peel the onion and cut it into quarters, leaving the base intact in each quarter.

2. Brush the zucchini, peppers and onion with olive oil. Place them on the grill about 2 to 3 inches from the hot coals. Barbecue for 8 to 12 minutes, turning frequently. As soon as each vegetable is tender-crisp remove from the grill. The onion will take the longest.

3. Meanwhile, prepare the dressing, whisking the vinegar, tarragon and garlic together in a large salad bowl. Gradually whisk in the oil. Add salt and pepper to taste. The dressing will be quite vinegary.

4. Once the vegetables are cooked, immediately slice them into bite-size pieces and toss with the dressing. Crumble the goat cheese over top, if using, and stir until partially melted. Then, add the lettuce and toss. Serve while still warm. Or, if unable to serve right away, leave the warm vegetables tossed with the dressing at room temperature. Just before serving, add the lettuce and toss.

PER SERVING: 112 calories, 2.3 g protein, 6.7 g carbohydrates, 9.3 g fat, 46.6 mg calcium, 1.4 mg iron, 2.6 g fiber.

EXOTIC CUMIN

• Many classic Middle Eastern, Moroccan and Indian dishes get their distinctive taste from this aromatic nutty-tasting spice.

• Cumin seeds, shaped like caraway seeds, are actually the dried fruit from a plant of the parsley family. They come in three colors — amber, white and black (which has a very pungent peppery taste).

• Cumin seeds will keep well for at least a year but ground cumin goes rancid quickly so smell before using.

OLIVE OIL

THE BEST POTATO SALAD

A no-fuss favorite with variations to suit any style of menu.

Preparation time: 15 minutes / Cooking time: 20 minutes

Makes: 8 servings

10 medium-size potatoes
1 cup vegetable oil
3 to 4 tbsp red wine vinegar
1 tbsp Dijon mustard
2 crushed garlic cloves
$\frac{1}{2}$ tsp each of dried basil, dried leaf oregano and salt
1 red onion, finely chopped
2 cups thinly sliced celery

1. Cook the unpeeled potatoes in boiling salted water just until tender, about 15 to 20 minutes. Meanwhile, in a large bowl, whisk the oil with the vinegar, Dijon, garlic and seasonings. Drain the potatoes when they are done. When just cool enough to handle, peel, if you like, and cut into $\frac{1}{2}$-inch cubes. As soon as each potato is cut, stir it into the dressing while still hot. Stir in the onion and celery. Serve warm. Or refrigerate, preferably overnight, before serving.

VARIATIONS

Creamy Dill
Use 1 cup mayonnaise in place of the oil, and 3 tablespoons lemon juice instead of vinegar. Omit the oregano. Stir in $\frac{1}{2}$ cup finely chopped fresh dill. Serve with barbecued chicken or fish.

Horseradish
Add 3 tablespoons horseradish to the dressing. Use 4 chopped whole green onions in place of the red onion. Serve with cold roast beef or brisket.

Zesty Italian
Use 1 cup olive oil in place of the vegetable oil. Increase the dried basil to 1 teaspoon or add $\frac{1}{4}$ cup chopped fresh basil. Stir in 1 chopped red pepper and $\frac{1}{2}$ cup finely chopped pepperoni. Serve with burgers or steak.

PER SERVING: 440 calories, 4.4 g protein, 46.5 g carbohydrates, 27.6 g fat, 27.9 mg calcium, 1 mg iron, 4 g fiber.

P O T A T O E S

MEAN BEAN TOSS

A three-bean bonanza — high fiber, no cooking, bold fiery flavor.

Preparation time: 10 minutes / Cooking time: 1 minute
Refrigeration time: 3 hours / Makes: 6 servings

DRESSING
½ cup vegetable oil
2 tbsp red wine vinegar
1 tbsp granulated sugar
2 crushed garlic cloves
¼ tsp each of Worcestershire and Tabasco sauce
1 tsp dried leaf oregano
¼ tsp dry mustard
Salt and freshly ground black pepper

SALAD
12-oz (350-g) pkg frozen or 19-oz (540-mL) can lima beans, drained
19-oz (540-mL) can chick-peas, drained
19-oz (540-mL) can red kidney beans, drained

1. Combine the dressing ingredients in a large bowl. Whisk together until blended.

2. Turn the frozen lima beans into a large pot of boiling water. Boil for 1 minute or until thawed. Then, plunge them into cold water to stop the cooking. Drain well and add to the dressing along with the chick-peas and kidney beans. Toss together until coated. Cover and refrigerate at least 3 hours, or preferably overnight. Serve on a bed of shredded lettuce.

PER SERVING: *367 calories, 13.1 g protein, 39.9 g carbohydrates, 19.9 g fat, 67.5 mg calcium, 3.7 mg iron, 11.2 g fiber.*

BEAUTIFUL BULGUR
Bulgur or cracked wheat consists of tiny tan-colored, irregularly shaped wheat nuggets that are precooked and cracked. They have a robust roasted wheat flavor. A half cup of cooked bulgur has 5.8 grams of protein, 4.9 grams of fiber and 180 calories.

TERRIFIC TABBOULEH WITH MINT

A refreshing way to add wholesome grains to your summer diet. For a party presentation, serve in scooped-out tomato halves.

Preparation time: 20 minutes / Standing time: 30 minutes
Makes: 4 to 6 servings

SALAD
1 cup bulgur (cracked wheat)
4 tomatoes, chopped
3 whole green onions, sliced
¼ cup chopped parsley

DRESSING

½ cup olive oil
3 tbsp freshly squeezed lemon juice
1 crushed garlic clove
1 tsp dried mint or 2 tbsp finely chopped fresh mint
¼ tsp salt
Freshly ground black pepper

1. Place the bulgur in a medium-size bowl and cover it with boiling water. Set aside for 30 minutes.

2. Meanwhile, combine the tomatoes, onions and parsley in a large bowl. Set aside. Combine the dressing ingredients in a small bowl and set aside. Then, drain the bulgur and wring out excess moisture, using a kitchen cloth. Add the bulgur to the tomato mixture. Whisk the dressing ingredients together and drizzle over top. Fold together until the salad is evenly coated with dressing. Taste and add more mint, if you like. Refrigerate, covered, if not serving right away.

PER SERVING: 293 calories, 4.2 g protein, 25.5 g carbohydrates, 20.9 g fat, 23.7 mg calcium, 1.7 mg iron, 7.4 g fiber.

GARLIC

MINT

LEMON

HEALTHY SALAD DRESSINGS

Some salad dressings are almost pure fat. Drizzling a ¼ cup of basic vinaigrette, for example, over a few greens can add 400 fat calories and little else to a seemingly innocent side salad. But there are lots of ways to whisk more nutritious ingredients into a healthier dressing, starting with calcium-rich buttermilk or protein-high cheese.

Buttermilk-Tarragon
Stir ¼ cup each of buttermilk and light sour cream with ¼ teaspoon dried or 1 teaspoon chopped fresh tarragon. Great with chicken salads. Makes ½ cup.

Fast Herbed Chèvre
Mash 3 tablespoons creamy goat cheese with 3 tablespoons yogurt. Stir in 1 tablespoon chopped fresh basil or ¼ teaspoon dried basil. Drizzle over romaine lettuce. Makes ⅓ cup.

Light Blue
Mash 2 tablespoons blue or Gorgonzola cheese with ⅓ cup light sour cream, 1 tablespoon lemon juice and a generous pinch of black pepper. Great with greens and chopped chives. Makes ½ cup.

Coleslaw Dressing
Stir together ½ cup plain yogurt, 1 tablespoon white vinegar, ½ teaspoon celery seed, ½ teaspoon regular prepared mustard and a generous pinch of granulated sugar. Makes ½ cup.

Potato Salad Dressing
Stir together ½ cup light sour cream, 1 tablespoon grated onion, 1 tablespoon cider vinegar and ¼ teaspoon crushed black pepper. Makes ½ cup.

Yogurt Poppy Seed
Stir finely grated peel of 1 orange into ½ cup plain yogurt, with ½ teaspoon honey and 1 teaspoon poppy seeds. Terrific tossed with fruit and greens. Makes ½ cup.

QUICK CLASSIC MAYO

There isn't a commercial variety of mayonnaise on the market that compares to the taste of homemade.

Preparation time: 5 minutes / Makes: 1¼ cups

1 egg yolk, at room temperature
1 tbsp white vinegar
1 tsp Dijon mustard
¼ tsp salt
½ tsp freshly ground black pepper
1 cup vegetable oil

By Hand

1. In a medium-size bowl, whisk the egg yolk, vinegar, Dijon, salt and pepper together.

2. Whisk in the oil, drop by drop at first, until the mixture begins to thicken. Then, whisk in the oil 1 teaspoon at a time, making sure the oil is completely absorbed before the next addition. Taste and add more salt and pepper, if you wish. Mayonnaise may be used right away. Or, if you prefer, cover and refrigerate for 2 to 3 days.

In a Blender or Food Processor

1. Place all the ingredients (except the oil) in a blender or food processor fitted with a metal blade. Whirl until well blended.

2. With the motor running, add the oil, drop by drop at first, until the mixture begins to thicken. Then, add the oil in a slow thin steady stream until the oil is absorbed. Taste and add salt and pepper, if needed. Use right away or cover and refrigerate 2 to 3 days.

PER TABLESPOON: *99 calories, 0.2 g protein, 0.1 g carbohydrates, 11.2 g fat, 1.6 mg calcium, 0.05 mg iron, 0.01 g fiber.*

Mayo Clinic

Making homemade mayonnaise is easy if you keep these points in mind: Start with room-temperature ingredients. Whisk the oil in drop by drop at first, then in a slow steady stream until the emulsion occurs.

If the mayonnaise curdles, don't panic. Just whisk another egg yolk in a clean bowl, then whisk the yolk into the curdled mayonnaise, drop by drop, then in a slow steady stream until combined.

In a pinch, you can give commercial mayonnaise homemade flavor by adding some fresh lemon juice.

Mayo Makeovers

Jazz up 1¼ cups of homemade or store-bought mayonnaise with the following stir-ins.

Zesty Chutney
Stir in 2 tablespoons mango chutney and the finely grated peel of 1 orange. Great on turkey sandwiches.

Chili
Stir in 2 tablespoons chili sauce, ¼ teaspoon Tabasco sauce and a pinch of cayenne pepper. Smear on burgers.

Provençale
Stir in 1 tablespoon finely chopped parsley, 1 teaspoon anchovy paste, 1 crushed garlic clove and a generous pinch of dried basil. Serve with steak or roast beef sandwiches.

Ginger-Onion
Stir in 2 tablespoons finely chopped preserved ginger and 1 finely chopped whole green onion. Spoon over grilled fish.

Lemon Tarragon
Stir in finely grated peel of ½ lemon and 1 teaspoon each of lemon juice and dried tarragon. Slather over chicken or fish.

Best-Ever Caesar Dressing

This dressing is requested so often, I keep a copy of the recipe taped to my office cupboard. Don't skip the anchovy paste — it's sold in tubes in most supermarkets. And use only good-quality, freshly grated Parmesan — not the ready-grated kind.

Preparation time: 5 minutes / Makes: 1 cup

GARLIC
PRESS

½ cup good-quality olive oil
2 tbsp freshly squeezed lemon juice
2 large crushed garlic cloves
1 tsp anchovy paste
½ tsp Worcestershire sauce
¼ tsp each of granulated sugar, dry mustard, salt and
   freshly ground black pepper
¼ cup freshly grated Parmesan cheese

1. Measure all the ingredients into a medium-size bowl and whisk together. Use right away or seal in a jar and refrigerate. The dressing will keep for at least a week in the refrigerator. Makes enough to toss with 2 small heads of romaine lettuce.

PER TABLESPOON: *69 calories, 0.9 g protein, 0.5 g carbohydrates, 7.2 g fat, 17.3 mg calcium, 0.08 mg iron, 0.01 g fiber.*

Short Notice Dressings

Here are fast dressings to match whatever type of salad you're in the mood for. If you want the taste of olive oil to star, use a good quality, otherwise a vegetable oil is fine.

Tarragon
Whisk ⅓ cup oil with 1 tablespoon tarragon vinegar, ¼ teaspoon Dijon mustard and a pinch of salt. Great over asparagus. Makes ½ cup.

Curried
Whisk ⅓ cup oil with 1 tablespoon lemon juice, 1 egg yolk, ¼ teaspoon curry powder and a pinch each of sugar and salt. Excellent over greens with hard-cooked eggs, chicken or seafood dishes. Makes ½ cup.

Greek
Whisk ¼ cup olive oil with 2 tablespoons red wine vinegar and a pinch each of dried leaf oregano and salt. Add crushed garlic and mashed feta cheese. Makes ⅓ cup.

Italian
Whisk ⅓ cup olive oil with 2 tablespoons red wine vinegar, 2 tablespoons freshly grated Parmesan cheese, 1 clove crushed garlic and a pinch each of granulated sugar, dried leaf oregano and salt. Makes ⅔ cup.

Fruit
Whisk 3 tablespoons oil with 1 tablespoon lime juice, 1½ teaspoons liquid honey and a pinch of salt. Add 1 teaspoon poppy seeds. Pour over fresh fruit on a bed of crisp lettuce. Makes ⅓ cup.

Dijon
Whisk ⅓ cup oil with 1 tablespoon vinegar, 1½ teaspoons Dijon mustard and a pinch of salt. Drizzle over smoked salmon, cold roast beef or chef's salad. Makes ½ cup.

Mexican
Whisk ⅓ cup oil with 1 tablespoon lemon juice, ¼ teaspoon ground cumin and big pinches each of chili powder and garlic salt. Great with avocado, tuna, chick-peas or tomatoes. Makes ½ cup.

MIGHTY VEGETABLES

Up until recently vegetables took a back seat. When we were growing up, the emphasis was always on meat. Vegetables were an afterthought, often overcooked to a flavorless mush. Then we experienced those nouvelle plates with not much more than a single snow pea artfully fanned. Now with our increased awareness of nutrition and the need to up the fiber and down the fat in our diets, veggies have become the natural stars. We adore them raw or lightly steamed with a twist of lemon, spritz of balsamic vinegar or a drizzle of olive oil. We're also dressing them up with fresh herbs and unusual cheeses. And those ever-so-basic root crops, the powerhouse squashes, rutabagas, parsnips and turnips, are enjoying a well-deserved renaissance. Microwaves and food processors allow us to cook and purée them effortlessly in minutes. We now appreciate our gifts from the garden not just for their nutritional pay-off, but for their unique fresh taste and texture.

SIMPLY SEASONAL

Canadians are fortunate in that each of the four seasons brings a different harvest of home-grown vegetables to our tables. Just when we've had our fill of late summer's vine-ripened beefsteak tomatoes and sweet corn-on-the-cob, autumn brings squash in the most incredible shapes and colors as well as leafy green and ruby red cabbages. When we're snug inside on snowy days, we savor the heartiness of earthy root vegetables — beets and carrots — with our more substantial winter suppers. For us, spring spells fresh asparagus. Come summer, roadside stands and farmers' market stalls overflow with a carnival of peppers and green beans. Our fast ways with vegetables are designed not to improve on nature, but to bring out the best seasonal taste.

ASPARAGUS PARMIGIANA

Simply sauté tender asparagus in butter then finish with a generous shaving of the finest Parmesan you can buy.

Preparation time: 5 minutes / Cooking time: 4 minutes

Makes: 4 to 6 servings

DIETER'S DREAM

A cup of cooked chopped asparagus spears has only 35 calories and it's extremely rich in vitamins A and C.

2 bunches asparagus, about 2 lbs (1 kg)
1 tbsp butter
Salt and freshly ground black pepper
2 to 3 tbsp coarsely grated fresh Parmesan cheese

1. Snap off and discard the woody ends from the asparagus. Slice each spear, diagonally, into 3 pieces. Melt the butter in a large frying pan set over medium heat. When bubbling, add the asparagus. Sprinkle with salt and pepper. Cook, stirring often, until tender-crisp, about 3 to 4 minutes. Turn onto a platter. Sprinkle with the Parmesan cheese. Serve hot or warm.

PER SERVING: 49 calories, 3.3 g protein, 4.2 g carbohydrates, 2.8 g fat, 43.2 mg calcium, 0.6 mg iron, 0.01 g fiber.

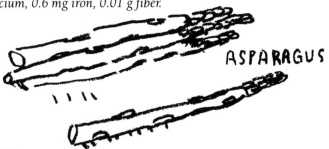
ASPARAGUS

PIQUANT GREEN BEANS

Green beans are refreshed with a balsamic vinegar glaze — a punchier, classier version of the old-fashioned cider-vinegar-and-brown-sugar treatment.

Preparation time: 5 minutes / Cooking time: 2 minutes

Makes: 4 servings

8 oz (250 g) green beans
1 cup water
2 tbsp red wine vinegar or balsamic vinegar
1 tbsp brown sugar
1 tbsp unsalted butter
Salt and freshly ground black pepper

1. Trim the beans. Bring 1 to 2 inches of water to a boil in a large frying pan. Add the beans. Boil, covered, for 2 minutes. Drain off the water. Add remaining ingredients and stir over medium heat for 1 to 2 minutes until glazed.

PER SERVING: *59 calories, 1.2 g protein, 8.7 g carbohydrates, 3 g fat, 32.7 mg calcium, 1 mg iron, 0.01 g fiber.*

ALL ABOUT BROCCOLI

Look for tight flowerets with a purple tinge, firm stalks and core. Broccoli should have a fresh but not a strong smell. Boil, uncovered, to avoid browning, for about 4 to 5 minutes for stalks and 3 to 4 minutes for flowerets. Microwave, covered, on high with 2 to 3 tablespoons of water. Place stalks near the outside of the dish as they take longer to cook.

QUICK WAYS WITH BROCCOLI

Broccoli is receiving accolades these days for its many health benefits. Here are some fast-fix ways to enjoy it.

Parmesan Toss
Cut 1 bunch broccoli into bite-size flowerets and cook until tender-crisp. Toss with 2 tablespoons freshly grated Parmesan cheese, 2 tablespoons toasted slivered almonds and freshly ground black pepper. Serves 4.

New Creamy Broccoli
Cut 1 bunch broccoli into small flowerets and cook until tender-crisp. Drain. Dab with 2 tablespoons creamy goat cheese and a generous pinch of freshly ground black pepper. Stir over low heat until the cheese is melted. Serves 4.

Warm Mustard Vinaigrette
Cut 1 bunch broccoli into bite-size flowerets. Cook until tender-crisp. Drain well and toss immediately with 2 tablespoons olive oil whisked with 1½ teaspoons Dijon mustard and 1 tablespoon red wine vinegar. Serves 4.

Balsamic Vinegar
Cut 1 bunch broccoli into bite-size pieces and cook until tender-crisp. Meanwhile, combine 1 tablespoon butter with 1 tablespoon balsamic vinegar and a pinch each of granulated sugar and salt. Heat until melted and toss with the hot drained broccoli. Serves 4.

Garlic Stir-Fry
Heat 2 cloves garlic in 1 tablespoon peanut oil. Add 1 bunch broccoli, cut into bite-size pieces, and ¼ cup water. Stir-fry over medium heat until tender-crisp, about 8 minutes. Serves 4.

Broccoli Soup
Purée 2 cups well-cooked broccoli flowerets with a 10-oz (284-mL) can of condensed chicken broth. Then, add ¼ cup yogurt or light sour cream. Makes 1½ cups.

Oriental Stir-Fry
Heat 2 teaspoons peanut oil with ½ teaspoon minced ginger. Add 1 bunch broccoli, cut into bite-size pieces, and ¼ cup water. Stir-fry for 6 minutes, until hot. Add 2 to 3 teaspoons teriyaki sauce and toss. Serves 4.

BLUSHING BEETS
Beets are a great buy.
The green tops are an
excellent source of
potassium and
calcium and have only
26 calories per cup.
Two cooked beets
contain 43 calories.

Buying
Choose smooth beets
with green leaves.

Storing
Cut off the greens,
leaving an inch of
stalk on the beet and
trim the roots, leaving
an inch of root on the
end. Store the greens
in a plastic bag in the
refrigerator. Use
within 2 days. Beets
will keep up to 3 to 4
weeks in the
refrigerator.

Sautéeing Greens
Wash and sauté in a
frying pan until
wilted. No extra water
is needed. Chop, then
add salt and pepper.

Boiling Beets
Place the beets in a
large pot of unsalted
water. Boil gently,
uncovered, for 30
minutes, until barely
tender. Drain, plunge
beets into cold water
and peel.

EASY HARVARD BEETS

When my grandmother made Harvard beets they tasted more like candy than a "must-eat" vegetable. Today sassy is undoubtedly a more appropriate description for our reduced-sugar version — but they're still just as satisfying, especially with Fancy Garlic Mashed Potatoes (see page 76) and roast beef or smoked pork.

Preparation time: 5 minutes / Cooking time: 7 minutes

Makes: 4 servings

¼ cup brown sugar
1 tbsp cornstarch
Generous pinches each of dry mustard, ground ginger and salt
2 tbsp white vinegar
14-oz (398-mL) can diced or sliced beets
Brown sugar and white vinegar (optional)

1. Measure the sugar, cornstarch and seasonings into a heavy-bottomed saucepan. Stir together until blended. Add the vinegar and the entire contents of the can of beets.

2. Stir over medium heat until the mixture starts to thicken, about 2 minutes. Then, continue to cook, stirring occasionally, about 5 minutes. Add more sugar and vinegar, if you wish.

PER SERVING: 79 calories, 0.6 g protein, 20.2 g carbohydrates, 0.1 g fat, 24.9 mg calcium, 1.7 mg iron, 1.2 g fiber.

CURRIED BEETS

What started off as an unpredictable combination of flavors turned out to be one of our favorite side-dish standbys, especially with stuffed pork tenderloin.

Preparation time: 30 minutes / Cooking time: 25 minutes

Makes: 4 to 6 servings

1½ lbs (750 g) beets, about 6 medium
1 onion
1 tbsp butter
½ tsp curry powder
¼ tsp ground cumin
Pinch each of cinnamon, salt and white pepper
1 tbsp red wine vinegar

1. Trim the tops of the beets but do not peel. Place the beets in a saucepan. Fill with cold water and cover. Set the pan over high heat and bring to a boil. Reduce heat and boil gently for about 15 to 25 minutes. The beets should be firm and slightly underdone.

2. Meanwhile, thinly slice the onion lengthwise. Melt the butter in a frying pan set over medium-low heat. Cook the onion, stirring often, until soft, about 3 minutes. Add the curry powder and cumin and continue cooking for 2 more minutes, until golden. Remove from the heat and set aside.

3. Drain the beets and rinse them under cold water. The skins should slip off easily without the use of a knife. Cube the beets.

4. Add the beets to the pan. Sprinkle with remaining seasonings and vinegar. Reheat over medium-low heat, stirring often, until well coated, about 2 minutes.

PER SERVING: 50 calories, 1.1 g protein, 7.3 g carbohydrates, 2 g fat, 16 mg calcium, 0.8 mg iron, 0.3 g fiber.

MAPLE-RUM CARROTS

What could be better than candied carrots? — this buttery maple-glazed version doused with rum.

Preparation time: 5 minutes / Cooking time: 10 minutes

Makes: 4 servings

2½ cups frozen carrots or thinly sliced fresh carrots
2 tbsp butter
2 tbsp maple syrup or brown sugar
1 tbsp rum
Salt and freshly ground black pepper

1. Cook the carrots in boiling salted water according to package directions or until just tender-crisp. Drain well. Measure the butter, syrup and rum into the saucepan and heat, stirring until the carrots are well coated and the glaze is bubbly. Add salt and pepper to taste.

VARIATION

Honey 'n' Lemon
In place of the mixture given above, add about 2 tablespoons each of lemon juice and honey to the saucepan.

PER SERVING: 121 calories, 1.2 g protein, 15.1 g carbohydrates, 5.8 g fat, 32.3 mg calcium, 0.9 mg iron, 0 g fiber.

PEEL ME AN ARTICHOKE

Buying
Look for plump, compact artichokes. Leaves will squeak when pressed.

Storing
Store, uncovered, in refrigerator crisper. Use within 3 days.

Trimming
Grasp artichoke by the stem. Swish in water to remove dirt between leaves. Cut off stem. Remove tough bottom leaves. Stretch apart centre leaves. Pull out hairy choke with a serrated spoon. Rub cut portions with half a lemon.

Steaming
Place artichokes on a rack in a pot with a couple of inches of boiling water. Cover and steam for 15 to 25 minutes until a middle leaf can easily be pulled out.

Microwaving
Place 2 artichokes in a dish with ¼ cup water. Microwave, covered, on high for 7 minutes. Let stand 3 minutes.

DIPPING SAUCE
Stir ⅓ cup melted butter with 2 tablespoons lemon juice and pinches of white pepper, tarragon and finely chopped chives.

GINGERED ORANGE CARROTS

The bite of ginger contrasts nicely with the sweetness of the carrots.

Preparation time: 10 minutes / Cooking time: 10 minutes

Makes: 8 servings

1½ lbs (750 g) carrots, peeled and sliced, about 5 cups
6 slices peeled fresh gingerroot, approximately 1 inch wide
    and ⅛ inch thick
¾ cup freshly squeezed orange juice
1½ tbsp butter
1½ tsp granulated sugar
Generous pinches each of salt and freshly ground black pepper

1. Place all the ingredients in a large wide frying pan. Bring to a boil. Cover, reduce heat, and simmer, uncovered, for 8 to 10 minutes or just until the carrots are tender-crisp. Shake the pan several times during the cooking. Remove the ginger and discard.

PER SERVING: *71 calories, 1.1 g protein, 12.3 g carbohydrates, 2.4 g fat, 30.3 mg calcium, 0.6 mg iron, 0.2 g fiber.*

LETTUCE-BUTTER SAUTÉ

Lettuce takes on a sophisticated character when sautéed, especially in this creamy French version. Be sure to remove the lettuce from the heat while it still has crunch. Perfect with barbecued swordfish steaks or veal chops.

Preparation time: 5 minutes / Cooking time: 3 minutes

Makes: 4 servings

1 head leaf lettuce
2 tbsp butter
½ small crushed garlic clove
2 tbsp sour cream or table cream
Freshly grated nutmeg

1. Separate lettuce leaves. Wash and dry. Cut into bite-size pieces. (Lettuce will measure about 8 cups.) Melt the butter in a wide saucepan over medium heat. Add the garlic and stir for a minute. Stir in lettuce just until evenly coated with butter. Add the sour cream and nutmeg and stir over medium heat until lettuce is warm but still crunchy.

PER SERVING: *68 calories, 1.3 g protein, 3.5 g carbohydrates, 6 g fat, 67.8 mg calcium, 1.4 mg iron, 1.3 g fiber.*

CABBAGE SAUTÉS

Come mid-winter, cabbage is undoubtedly one of the best-buy fresh vegetables available. Here are quick ways to sauté it.

Danish Cabbage
Sauté ½ head shredded cabbage in 2 tablespoons butter until tender-crisp. Stir in ½ cup sour cream, 1 tablespoon chopped fresh or ½ tsp dried dillweed, salt and pepper to taste.

Chinese Cabbage
Stir-fry ½ head shredded cabbage in 1 tablespoon oil for 5 minutes. Stir in 3 tablespoons soy sauce, 2 tablespoons sherry, 1 tablespoon granulated sugar, pinches garlic powder and ground ginger. Stir-fry until tender-crisp.

Curried Cabbage
Sauté 1 clove crushed garlic in 2 tablespoons butter. Stir in 2 teaspoons each of curry powder and granulated sugar, and ½ head shredded cabbage. Stir frequently over medium-high heat for 5 minutes.

Buttery Corn-on-the-Cob Topper

When you've had your fill of corn "au naturel," add an extra bit of zip with this peppery hot butter.

Preparation time: 5 minutes

Makes: 8 servings

3 tbsp snipped chives or sliced whole green onions
¼ tsp each of freshly ground black pepper, chili powder
   and white pepper
¼ tsp cayenne pepper (optional)
Salt (optional)
½ cup butter, at room temperature
8 cobs of corn, cooked

1. Prepare the butter by stirring the chives and seasonings into the butter. Add the cayenne pepper if you want fiery hot flavor and ¼ teaspoon salt if using unsalted butter. Use right away or cover and refrigerate for up to a week. Spread on hot corn-on-the-cob.

PER SERVING: 186 calories, 2.7 g protein, 19.5 g carbohydrates, 12.5 g fat, 7.2 mg calcium, 0.6 mg iron, 2.8 g fiber.

Corn Cookery

Remove the husks and cook in boiling water for 5 to 8 minutes. To microwave 4 ears, leave the husks intact and place the corn cobs in a microwave-safe dish in 1 layer. Cook, uncovered, on high for 10 to 12 minutes, turning once.

Quick Ways with Corn

For the following recipes, use a 12-oz (341-mL) can of drained kernel corn or 1½ cups frozen corn. Each recipe serves 4.

Skillet Ratatouille
In a large frying pan, sauté 2 crushed garlic cloves and 1 large chopped onion in 1 tablespoon olive oil. Add a 28-oz (796-mL) can of drained tomatoes, 2 sliced zucchini, corn and 1 teaspoon Italian seasoning. Simmer, covered, for 10 minutes. Stir often.

Balsamic Buttered Corn
Heat corn. Stir in 2 teaspoons each of butter and balsamic vinegar.

Fiery Chili
Heat corn with ¼ cup water and ¼ teaspoon crushed dried chilies until hot. Then, stir in ½ cup sour cream.

Vegetable Medley
Sauté 1 crushed garlic clove in 1 tablespoon butter. Add 2 coarsely chopped tomatoes, 1 sliced zucchini, corn and a pinch of dried basil. Heat.

Caesar Toss
Heat corn. Stir in 3 tablespoons creamy Caesar salad dressing and 2 sliced whole green onions. Serve with steak or burgers.

French Parsley
Melt 1 tablespoon butter over medium-low heat. Add 2 large crushed garlic cloves and ¼ cup finely chopped parsley. Stir frequently for 3 minutes. Add corn and stir until hot.

Fast Curry
Heat 1 teaspoon butter in a frying pan. Add corn, 1 teaspoon curry powder and ⅛ teaspoon cayenne pepper. Stir constantly until hot.

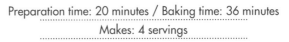

ORIENTAL MUSHROOM SAUTÉ

We've updated fried mushrooms with a light bath of soy sauce and gratings of fresh gingerroot. Fabulous with grilled steak, veal chops or chicken.

Preparation time: 10 minutes / Cooking time: 5 minutes

Makes: 4 servings

1 lb (500 g) fresh mushrooms
1 tbsp each of butter and vegetable oil
1 tbsp soy sauce
2 whole green onions, thinly sliced
2 tsp finely grated fresh gingerroot
Pinch of freshly ground black pepper

1. Clean the mushrooms and slice them. Set aside.

2. In a medium-size frying pan, heat the butter and oil over medium heat. Add mushrooms, soy sauce, green onions and gingerroot. Sauté for 3 to 5 minutes or until the mushrooms are tender. Season with pepper.

PER SERVING: 89 calories, 2.9 g protein, 6.4 g carbohydrates, 6.8 g fat, 8.9 mg calcium, 1.7 mg iron, 1.7 g fiber.

ROASTED MARINATED PEPPERS

Take a jar of roasted peppers to your next picnic or keep them in the refrigerator at the cottage. Simply roast the peppers to bring out their sweetness, then store in homemade vinaigrette or store-bought salad dressing. They instantly dress up sandwiches or salads and are wonderful on grilled steaks or burgers.

Preparation time: 20 minutes / Baking time: 36 minutes

Makes: 4 servings

2 red peppers
2 yellow or green peppers
½ cup homemade or bottled Italian salad dressing
2 whole green onions, thinly sliced

1. To roast the peppers, spread them in a single layer on a baking sheet with shallow sides. Pierce each pepper near the stem with a knife. Bake in a preheated 375F oven for 18 minutes. Turn and bake for an additional 18 minutes or until the peppers are blistered. Immediately place them in a plastic bag. Seal and set aside for 10 minutes to allow the skins to loosen.

TOP OF THE FIBER CROP

The Canadian Cancer Society recommends eating high-fiber foods to help prevent some forms of cancer. These vegetables are all good sources of fiber and here's how they stack up.

Vegetable (1 cup/ 250 mL, cooked)	Crude Fiber Content (g)
Corn	4.8
Winter squash	3.6
Green peas	3.4
Parsnips	3.3
Lima beans	3.2
Brussels sprouts	2.6
Broccoli	2.5
Cauliflower	2.2
Rutabaga	2.0

Source: Canadian Nutrient File, Food Advisory Division, Agriculture Canada

2. Then, peel off the skins and remove the seeds. Cut the peppers into bite-size strips. Place them in a container with a tight-fitting lid. Stir in the Italian salad dressing and green onions. Refrigerate until ready to use, up to 2 weeks.

PER SERVING: *158 calories, 0.7 g protein, 7.9 g carbohydrates, 14.3 g fat, 10.2 mg calcium, 0.4 mg iron, 1.3 g fiber.*

SUMPTUOUS SPINACH

Here's a fast route to a sin-free splurge of creamy spinach.

Preparation time: 2 minutes / Cooking time: 5 minutes

Makes: 4 servings

SPINACH

12-oz (375-g) pkg frozen chopped spinach
1 tsp butter
1 tbsp finely chopped shallots or ½ crushed garlic clove
¼ cup regular or light sour cream
1 tbsp freshly squeezed lemon juice
Generous pinch of salt

1. Place the spinach in boiling water and cook just until the spinach can be separated, about 3 minutes. Drain very well and squeeze out all the liquid.

2. Melt the butter in a large frying pan. Add the shallots and stir for 2 minutes. Stir in the spinach and remaining ingredients.

PER SERVING: *65 calories, 3.2 g protein, 5.9 g carbohydrates, 4.1 g fat, 143 mg calcium, 1.3 mg iron, 1.9 g fiber.*

SPEEDY WAYS WITH FRESH SPINACH

Always choose spinach that has crisp, bright green leaves and a light earthy aroma. If it smells like cabbage, it's old. Wash well, then trim the stems. Follow one of these quick and easy suggestions. All make about 4 servings.

Spinach and Cream
Place ¼ cup half-and-half cream, 4 cups spinach leaves and 1 teaspoon dried tarragon in a large frying pan. Stir over medium heat until piping hot. Add salt and pepper to taste.

Orange Salad
Peel and cut 2 oranges into bite-size pieces. Toss with 4 cups spinach, ¼ cup bottled blue cheese salad dressing and ½ teaspoon dried dillweed.

Fresh Bacon Salad
Cut 4 slices of bacon into 1-inch pieces. Cook in a large frying pan until crisp. Don't drain. Stir in 2 tablespoons lemon juice, 1 teaspoon granulated sugar and 1 teaspoon Worcestershire sauce. Toss with a 10-oz (284-g) package (7 cups) spinach leaves.

Quick Coleslaw
Stir 2 cups shredded cabbage with 2 cups shredded spinach, ¼ cup coleslaw dressing and ¼ teaspoon caraway seeds.

Sautéed French Spinach
Sauté 2 crushed garlic cloves in 2 tablespoons butter for 1 minute. Whisk in 2 teaspoons Dijon mustard. Add a 10-oz (284-g) package (7 cups) spinach leaves. Stir just until wilted, about 4 minutes.

HERBED SPAGHETTI SQUASH TOSS

As a side dish, we love this golden spaghetti squash tossed with butter and scented with thyme. For a vegetarian dinner, add lots of freshly grated Parmesan cheese.

Preparation time: 10 minutes

Baking time: 45 minutes or Microwave time: 15 minutes / Makes: 6 servings

1 spaghetti squash, about 3½ lbs (1.75 kg)
4 whole green onions, thinly sliced
2 to 4 tbsp butter
½ tsp dried leaf thyme or ¼ tsp ground nutmeg
¼ tsp each of salt and freshly ground black pepper

1. Preheat oven to 350F. Pierce the squash in several places and place it on a baking sheet. Bake in the centre of the preheated oven, turning halfway through, until tender when pierced with a fork, about 35 minutes. Or cook on high in the microwave for 15 minutes.

2. Slice in half lengthwise. Scoop out and discard the seeds. Using a fork, scrape the pulp into a bowl, separating the strands but being careful not to mash them. Gently toss with remaining ingredients.

PER SERVING: *119 calories, 2 g protein, 19.1 g carbohydrates, 4.6 g fat, 67.5 mg calcium, 1.1 mg iron, 4.2 g fiber.*

SPAGHETTI SQUASH — THE GREAT IMPOSTER

Spaghetti squash is an amazing vegetable. When baked it separates into moist strands that look like pale orange spaghetti, with enough texture to make it the ideal dieter's stand-in for pasta. Two heaping cups of spaghetti squash contain 92 calories compared to 318 for the same amount of pasta.

SATISFYING WAYS WITH SQUASH

Gingered
Thinly slice peeled squash and cut it into bite-size pieces. Sauté in butter with 1 crushed garlic clove and 3 thin slices of fresh gingerroot. Add salt and pepper to taste.

Fall Purée
Heat a 13-oz (400-g) package of frozen cooked puréed squash according to package directions. Stir in 1 teaspoon each of brown sugar and butter and generous pinches of ground ginger, cinnamon and cayenne pepper.

Tomato Medley
Cook 1 chopped onion in 2 tablespoons butter. Add 3 cups cubed squash, 2 chopped tomatoes, pinches of granulated sugar, salt and pepper. Cook, covered, 3 to 5 minutes, stirring often.

Herbed Sauté
Cook 3 slices of bacon until crisp. Remove from the pan. Add 3 cups cubed squash. Sprinkle with dried sage, dried leaf thyme, salt and pepper. Stir-fry for 2 minutes. Add ½ cup chicken bouillon. Simmer, uncovered, until tender. Drain and sprinkle with the bacon.

Maple Bake
Slice an acorn squash in half. Scoop out the seeds. Sprinkle with maple syrup. Dot with butter. Bake at 350F for 35 minutes. Sprinkle with chopped pecans during the last 5 minutes of baking.

Curried Bisque
Heat a 13-oz (400-g) package of frozen cooked puréed squash with 1 cup chicken bouillon, 1 crushed garlic clove, ¾ teaspoon curry powder and ½ teaspoon ground cumin. When hot, stir in ½ cup sour cream.

New-Style Sautéed Tomatoes

When assistant food editor Lucie Richard created this clever version of fried tomatoes we stood at the counter and devoured the entire panful.

Preparation time: 5 minutes / Cooking time: 5 minutes
Makes: 4 servings

4 large ripe tomatoes
1 tbsp olive or vegetable oil
2 tbsp red wine or 1 tbsp red wine vinegar
⅓ cup sour cream
1 tbsp chopped fresh or ¼ tsp dried tarragon or basil
Salt and freshly ground black pepper

1. Cut the tomatoes into ½-inch-thick slices. Heat the oil in a shallow wide-bottomed pan set over medium-high heat. Add the tomatoes, in 2 batches if necessary, and sauté for about 1 minute per side, just until heated through. Transfer the tomatoes to a platter. Immediately add the wine to the pan, scraping the bottom gently to remove any tomato bits.

2. When the wine is reduced by half, stir in remaining ingredients. As soon as the sour cream is hot, spoon the sauce over the tomatoes. Serve warm or at room temperature.

PER SERVING: *124 calories, 2.6 g protein, 11.5 g carbohydrates, 8.1 g fat, 35.3 mg calcium, 1.1 mg iron, 3 g fiber.*

Frozen Paste

Cook peeled chopped tomatoes into a thick paste then freeze in ice-cube trays. Store the frozen cubes in a large freezer bag and use as flavor boosts in meat sauces, gravies and soups.

Terrific Tomatoes

Tomato Bake
Seed and chop 2 large tomatoes. Sprinkle them over flat bread with 2 tablespoons crumbled goat cheese or Stilton. Bake at 400F until the bread is toasted.

Mexican Salad
Blend ¼ cup sour cream with ½ teaspoon ground cumin, generous pinches each of chili and garlic powders. Fold in 2 coarsely chopped tomatoes. Perfect atop frilly lettuce.

Fried Green
Slice and fry green tomatoes and serve them alongside eggs or hamburgers.

Middle Eastern
Sauté minced garlic and hot peppers in olive oil. Add sliced tomatoes and heat. Serve in pitas or as a side dish with grilled chicken.

Chèvre Broil
Cut tomatoes into thick slices and arrange them in a baking dish. Cover with thin slices of chèvre and chopped basil, then broil until the cheese is melted.

Avocado Appetizer
Coarsely chop 2 tomatoes and 2 whole green onions. Toss with 2 tablespoons bottled Italian salad dressing and a generous sprinkling of dried basil, dried leaf oregano, salt and pepper. Serve in avocado halves.

FREEZER TOMATO AND FRESH BASIL SAUCE

This is one of the best possible uses for a basket of ripe tomatoes and a bunch of garden basil. It's a marvelous topper on everything from pasta to poultry. Add a little fresh garlic and sprinkle of basil when you thaw and reheat.

Preparation time: 20 minutes / Cooking time: 25 minutes

Makes: 5 cups

3 lbs (1.5 kg) ripe tomatoes, about 10
$\frac{1}{4}$ cup olive oil
2 onions, coarsely chopped
2 garlic cloves, thinly sliced
$\frac{1}{2}$ tsp freshly ground black pepper
$\frac{1}{4}$ tsp salt
$\frac{1}{8}$ to $\frac{1}{4}$ tsp chili pepper flakes
$\frac{1}{4}$ cup chopped fresh basil

1. Bring a large pot of water to a full rolling boil. Neatly cut the stem ends from the tomato tops. Then, make a small slit through each bottom. (The slits will make peeling the tomatoes easier after blanching.)

2. Plunge the tomatoes into the boiling water. Boil for 30 to 40 seconds. Drain immediately, then immerse in ice-cold water. The skins will now peel off easily.

3. Heat the oil in a large saucepan set over medium-low heat. Add the onions and garlic. Cook, stirring occasionally until softened, about 5 minutes.

4. Meanwhile, coarsely chop the tomatoes. Stir them into the onions in the saucepan, along with the pepper, salt and chili flakes. Bring the sauce to a boil. Then, reduce heat and simmer, uncovered, for 15 minutes, stirring occasionally. Stir in the basil. Taste and add more seasonings, if needed. Continue simmering for 5 minutes. The sauce can be refrigerated or frozen.

PER CUP: 174 calories, 3.1 g protein, 17.3 g carbohydrates, 11.9 g fat, 28 mg calcium, 1.5 mg iron, 4.5 g fiber.

EASY FREEZE TOMATOES

Simply wash whole tomatoes and pack them into plastic freezer bags. When you want to use them, run hot water over the tomatoes until the skins crack, making peeling easy. You can also add them still frozen to sauces, soups and stews, but you may want to remove the skins when they come to the surface.

Conserve freezer space by cooking the tomatoes down into thick rich sauces before freezing. Hold the spices and onions until you're ready to use the sauce because they lose their strength in the freezer.

TOMATOES   BASIL

DRESSED-UP VEGGIES

For those times when you want to add a little swank and sparkle to your vegetables, try our extra flourishes — a spritz of cream, a dash of cognac, or a sprinkling of herbs. Drizzle tender asparagus with soy and sesame oil or bathe sweet parsnips and grated carrots in a nutmeg-scented cream and bake to bubbly perfection. Just as we strive to not overcook vegetables, we don't want to overpower their freshness or unique textures. All our dress-up additions are meant to simply complement and enhance.

SPRUCED-UP SPROUTS

Crunchy water chestnuts and earthy thyme stand up beautifully to brussels sprouts.

Preparation time: 10 minutes / Cooking time: 10 minutes

Makes: 4 servings

1 lb (500 g) small brussels sprouts, about 3 cups
2 cups chicken bouillon
10-oz (284-mL) can water chestnuts, drained
2 tbsp butter
Generous pinch of granulated sugar
$\frac{1}{2}$ tsp dried leaf thyme
Salt and freshly ground black pepper
Freshly squeezed lemon juice (optional)

1. Trim the ends of the sprouts as necessary. Cut a shallow cross in the base of each sprout with the tip of a sharp knife. Bring the chicken bouillon to a boil in a large saucepan. Add the sprouts and boil gently, uncovered, until almost fork-tender, about 5 to 10 minutes, depending on the size of the sprouts. While the sprouts are cooking, slice the chestnuts.

2. When sprouts are almost fork-tender, drain well. If the sprouts are large, you may wish to slice them in half and return to pan. Then, add the butter, a very generous pinch of sugar, seasonings and chestnuts to pan. Sauté over medium heat until the chestnuts are warm and the sprouts are glazed. Drizzle with a little freshly squeezed lemon juice, if you wish.

PER SERVING: *121 calories, 3.9 g protein, 16.3 g carbohydrates, 6.4 g fat, 55 mg calcium, 2.1 mg iron, 0.01 g fiber.*

FRESH BRUSSELS SPROUT POWER

A cup of sprouts has only 55 calories and comes packed with four times the vitamin C of a glass of orange juice. Top with a teaspoon of butter and you add 33 calories to the total.

Trimming

To remove the tough bottoms from asparagus, gently bend the ends. They'll break off where the tough woody section begins. You may also want to peel the fibrous green portion from the bottom part of the stalks.

Cooking

Lay the asparagus in a large wide saucepan half-filled with boiling salted water. Return the water to a gentle boil and cook for 5 to 8 minutes or until the asparagus is bright green but not limp. Do not overcook. To steam, wind string loosely around bundles of 6 to 10 spears and stand, stalk-end down, in a tall narrow pot with a few inches of water. Cover tightly and boil for 10 to 15 minutes. The tough ends cook in the water while the tender tops steam.

PHOTO: Asparagus Chinoise, see recipe above right.

ASPARAGUS CHINOISE

When you have a yen for something Oriental, treat your asparagus to a drizzle of sesame oil, soy sauce and orange zest.

Preparation time: 5 minutes / Cooking time: 4 minutes

Makes: 2 to 4 servings

1 bunch asparagus, about 1 lb (500 g)
1 tsp sesame oil
1 tsp soy sauce
Finely grated peel of 1 small orange
Freshly ground black pepper

1. Bring a large pot of salted water to a full rolling boil. Meanwhile, snap off and discard the woody ends from the asparagus. Plunge the asparagus into the water and boil, uncovered, until tender-crisp, about 4 minutes. Measure the oil, soy sauce and orange peel into a small bowl. Whisk until blended. Then, drain the asparagus. (Rinse under cold water if you wish to serve it as a cold salad.) Pat dry and arrange on a platter or individual plates. Drizzle with the soy dressing. Sprinkle with pepper.

PER SERVING: 30 calories, 2.1 g protein, 3.8 g carbohydrates, 1.4 g fat, 20.6 mg calcium, 0.6 mg iron, 0.01 g fiber.

BROCCOLI WITH BUTTERED PECANS

Just the elegant green to accompany a highly seasoned main course. It's got crunch and color.

Preparation time: 15 minutes / Cooking time: 5 minutes

Makes: 8 servings

2 lbs (1 kg) broccoli
¼ cup butter
½ cup coarsely chopped pecans
¼ tsp each of salt and freshly ground black pepper

1. Cut the broccoli into flowerets. Cut the stems into bite-size pieces. Bring 3 inches of salted water to a boil. Add the broccoli and cook, covered, for 4 to 5 minutes or until tender. Then, drain well and transfer to serving dish to keep warm.

2. Melt the butter in a small saucepan over medium heat just until it begins to turn brown. Add the pecans and sauté until golden brown. Pour the pecan butter over the broccoli. Sprinkle with salt and pepper.

PER SERVING: 131 calories, 4.3 g protein, 7.6 g carbohydrates, 10.8 g fat, 62.4 mg calcium, 1.2 mg iron, 0.5 g fiber.

BAKED COGNAC CARROTS

The common carrot bakes eloquently in a cognac butter. An admirable companion to almost any party entrée from stuffed turkey to veal chops. Sprinkle with lots of chopped coriander or green onions.

Preparation time: 15 minutes / Cooking time: 45 minutes to 1 hour

Makes: 10 servings

¼ cup melted butter
1 tsp granulated sugar
½ tsp salt
6 cups carrots cut into 2-inch pieces, or 6 cups small
   thick carrots
¼ cup cognac
1 bunch green seedless grapes

1. Preheat oven to 350F. Combine the butter, sugar and salt in a large shallow baking dish. Stir in the carrots and pour the cognac over top. Cover and bake in the preheated oven for 45 minutes to 1 hour or until the carrots are done as you like. Stir once during baking. Stir in the grapes and serve.

PER SERVING: 130 calories, 1.2 g protein, 14.8 g carbohydrates, 6.5 g fat, 31.8 mg calcium, 0.6 mg iron, 0.2 g fiber.

CARROTS

HONEY-DIJON BUTTER

Heat 2 tablespoons butter in a small saucepan. Stir in 1 tablespoon honey, 1 teaspoon Dijon mustard, ¼ teaspoon finely grated lemon peel and 1 teaspoon lemon juice. Heat, then drizzle over hot carrots, parsnips, asparagus or beets.

PHOTO: Hot 'n' Tangy Black Beans, see recipe on page 89.

ENTERTAINING WAYS WITH ASPARAGUS

Lemon Herbed
Heat ¼ cup butter with 1 tablespoon lemon juice, ½ teaspoon granulated sugar, ¼ teaspoon dried tarragon, salt and pepper. Great as a sauce or hot dip for cold spears.

Asparagus Italiano
Wrap spears of cold asparagus with prosciutto. Serve with a Dijon mustard-mayonnaise blend for dipping.

French Sophisticate
Whisk ½ cup oil with 2 to 3 tablespoons white vinegar and 2 finely chopped shallots. Sieve the whites, then the yolks of 2 hard-cooked eggs. Whisk the egg into the dressing with dried tarragon, chervil, salt and pepper. Spoon over spears.

Mediterranean Salad
Whisk ¼ cup olive oil with 1½ tablespoons freshly squeezed lemon juice, salt and pepper. Add chopped green onion and slivered black olives. Drizzle over cold asparagus on lettuce.

CARROT AND PARSNIP GRATIN

Parsnips' rather assertive flavor is mellowed by carrots, cream and Parmesan cheese in this most sophisticated of gratins. Always choose small parsnips: they're sweeter and nuttier.

Preparation time: 15 minutes / Cooking time: 5 minutes
Baking time: 1 hour / Makes: 8 to 12 servings

1 lb (500 g) carrots
1 lb (500 g) parsnips
2 tbsp all-purpose flour
1 cup freshly grated Parmesan cheese
$\frac{1}{4}$ cup butter
$\frac{1}{4}$ cup all-purpose flour
2 cups homogenized milk
$\frac{1}{2}$ cup whipping cream
2 eggs
$\frac{1}{4}$ tsp salt
$\frac{1}{8}$ tsp freshly ground white pepper
Pinch of freshly grated nutmeg

1. Preheat oven to 350F. Generously butter a shallow 9x13-inch baking dish. Peel, then grate the carrots and parsnips. (This can be done in a food processor.)

2. Measure 6 cups grated vegetables into a large bowl. Stir 2 table-spoons flour and $\frac{1}{2}$ cup grated Parmesan cheese together. Then, stir the flour and cheese into the vegetables. Set aside.

3. Melt the butter in a saucepan over medium heat. Sprinkle in $\frac{1}{4}$ cup flour and cook for 2 minutes, stirring constantly. Gradually whisk in the milk and stir continuously until it starts to bubble. Remove from the heat. In a small bowl, whisk the cream, eggs and seasonings together. Gradually stir this mixture into the hot milk mixture. Stir for 1 minute. Pour over the carrots and parsnips. Stir well and pour into a buttered dish. Evenly sprinkle with remaining Parmesan. If making ahead, leave at room temperature for up to an hour or refrigerate for several hours before baking.

4. Bake in the centre of the preheated oven for 1 hour, until golden and bubbly. Let stand for 10 minutes before serving.

PER SERVING: 201 calories, 7.7 g protein, 17.5 g carbohydrates, 11.7 g fat, 169.1 mg calcium, 0.8 mg iron, 2.1 g fiber.

FAST FIX CARROTS

Creamy Cumin
Toss 2 cups cooked sliced carrots with $\frac{1}{2}$ cup sour cream and $\frac{1}{2}$ teaspoon ground cumin. Serves 4.

Light Oriental
Sauté 2 cups grated carrots with 1 crushed garlic clove, 1 teaspoon soy sauce, 1 teaspoon granulated sugar and $\frac{1}{2}$ teaspoon lemon juice. Serves 4.

Dilled Purée
Cook 2 cups sliced carrots in 2 cups chicken bouillon and $\frac{1}{2}$ teaspoon dill seed. Drain and purée. Stir in $\frac{1}{4}$ cup sour cream. Serves 4.

Italian Salad
Toss 3 cups grated carrots with $\frac{1}{4}$ cup Italian salad dressing and 1 teaspoon capers. Serves 6.

All-Spiced
Drain 2 cups cooked sliced carrots. Return the carrots to pan and add $\frac{1}{2}$ cup orange juice and $\frac{1}{4}$ teaspoon allspice. Sauté until the juice is syrupy. Serves 4.

TINY CREAMED ONIONS

For many of us, creamed onions are a mandatory part of Christmas dinner. There's something wonderfully comforting yet luxurious about them. They're not difficult to prepare — especially if you can find someone else to peel them!

Preparation time: 25 minutes / Cooking time: 20 minutes
Baking time: 15 minutes / Makes: 5 cups

2 lbs (1 kg) fresh pearl onions
2 cups chicken broth or bouillon
1 bay leaf
¼ cup butter
¼ cup all-purpose flour
1 cup (250-mL container) milk, or half-and-half or table cream
¼ tsp poultry seasoning or dried tarragon
⅛ tsp salt
⅛ tsp white pepper
Pinch of freshly grated nutmeg
2 tbsp freshly grated Parmesan cheese

1. Fill a large saucepan with water and bring to a boil. Trim the onion tops but do not remove the root ends or the onions may fall apart during cooking. Plunge the onions into the water and boil for 3 minutes. Drain. Immerse in cold water, then peel.

2. Preheat oven to 350F. Return the onions to the saucepan. Add the chicken broth and bay leaf. Cover and bring to a boil. Then, reduce heat and simmer, covered, until the onions are just fork-tender, about 12 minutes. Drain, reserving broth. Discard the bay leaf.

3. Make the cream sauce by melting the butter in a saucepan set over medium heat. Blend in the flour and cook, stirring constantly, for 1 minute. Very gradually whisk in the milk and 1 cup of the reserved cooking broth. Cook the sauce, stirring frequently, until it is thick and just comes to a boil.

4. Stir in the seasonings and onions. Pour into a 6-cup (1.5-L) casserole dish. Sprinkle with the cheese. Bake for 15 minutes, until the sauce bubbles around the edges of the casserole. The dish can be prepared ahead, refrigerated and reheated, uncovered, in the oven. Great with fish or chicken.

PER ½ CUP: *107 calories, 3.6 g protein, 10.5 g carbohydrates, 5.9 g fat, 67.5 mg calcium, 0.5 mg iron, 1.3 g fiber.*

PEARL
ONIONS

TURNIP WITH FRESH DILL

For a fast dressed-up turnip dish, slice 1½ lbs (750 g) turnip or rutabaga into julienne strips. Cook in boiling salted water with 1 tablespoon granulated sugar added until fork-tender. Drain well, then add 1 tablespoon each of butter, granulated sugar and white vinegar, 2 tablespoons chopped fresh dill or ½ teaspoon dried dillweed, salt and white pepper. Stir over medium heat until the turnip is glazed, about 2 minutes. Wonderful with the holiday bird. Serves 4.

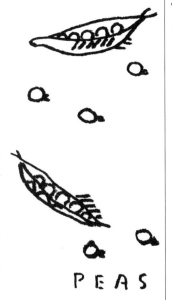

PEAS

5-MINUTE PARTY PARSNIPS

An unparalleled parsnip purée with an assertive grown-up taste. If parsnips are hard to cut, pop in a microwave for 30 seconds.

Preparation time: 15 minutes / Microwave time: 5 minutes

Makes: 4 servings

4 large parsnips, about 1 lb (500 g)
2 tbsp butter
2 tbsp water
¼ cup sour cream or yogurt
Pinches of freshly grated nutmeg or curry powder,
 salt and pepper

1. Peel the parsnips and thinly slice. Arrange them in a shallow microwave-safe dish. Dot with butter. Add the water. Microwave, covered, on high for 5 minutes or until tender. Then, in a food processor, purée the parsnips with remaining ingredients.

PER SERVING: *162 calories, 1.8 g protein, 20.2 g carbohydrates, 9 g fat, 55.9 mg calcium, 0.6 mg iron, 4.9 g fiber.*

PURÉED PEAS PARISIENNE

The gentle taste and bright green of puréed peas is irresistible. Especially stunning spooned into hollowed-out tomato halves.

Preparation time: 5 minutes / Cooking time: 15 minutes

Makes: 2 cups

2 tbsp butter
2 tbsp each of chopped onion and green pepper
3 cups fresh or frozen green peas
½ tsp salt
Pinch each of pepper and freshly grated nutmeg
2 tbsp sour cream (optional)

1. Heat the butter in a large frying pan over medium-low heat. Add the onion and green pepper and cook, stirring often, for about 5 minutes. Add the peas and ¼ cup water. Cover tightly and cook for 5 minutes or until done as you like. Uncover and stir until the water is evaporated. Add the salt, pepper and nutmeg. Purée in a blender or food processor until fairly smooth. Blend in the sour cream, if you like.

PER ½ CUP: *147 calories, 6.3 g protein, 17.9 g carbohydrates, 6.1 g fat, 33.8 mg calcium, 1.9 mg iron, 4.7 g fiber.*

SIDE DISH STARS

When we were growing up, potatoes or rice was a mandatory part of the meal. We didn't give it much thought. More often than not, we'd throw the starch of our choice in a pot and serve it boiled and boring. Today the humble potato is wearing several new jackets and proudly taking a more prominent place on the dinner plate. We've increased our rice repertoire to include brown, basmati and Arborio. Now rice comes to dinner all dolled up with spices or herbs, stirred or simmered with rich stock or flavored with cheese or chilies. Even the lowly bean has a terrific new image and graces the menus of the best chefs in town. All this is as it should be. We've learned to embellish these mild-tasting complex carbohydrates to bring out the best of everything they're served with and they've earned quite a reputation on their own for being not just healthy but hip.

POSH POTATOES

Fattening and bland was the way we used to regard potatoes. No more! In our surge toward homey wholesome food in the '90s, spuds are premier players. The bad rap that plagued the potato had nothing to do with the potato and everything to do with the calorie-laden gravy or butter we heaped on it. Then, nouvelle cuisine minced in, sending potatoes onto the back burner. Today, with our renewed interest in simple foods, pure flavors and lower fat intake, potatoes have a terrific new image. Nutritionists are touting the tuber as an almost perfect food — high in fiber, complex carbohydrates and satisfaction. At the same time, chefs are capitalizing on potatoes' earthy flavor as the basis for good ol' comfort cuisine, or gussying them up as impressive side dishes. Bye-bye fattening and bland. Step aside for the seductive spud.

ROASTED POTATOES WITH GARLIC AND PARMESAN

Terrific casual-dinner potatoes: thick, roasted wedges tossed with Parmesan, garlic and pepper.

Preparation time: 10 minutes / Baking time: 20 minutes

Makes: 4 servings

¼ cup butter, at room temperature
1 crushed garlic clove
3 medium potatoes
¼ cup freshly grated Parmesan cheese
Salt and freshly ground black pepper
Sour cream (optional)

1. Preheat oven to 425F. In a small bowl, combine the butter and garlic. Cut each potato in half lengthwise, then each half into 4 long wedges.

2. Place the wedges on a baking sheet. Brush with the butter mixture. Sprinkle with the cheese, salt and pepper. Bake 20 minutes or until the potatoes are tender, turning several times. Serve drizzled with sour cream, if you like.

PER SERVING: *268 calories, 8 g protein, 27 g carbohydrates, 15 g fat, 130 mg calcium, 0.5 mg iron, 2 g fiber.*

WHOLESOME SPUDS

Nutritionally, spuds pack a wallop. A large baked potato contains about 225 calories, 5 g of protein, no cholesterol and only a trace of fat. In addition, it delivers 2.8 g of iron, about half the potassium and vitamin C we require in a day and 3.5 g of fiber.

GOLDEN CRISP ROSEMARY PARTY POTATOES

Thinly sliced potatoes tossed with garlic and rosemary are over-lapped in a baking dish and roasted until golden.

Preparation time: 10 minutes / Cooking time: 5 minutes
Baking time: 30 minutes / Makes: 4 servings

4 large potatoes
¼ cup butter
1 small crushed garlic clove
½ tsp dried rosemary, crumbled
Generous pinch each of salt and freshly ground black pepper

1. Preheat oven to 450F. Peel the potatoes and thinly slice. Pat them dry with paper towels. Place in a large bowl.

2. Then, melt the butter in a medium-size frying pan. Add the garlic, rosemary, salt and pepper. Sauté for about 5 minutes to develop the garlic flavor.

3. Pour the butter-and-garlic mixture over the potatoes and gently toss until coated.

4. Butter a 10-inch pie plate or quiche pan. Overlap the buttery potatoes in the pie plate to form 2 or 3 layers. Drizzle with any butter remaining in the bowl. If not baking right away, cover with clear wrap and leave at room temperature up to an hour. Bake in the centre of the preheated oven for 30 minutes or until the potatoes are cooked and crispy brown on top.

PER SERVING: *298 calories, 4.2 g protein, 45.5 g carbohydrates, 11.9 g fat, 27.5 mg calcium, 0.8 mg iron, 0 g fiber.*

BAKED POTATO PANACHE

Caesar Spuds

Cut a hot baked potato into cubes. Drizzle with Caesar salad dressing and toss. Sprinkle with Parmesan cheese and bacon bits.

Italian Grill

Cut a baked potato in half. Cover with grated mozzarella or Parmesan cheese and pinches of dried leaf oregano, dried basil and garlic powder. Grill.

Chili 'n' Cheese

Cover baked potato halves with cottage cheese or ricotta spiced with chili powder or ground cumin. Top with chopped red onions.

POTATOES

POTATO PRIMER

Buying

Look potatoes over carefully — even if they're in sealed bags, you can feel and smell them. They should be firm, with no soft spongy spots, and have smooth skins. A smell may mean they're spoiled. Pass on potatoes with large eyes, sprouts, green areas or blemishes.

Storing

Do not keep potatoes under the sink. The ideal location is dark, dry and well ventilated, and between 46 and 50F (8 and 10C). In an apartment, try a closet away from a heat vent or radiator. When potatoes get warm, they sprout; when cold, they change flavor; and in bright light — or even daylight — they tend to turn green or develop a bitter taste. In hot weather, if you don't have ideal conditions, the refrigerator is probably your best bet. If you have good storage conditions, stock a month's supply; if not, buy no more than a week's worth. Don't stock up on new potatoes; they do not keep well. Don't wash potatoes before storing, but pick out bruised, blemished or sprouted spuds and use them first.

Cooking

Inspect each potato and remove green or damaged areas. Scrub under cold running water. Don't peel unless absolutely necessary — the skin contains nutrients and fiber and also prevents the water-soluble nutrients from flowing into the boiling water. If you must peel, do so just before cooking and immediately cover the potatoes with cold water.

Steaming

Place a wire rack or steamer basket in the bottom of a large saucepan. Pour in water to come within an inch of the bottom of the rack and bring to a boil. Add the potatoes; adjust the heat to keep the water boiling without touching the potatoes. Cover tightly. The potatoes will take from 20 to 30 minutes to cook.

Boiling

Immerse the potatoes in boiling salted water. (While many cooks swear by the French method of starting the potatoes in a pot of cold water and rapidly bringing it to the boil, the potatoes take longer to cook and you lose more nutrients.) Tightly cover and cook over medium heat until tender when pierced with a fork or the point of a sharp paring knife. Whole mature potatoes take about 30 minutes, new potatoes 15 to 20 minutes. Drain, then place the saucepan back on the burner and shake over medium heat until the outsides of the potatoes are thoroughly dry.

Pan Roasting

Beautiful golden-brown roasted potatoes are easy. Peel and cut the potatoes into halves or quarters. One to 1¼ hours before the meat is cooked, scatter the potatoes around the roast and turn them until they're coated with pan drippings. Baste and turn often. Delicious pan roasting is also possible without meat: Parboil the potatoes for 10 minutes; drain, peel, cut in halves or quarters and place in a shallow pan. Brush with melted butter, olive or vegetable oil. Roast, uncovered, in a preheated 400F oven until fork-tender and golden brown, about 40 minutes. Turn often and baste, adding more butter if necessary.

Baking

Scrub the potatoes. Prick the skins with a fork so steam can escape, or the potatoes may burst during the baking. If you like crusty skin, place the potatoes directly on the oven rack or a baking sheet in a 425F oven. In 40 to 50 minutes they should feel soft when gently squeezed with mitted hands or tender when pierced with a thin skewer or the point of a sharp knife. For soft skins, rub the potatoes with vegetable oil or butter and bake at 350F for an hour. (Foil wrapping steams rather than bakes.)

Microwaving

Choose uniform shapes. Pierce the potatoes to allow steam to escape. Place them on a double thickness of paper towel in spoke fashion, with small ends toward the centre, or use a microwave roasting rack. A single potato bakes in about 4 minutes on high; for each additional potato, add 2 to 3 minutes. Turn the potatoes over halfway through cooking. Standing time finishes the cooking, so potatoes should be easy to pierce but still firm when they come out of the microwave. During standing time, wrap in a kitchen cloth or in foil, shiny-side in. One potato needs about 4 minutes' standing time; allow 5 to 10 minutes for 3 or 4.

LEMON DILLED POTATOES

A lemon and dill treatment dresses up simple boiled potatoes. For an even prettier presentation, use baby new potatoes or the small rounded peeled potatoes sold in many supermarkets.

Preparation time: 5 minutes / Cooking *or* Microwave time: 10 minutes

Makes: 4 servings

6 medium-size potatoes, quartered
2 tbsp butter, at room temperature
1 tsp freshly squeezed lemon juice
Finely grated peel of 1 small lemon
Pinch of salt
Generous grinding of black pepper
2 tbsp finely chopped fresh dill

1. Scrub the potatoes and peel, if you wish. Place them in a large saucepan. Add enough water to cover the potatoes. Bring to a boil over high heat. Then, reduce the heat to medium-low. Partially cover and boil gently just until the potatoes can be pierced with a fork, about 10 minutes. Drain well.

2. To microwave, place the potatoes in a shallow microwave-safe dish. Add about ¼ cup water. Microwave, covered, on high for about 8 minutes. Stir once during cooking. Let stand, covered, for about 2 minutes. Then, drain well.

3. Meanwhile, in a small bowl, stir the butter with the lemon juice, peel, salt and pepper. Once the potatoes are cooked, immediately toss them with the butter mixture. Then, sprinkle with fresh dill and serve.

PER SERVING: 276 calories, 4.8 g protein, 52.8 g carbohydrates, 5.9 g fat, 18.5 mg calcium, 1.1 mg iron, 4.1 g fiber.

NEW POTATO TOSSES

Cook new potatoes in boiling salted water for 15 minutes. Drain well and toss with one of these flavor-boosters:

• Garlic butter and snipped chives

• Caesar, Roquefort or garlic salad dressing

• Boursin or herbed cream cheese

• Grated Parmesan cheese, butter and sliced whole green onions

• Knockout Garlic Dip (see page 11)

• Butter, paprika and black pepper

• Salsa and sliced whole green onions

• Pesto and grated Parmesan cheese

• Olive oil and chopped basil, coriander or mint

DILL

LEMON

MEXICAN
SALSA
SPUDS

MEXICAN SALSA SPUDS

A zesty salsa-and-cheddar sauce turns a plain baked potato into a main event.

Preparation time: 5 minutes / Makes: 2 servings

2 large baked potatoes
$\frac{1}{2}$ cup grated old cheddar cheese
$\frac{1}{4}$ cup light sour cream
2 tbsp mild, medium or hot salsa
1 whole green onion, thinly sliced
1 tbsp chopped coriander (optional)

1. Slice the hot baked potatoes in half lengthwise. Sprinkle them with the cheese. Spoon 1 tablespoon sour cream on each half, followed by $\frac{1}{2}$ tablespoon salsa and a sprinkling of green onion and coriander. If necessary, return to a 400F oven for 5 minutes to completely melt the cheese. Or microwave, uncovered, on high for 30 seconds.

PER SERVING: *384 calories, 14 g protein, 58 g carbohydrates, 12 g fat, 251 mg calcium, 1.3 mg iron, 4.1 g fiber.*

HEAVENLY WHIPPED POTATOES

Dedicated mashed potato fanciers always have their own special tricks for perfect mashed potatoes. We used them all together in this easy version to assure you of the creamiest creation.

Preparation time: 20 minutes / Cooking time: 20 minutes
Makes: 10 servings

10 potatoes
1 tsp salt
$\frac{1}{4}$ to $\frac{1}{2}$ cup milk
$\frac{1}{2}$ cup butter
$\frac{1}{2}$ cup sour cream
2 tsp grated onion
Freshly grated nutmeg
Salt and freshly ground black pepper

1. Peel the potatoes. Cut them in half and place them in a saucepan with the salt. Cover generously with cold water. Bring to a boil. Cover and simmer until the potatoes are tender, about 20 minutes. Drain off the water. Return the pan to the burner and shake the pan until the potatoes are very dry.

2. Meanwhile, heat $\frac{1}{4}$ cup milk and remaining ingredients together until warmed through. This will help to keep the potatoes fluffy. Put the warm milk mixture and the potatoes in the large mixing bowl of an electric mixer. Whip them with the electric mixer until light and creamy, adding another $\frac{1}{4}$ cup milk, if necessary.

PER SERVING: *238 calories, 3.2 g protein, 30.8 g carbohydrates, 11.9 g fat, 37.2 mg calcium, 0.5 mg iron, 0.02 g fiber.*

SWEET POTATO PURÉE

A touch of orange and ginger spice up a classic purée.

Preparation time: 15 minutes
Cooking time: 20 minutes *or* Microwave time: 15 minutes
Baking time: 20 minutes / Makes: 6 servings

3 lbs (1.5 kg) sweet potatoes, about 4
1 tbsp butter
$\frac{1}{4}$ cup half-and-half cream, at room temperature
1 tbsp orange juice concentrate
Pinch of ground ginger
$\frac{1}{4}$ tsp ground white pepper

1. Peel the potatoes, cut into quarters and place them in a saucepan. Cover with water. Set over high heat and cover the pan. Bring to a boil, then reduce heat and simmer until the potatoes are very tender, about 20 minutes. Or cook the potatoes in the microwave. Prick all over with a fork and place 1 inch apart on a paper towel. Microwave on high for 10 to 15 minutes, turning halfway through baking. When the potatoes are cooked, peel them and cut into small pieces.

2. Purée the potatoes in a food processor fitted with a metal blade. Add the butter, cream, orange juice concentrate, ginger and pepper. Whirl, using an on-and-off motion, just until the mixture is smooth. Scrape down the sides of the processor bowl often to ensure a smooth purée.

3. Transfer the sweet potato mixture to an 8-cup (2-L) baking dish and smooth the top. Bake, uncovered, in a preheated 350F oven for 20 minutes or until the mixture is piping hot.

PER SERVING: *234 calories, 3.7 g protein, 48.7 g carbohydrates, 3.3 g fat, 66.7 mg calcium, 0.9 mg iron, 0.02 g fiber.*

SWEET POTATO SAVVY
Despite the name, a whole baked sweet potato has only 118 calories and a generous amount of vitamin A, potassium and vitamin C.

Easy Bake
Place sweet potatoes on a shallow tray and bake at 400F for 45 minutes. Turn halfway through baking time.

Stir-Ins
Mash baked or boiled sweet potatoes with butter and stir in a little bourbon, orange marmalade, curry powder, or candied ginger and grated orange peel.

FANCY GARLIC MASHED POTATOES

The height of comfort food yet full flavored and with enough sophisticated ingredients to make an appearance at a black-tie affair. The inspiration for these comes from Chef Bob Bermann of Toronto's Avocado Club.

Preparation time: 20 minutes / Cooking time: 20 minutes

Makes: 6 servings

3 lbs (1.5 kg) russet potatoes, about 6 large
2 small sweet peppers, preferably 1 red and 1 green
3 tbsp chopped green and/or black olives
1 tbsp olive or vegetable oil
2 crushed garlic cloves
$\frac{1}{2}$ cup half-and-half or table cream
$\frac{1}{3}$ cup butter
$\frac{1}{4}$ tsp salt
$\frac{1}{4}$ tsp freshly ground black pepper

1. Peel the potatoes and cut them into quarters. Place the potatoes in a saucepan and fill with water to cover. Add a pinch of salt, set over high heat and bring to a boil. When the water is boiling, cover and boil gently for 15 to 20 minutes or until potatoes can be easily pierced with a fork.

2. While the potatoes are cooking, finely chop the sweet peppers and olives. Set aside. Heat the olive oil in a frying pan set over medium heat. Add the peppers, olives and garlic. Sauté, stirring often, for about 5 minutes, until the peppers are soft.

3. Then, add the cream and butter and increase heat to medium-high. When the cream is hot and the butter has melted, remove from the heat and set aside.

4. When the potatoes are cooked, drain well. Mash the potatoes in a bowl, using a potato masher, until very smooth. Stir in the olive-and-cream mixture. Taste and add the salt and pepper as needed. This dish goes very well with steak or lamb chops.

PER SERVING: 373 calories, 5.2 g protein, 51.9 g carbohydrates, 17.3 g fat, 49.3 mg calcium, 1 mg iron, 0.4 g fiber.

MARVELOUS MASHED POTATOES

Here are some tips to keep your whipped potatoes light and heavenly.

• Always heat the milk and butter before gradually adding to the potatoes.

• Whip with a potato masher or an electric mixer. (Food processors turn potatoes into a thick, gluey mixture.)

• For fluffier potatoes, use an up-and-down motion with a potato masher, instead of a stirring action, to incorporate more air.

• Instead of traditional butter and milk, consider stirring in chopped sun-dried tomatoes, light sour cream, chopped basil, grated cheese or garlic oil.

Symphony Scalloped Potatoes

There's a beautiful harmony about the way all these ingredients work together to create the best scalloped potatoes we've ever had.

Preparation time: 30 minutes

Cooking time: 1½ hours

Makes: 8 servings

2 tbsp butter
1 large crushed garlic clove
2 tbsp all-purpose flour
2½ cups half-and-half cream
1½ cups grated Swiss cheese
½ fresh lemon
8 medium potatoes
6 whole green onions, sliced
Generous pinch each of salt, pepper and freshly grated nutmeg

1. Preheat oven to 325F. Melt the butter in a heavy-bottomed saucepan. Stir in the garlic and cook for about 1 minute. Blend in the flour and cook, stirring constantly, until very bubbly, about 2 minutes. Gradually add the cream, stirring until fairly thick and smooth. Stir in the cheese until melted. Cover and set aside.

2. Prepare the potatoes by squeezing the juice from the lemon, about 2 tablespoons, into a large bowl. Stir in 3 cups cold water. Peel the potatoes, immersing them in this lemon solution as they're peeled to prevent discoloring. Then, thinly slice the potatoes using a sharp knife or a food processor, returning the potatoes to the lemon solution as they're sliced.

3. Generously butter or grease an 8-cup (2-L) baking dish. Drain the potatoes and pat dry with paper towels. Overlap a third of the potatoes on the bottom of the dish. Top with a third of the onions. Then sprinkle generously with salt, pepper and nutmeg. Cover with a third of the sauce. Repeat layers, ending with the sauce. Cover and bake in the preheated oven for 1 hour. Uncover and continue baking for another half hour or until the potatoes are tender when pierced and the top is golden.

PER SERVING: *341 calories, 11.2 g protein, 36 g carbohydrates, 17.5 g fat, 299 mg calcium, 0.7 mg iron, 0.2 g fiber.*

Roasted Rosemary Potatoes

Slice potatoes into quarters or eighths, depending on their size. Toss with enough olive oil to lightly coat. Sprinkle liberally with salt, freshly ground black pepper and dried rosemary. Spread out on a baking sheet and bake at 375F for about 45 minutes, until golden. Stir occasionally.

SYMPHONY SCALLOPED POTATOES

SIDE DISH STARS

TRIPLE TESTED

RACY RICE AND GRAINS

Canadians are realizing that it's time to stop just dumping on rice. We literally used to heap our curries and Oriental stir-fries over a steamed bed of it. Now instead of being a wallflower on the sidelines, rice is married with classic and authentic spices and flavorings from Thailand, Italy, India and Morocco. Once you've tasted our racy Hot Pepper Risotto and our Fragrant Basmati Rice with cardamom and cumin, you'll never take rice for granted again.

BROWN AND WILD RICE WITH PECANS AND PEPPERS

Buttery pecans, green onions and red peppers add party color and crunch to this duo of rices.

Preparation time: 20 minutes / Cooking time: 40 minutes

Makes: 8 to 10 servings

3 cups cold water
½ tsp salt
1 cup each of brown and wild rice
⅓ cup coarsely chopped pecans
2 tbsp butter
½ cup finely chopped red pepper
4 whole green onions, thinly sliced
⅛ tsp each of salt and freshly ground black pepper

1. Rinse the rices in cold water. Then, place them in a saucepan with 3 cups cold water and ½ teaspoon salt. Bring to a boil. Reduce heat and simmer gently, covered, for about 35 minutes.

2. Meanwhile, stir the pecans in a small ungreased frying pan set over medium heat. When the nuts are fragrant and hot, remove them from the pan and set aside. Add the butter, red pepper and green onions to the pan and sauté for 3 minutes. When the rice is tender, drain off any excess water. Stir in the pecans, red pepper, onions, salt and pepper.

PER SERVING: *182 calories, 3.1 g protein, 30.2 g carbohydrates, 5.4 g fat, 13.4 mg calcium, 1.2 mg iron, 1.6 g fiber.*

UNBEATABLE STEAMED RICE

Here's an easy way to duplicate at home those bowls of steamed rice we first learned to love in Chinese restaurants.

Preparation time: 5 minutes / Cooking time: 18 minutes

Makes: 6 servings

3 cups water or chicken broth or bouillon
1 cup long-grain white rice
Generous pinch of salt

1. Measure the water, rice and salt into a medium-size saucepan. Tightly cover and bring to a boil over medium-high heat. Then, reduce heat to low and simmer, tightly covered, for 8 minutes. Drain the rice into a metal sieve, discarding all the cooking liquid. Place 1 inch of water in a saucepan that is large enough to accommodate the sieve. Bring the water to a boil. Then, reduce the heat to low. Place the metal sieve with the rice over the water. Cover with a paper towel and then set the pot lid on top of the sieve. Steam for 10 minutes. Fluff with a fork and serve.

PER SERVING: *113 calories, 2.2 g protein, 24.7 g carbohydrates, 0.2 g fat, 11.3 mg calcium, 1.3 mg iron, 0.3 g fiber.*

RICE

There are three kinds of rice grains — long, medium and short. Long-grain rice produces separate fluffy grains when cooked and is perfect for soups and pilafs. The fragrant basmati rice, grown in the foothills of the Himalayas and Pakistan, is a long-grain rice that improves with age and is usually carefully matured. Medium-grain and short-grain rice tend to stick together when cooked, making them more suited to puddings, rice rings and risottos. The Italian Arborio rice, a stubby short-grain rice with a pearly spot, falls into this category.

Parboiled rice undergoes a vacuum heating before the outer layers are removed, forcing some of the nutrients from the outer layers into the rice grain. Then, the hull and bran layers are removed.

Brown rice is still encased in its nutritional bran layer, with only the outer bark removed. It has a nutty flavor and chewy texture and takes longer to cook than white rice. Wild rice is actually the seed of a grass that grows wild in North America and is closer in nutritional makeup to wheat.

Cooking

Follow package directions for processed rice, including quick-cooking varieties. For regular long-grain rice, begin by stirring the rice in a saucepan with enough melted butter or hot vegetable oil to coat each grain. This keeps the grains separated and the rice from sticking to the pan. Add 2 to 2½ cups boiling water or bouillon for each cup of uncooked rice. Salt is a personal choice, but most recipes call for ¾ to 1 teaspoon for each cup of uncooked rice. Once the water comes to a boil, cover the pot and cook over low heat for about 25 minutes for white rice; about 40 minutes for brown rice. Rice should be swollen and just tender. Uncover the pot and continue cooking over low heat for a few minutes, shaking the pot occasionally until all the grains are separated.

BAKED PARTY LEMON RICE

Stir everything together in a casserole, pop into the oven and forget about it — the perfect party dish.

Preparation time: 5 minutes / Baking time: 35 minutes

Makes: 8 servings

2 cups long-grain rice
4$\frac{1}{2}$ cups chicken broth or bouillon
4 whole green onions, chopped (optional)
3 tbsp butter
3 tbsp freshly squeezed lemon juice
Finely grated peel of 1 lemon
$\frac{1}{2}$ tsp salt and pinch of white pepper

1. Preheat oven to 375F. Place the rice in an 8-cup (2-L) casserole dish. Heat the broth until boiling and add along with remaining ingredients to the casserole. Mix well. Cover tightly and bake in the preheated oven for 35 minutes or until all the liquid is absorbed.

PER SERVING: *227 calories, 3.6 g protein, 38.8 g carbohydrates, 6 g fat, 35.3 mg calcium, 1.7 mg iron, 0.9 g fiber.*

UPSCALE WILD RICE PILAF

Aromatic overtones of cinnamon and cardamom give intriguing character to this pilaf, making it a noble companion for duck or free-range chicken.

Preparation time: 10 minutes / Standing time: 1 hour

Cooking time: 45 minutes / Makes: 6 servings

$\frac{3}{4}$ cup wild rice
1 tbsp butter
1 onion, finely chopped
$\frac{3}{4}$ cup long-grain rice
4 cardamom pods
2 (3-inch) cinnamon sticks
2 cups chicken bouillon
Pinch of freshly ground black pepper
2 tbsp finely chopped whole green onion (optional)

1. Place the wild rice in a medium-size saucepan and cover with about 1$\frac{1}{2}$ cups cold water. Soak the rice at room temperature for 1 hour. Then, place saucepan over medium heat. Bring to a boil, reduce heat

EVER-READY RICE

If you have extra cooked rice, you can pop it into the freezer for later use. To reheat, add 1 or 2 tablespoons of liquid such as chicken broth or water and reheat the frozen rice in foil packets in the oven or in a small covered microwave-safe dish on defrost in the microwave. Frozen rice can also be added to hot soups, stews and curries — a fast way to complete a last-minute meal.

and simmer gently, uncovered, for 20 minutes. Drain the rice well and set aside.

2. In a large wide saucepan, melt the butter over medium heat. Add the onion and sauté for 5 minutes or until soft. Stir in the partially cooked wild rice, long-grain rice, cardamom and cinnamon sticks. Stir until the rice is coated with butter.

3. Add the bouillon. Bring the mixture to a boil, cover and reduce heat to low. Simmer gently for 20 minutes or until the rice is tender and the liquid is absorbed. Remove the saucepan from the heat and remove the cinnamon sticks. Season the rice with pepper. Serve sprinkled with the green onion.

PER SERVING: *191 calories, 6.4 g protein, 35 g carbohydrates, 2.8 g fat, 17.6 mg calcium, 1.6 mg iron, 0.5 g fiber.*

WILD RICE WITH A HINT OF HORSERADISH

Designed to go with a handsome prime rib, this mix of wild and brown rice gets an unexpected and most compatible flavor burst from horseradish.

Preparation time: 10 minutes / Cooking time: 40 minutes

Makes: 8 to 10 servings

2 tbsp butter
1 cup wild rice
1 cup brown rice
3½ cups water or chicken broth or bouillon
1 tbsp horseradish
½ tsp salt
¼ cup coarsely chopped Italian parsley

1. Melt the butter in a large saucepan set over medium heat. When bubbling, add all the rice and stir until the grains are coated with butter, about 2 minutes. Then, stir in the water, horseradish and salt.

2. Cover and cook until the water is boiling, then reduce heat to low and simmer until the rice is tender, about 40 minutes. Stir in the parsley and serve.

PER SERVING: *293 calories, 7.8 g protein, 53.1 g carbohydrates, 6 g fat, 27.3 mg calcium, 1.4 mg iron, 2.3 g fiber.*

COCONUT RICE

Rich coconut flavor permeates this creamy rice, the perfect complement for Thai dishes, curries or simple sautéed chicken.

Preparation time: 5 minutes / Cooking time: 20 minutes

Makes: 4 servings

1 tbsp butter
1 onion, finely chopped
½ tsp curry powder
¾ cup long grain rice
14-oz (400-mL) can unsweetened coconut milk
Salt and freshly ground black pepper (optional)

1. In a large saucepan, melt the butter over medium heat. Add the onion and curry powder and sauté for 5 minutes, until the onion is soft. Then, stir in the rice until coated with butter.

2. Vigorously shake the can of coconut milk. Then, add the entire contents to the rice and stir until evenly blended. Increase heat and bring the mixture to a boil. Cover, reduce heat to low and simmer gently for 15 to 20 minutes, until the coconut milk is absorbed. Add salt and pepper, if you wish.

PER SERVING: *397 calories, 5.2 g protein, 36.1 g carbohydrates, 27.3 g fat, 34.4 mg calcium, 3.3 mg iron, 0.9 g fiber.*

COCONUT MILK: HOW SWEET IS IT?

Coconut milk is the liquid from grated and soaked coconut pulp, not the liquid that forms in a coconut. Cans of unsweetened coconut milk are sold in ethnic food stores and most supermarkets, but be sure to check the label since sweetened coconut milk and coconut cream used in piña coladas are much too sweet for coconut rice or curries.

BOLD 'N' SPICY RICE

When you want a fiery sidekick to saddle up to a conservative entrée like a grand prime rib or roasted capon, this is it.

Preparation time: 15 minutes / Cooking time: 30 minutes

Makes: 8 servings

3 tbsp butter
2 onions, finely chopped
4 crushed garlic cloves
2 cups long-grain rice
5 cups chicken broth or bouillon
2 canned jalapeno peppers, seeded and chopped
½ tsp cayenne pepper
Freshly ground black pepper

1. Heat the butter in a large saucepan. Add the onions and garlic and sauté until the onions are soft, about 5 minutes. Stir in the rice until all the grains are coated with butter. Stir in the chicken broth, jalapeno peppers, cayenne and black pepper. Bring to a boil. Then, cover, reduce heat to low and simmer for 20 to 25 minutes, until the liquid is absorbed.

PER SERVING: 245 calories, 6.9 g protein, 40.9 g carbohydrates, 5.6 g fat, 29.7 mg calcium, 2.5 mg iron, 0.9 g fiber.

FRAGRANT BASMATI RICE

Basmati rice with its nutty flavor has become the "gourmet" grain. Simmering it with whole spices gives it a sophisticated, mild flavor that suits curries, grills and just about everything in between. Always rinse basmati rice several times to remove extra starch, and stir gently since the grains are fragile.

Preparation time: 10 minutes / Cooking time: 20 minutes

Makes: 4 servings

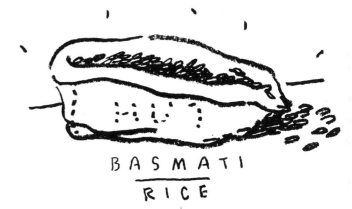

BASMATI RICE

1 onion
1 cup rice, preferably basmati
2 tbsp vegetable oil
2 crushed garlic cloves
1 tsp cumin seeds
4 cardamom pods
3-inch cinnamon stick
2 whole cloves
2¼ cups water
¼ tsp salt
2 bay leaves

1. Peel and finely chop the onion and set aside. Place the rice in a sieve and rinse under cold running water for about 30 seconds.

2. Heat the oil in a large saucepan over medium heat. Add the onion and garlic and sauté for 5 minutes or until the onion is soft. Stir in the cumin seeds, cardamom, cinnamon stick and cloves. Cook for about 1 minute to develop flavors. Stir in the rice until evenly coated with oil.

3. Add 2¼ cups water, salt and bay leaves. Bring to a boil. Then, cover, reduce heat to low and simmer until the water is absorbed, about 15 minutes. Remove from the heat and let stand, covered, for 5 minutes. Remove the bay leaves. Fluff the rice with a fork and serve immediately. Excellent served with chicken, pork or shrimp.

PER SERVING: 247 calories, 3.9 g protein, 40.7 g carbohydrates, 7.4 g fat, 36.4 mg calcium, 2.9 mg iron, 0.9 g fiber.

Cool Minted Vegetable Couscous

A summertime, make-ahead couscous cooled with a lemony mint vinaigrette. We love it with grilled lamb. In springtime, add sautéed asparagus.

Preparation time: 20 minutes / Cooking time: 5 minutes

Makes: 6 servings

12-oz (340-g) pkg couscous
$\frac{1}{4}$ English cucumber
2 ripe tomatoes, seeded
4 whole green onions, thinly sliced
$\frac{1}{4}$ cup finely chopped fresh mint
$\frac{1}{4}$ cup finely chopped fresh basil or parsley
2 tbsp olive oil
3 to 4 tbsp freshly squeezed lemon juice
Generous pinch each of salt and freshly ground black pepper
1 head Boston or Bibb lettuce
Fresh mint and basil leaves (optional)

1. Prepare the entire package of couscous following package directions. This will make about $4\frac{1}{2}$ cups cooked couscous.

2. After the couscous has sat, covered, for 5 minutes as directed on the package, gently fluff it with a fork. Then let sit, uncovered, until cooled to room temperature. Do not stir during this time.

Rice in Minutes

Start with 3 cups of hot cooked rice and spark it up with any of the following.

Parmesan Plus
Stir in $\frac{1}{4}$ cup freshly grated Parmesan cheese and 2 teaspoons butter. Great with veal or chicken.

Snappy Spinach
Stir in 1 cup chopped spinach, fresh or cooked, and 2 teaspoons freshly squeezed lemon juice. Serve with fish or chicken.

Savory Stuffing
Stir in 1 tablespoon butter, $\frac{1}{2}$ teaspoon poultry seasoning and 2 stalks thinly sliced celery. A terrific dish with chicken and turkey.

Curried Almond
Stir in 1 teaspoon curry powder and $\frac{1}{2}$ cup chopped almonds. Perfect with chicken.

Lemon-Dill
Stir in $\frac{1}{4}$ cup chopped fresh dill and 2 teaspoons grated lemon peel. Good with fish.

Country Bacon
Stir in 4 slices crumbled cooked bacon and 1 cup cooked peas. Great served with burgers.

Hot Pepper
Stir in $\frac{1}{4}$ teaspoon Tabasco sauce and $\frac{1}{2}$ red pepper, seeded and chopped. Excellent with steak.

Herbed Vegetable
Stir in 1 cup cooked frozen mixed vegetables and 1 teaspoon dried basil. Serve with burgers or veal.

3. Slice the cucumber in half lengthwise and discard the seeds. Then, cut the cucumber into ½-inch pieces. (They should measure about 2 cups.) Place in a large bowl.

4. Cut the seeded tomatoes into ½-inch pieces and add to the cucumber along with the green onions, mint and basil. Add the oil and 3 tablespoons lemon juice and gently toss to combine. Set aside.

5. Then, add the couscous to the vegetable mixture. Stir with a fork until combined. Taste and add salt, pepper and more lemon juice, if needed. Serve immediately or cover and refrigerate for up to 4 hours. If you wish to make a day ahead, do not add the tomatoes until just before serving.

6. To serve, wash and dry the lettuce, leaving leaves whole. Arrange in a circular fashion on a large platter. Mound the couscous mixture in the centre of the leaves. Garnish with mint or basil leaves.

QUICK-COOKING COUSCOUS

Couscous takes less time than rice to prepare. Simply stir 1 cup couscous with 1¼ cups boiling water, 1 tablespoon butter and ¼ teaspoon salt. Cover and leave for 5 minutes. Then, fluff with a fork.

VARIATION

Dried Herb
Stir in 2 teaspoons dried basil and 2 teaspoons dried mint in place of fresh herbs and increase the chopped parsley to ½ cup.

PER SERVING: *237 calories, 7.1 g protein, 40.9 g carbohydrates, 5.1 g fat, 34.4 mg calcium, 1.6 mg iron, 8.5 g fiber.*

MINT

QUICK WAYS WITH COUSCOUS

Fast ways to add extra punch to this five-minute wonder grain.

Baked Stuffed Peppers
Stir ½ cup freshly grated Parmesan cheese and ¼ teaspoon each of paprika and dried leaf thyme into 2 cups cooked couscous. Spoon into 4 scooped-out sweet peppers. Bake at 350F for about 20 minutes. Serves 4.

Pretty Stuffed Tomatoes
Scoop out 4 tomatoes. Coarsely chop the pulp and mix with ½ cup cooked couscous, ½ teaspoon dried basil and ½ cup chopped cucumber. Spoon into the tomatoes. Serves 4.

Spanish Couscous
Stir ¼ cup sliced stuffed green olives, 1 chopped tomato, 1 crushed garlic clove and generous pinches each of dried leaf thyme and oregano into 2 cups cooked couscous. Serve hot, warm or cold. Makes 3 cups.

Spiced Couscous
Heat 1 tablespoon olive oil in a large frying pan. Add 1 cup couscous. Stir for 1 minute over medium heat. Stir in 1¼ cups water, ¼ teaspoon salt and pinches of allspice and mace. Stir with a fork until all the liquid is absorbed. Makes 2 cups.

Lamb Go-With
Sauté 1 chopped onion in 1 tablespoon butter in a small saucepan. Add 1¼ cups water, ¾ cup frozen peas and a pinch of salt. Cover and bring to a boil. Stir in 1 cup couscous. Remove from heat. Let stand, covered, for 5 minutes. Stir in 2 tablespoons chopped fresh mint. Makes 4 cups.

Zippy Side Dish
Sauté 1 crushed garlic clove and 1 chopped zucchini in 1 to 2 teaspoons olive oil. Stir into 2 cups hot cooked couscous along with 1 teaspoon finely grated lemon peel, ¼ teaspoon dried basil, salt and freshly ground black pepper. Makes 3 cups.

Couscous Salad with Snow Peas

Our upscale Oriental extras give a unique twist to this unusual couscous salad.

Preparation time: 20 minutes / Cooking time: 5 minutes
Refrigeration time: 2 hours / Makes: 4 to 6 servings

Protein-Rich Couscous

Couscous is another name for semolina, the milled centre of durum wheat. It looks like pale golden, granular rice. A cup of cooked couscous has 7.6 grams of protein, no cholesterol and about 224 calories.

$1\frac{1}{4}$ cups couscous
$1\frac{1}{4}$ cups boiling water
1 tbsp butter
$\frac{1}{4}$ tsp salt
$\frac{1}{2}$ lb (250 g) fresh snow peas or 1 cup frozen peas
$\frac{1}{4}$ cup vegetable oil
Freshly squeezed juice of 1 orange
1 tbsp soy sauce
$\frac{1}{4}$ tsp ground ginger
1 red pepper

1. Place the couscous in a large bowl. Pour the boiling water over top and stir in the butter and $\frac{1}{4}$ teaspoon salt. Cover and set aside for the couscous to absorb the liquid, about 5 minutes.

2. Meanwhile, trim the snow peas. Blanch the snow peas or frozen peas in a large pot of boiling water, about 1 minute. Then, drain and rinse with cold water to stop the cooking.

3. Combine the oil and orange juice in a large bowl. Whisk in the soy sauce and ginger. Cut the red pepper into thin julienne bite-size strips. Add the pepper to the oil mixture. Stir in the drained peas.

4. Fluff up the couscous with a fork to break up any lumps. Add to the vegetables and toss together until evenly mixed. Refrigerate until chilled, about 2 hours, or ready to serve. Once the salad has chilled, cover tightly. It will keep well in the refrigerator for at least a day.

PER SERVING: 260 calories, 6.1 g protein, 33.5 g carbohydrates, 11.3 g fat, 25.5 mg calcium, 1.3 mg iron, 6.1 g fiber.

SNOW PEAS

HOT PEPPER RISOTTO WITH CHÈVRE

Distinctive goat cheese and hot peppers give richness and zing to this creamy risotto. Outstanding with grilled lamb and roast chicken.

Preparation time: 10 minutes / Cooking time: 30 minutes

Makes: 4 servings

$\frac{1}{4}$ cup butter
1 onion, preferably Spanish, finely chopped
1 crushed garlic clove
1$\frac{1}{2}$ cups Arborio rice
$\frac{1}{2}$ cup dry white wine
$\frac{1}{4}$ to $\frac{1}{2}$ tsp dried hot pepper or chili flakes
2 (10-oz/284-mL) cans undiluted chicken broth
2 cups water
$\frac{1}{2}$ cup chèvre
Salt and freshly ground black pepper (optional)

1. Melt the butter in a large wide saucepan. Add the onion and garlic and reduce heat to low. Sauté, stirring often, until the onion is soft, about 5 minutes. Then, add the rice and increase heat to medium. Stir the mixture until the rice is coated with butter.

2. Immediately add the wine while constantly stirring the rice mixture. Add $\frac{1}{4}$ teaspoon chili flakes (if you like food extremely fiery, add $\frac{1}{2}$ teaspoon) and stir gently until the rice absorbs the wine.

3. Then, add the undiluted chicken broth and water, about $\frac{1}{4}$ cup at a time. Stir constantly and wait until the liquid is absorbed before adding the next $\frac{1}{4}$ cup. This process is necessary in order to achieve the proper texture. Continue additions until all the liquid is absorbed and the rice is cooked, about 20 to 25 minutes. When cooked, the rice should be tender but not soft.

4. Stir in the cheese until evenly distributed. Taste and add salt and pepper, if needed.

PER SERVING: *470 calories, 14.4 g protein, 59.8 g carbohydrates, 16.5 g fat, 63.3 mg calcium, 4.1 mg iron, 1.2 g fiber.*

ARBORIO RICE

In order to make a great risotto, you must start with a thick, stubby Italian-style rice. The most common variety is Arborio. This rice can be purchased in Italian grocery stores, specialty food shops and supermarkets.

THE NEW BEAN CUISINE

In our quest for healthful dishes and dollar-value, beans are emerging as leading players in the '90s kitchen. They're high in protein but don't contain the fat and cholesterol of many other high-protein foods. And what a high-fiber power-house — $\frac{1}{2}$ cup of kidney beans holds three times as much fiber as $\frac{1}{2}$ cup of cooked oatmeal. Health-smart and easy on the budget they always were, but now we've smartened them up to the point that they are positively stylish.

ALL ABOUT BEANS

BEAN/PEA	APPEARANCE	USES FOR UNCOOKED (SOAKED)	USES FOR COOKED
Broad (fava)	Large, flat, kidney-shaped; light brown	Cook in a spicy tomato sauce with Mexican seasonings.	In salads with olive oil and lemon dressing; sauté in butter with onions.
Chick-pea (garbanzo)	Small, heart-shaped and tan-colored	Add to soups and stews; use as a base for hot curries.	In salads with spicy dressing; puréed with garlic for a dip, or fry in patties.
Great Northern (haricot or cannellini)	Small, kidney-shaped; creamy white	A wonderful baking bean, used in Boston baked beans; bake with canned tomatoes and herbs, topped with grated cheese.	Sauté with bacon, onions and thyme; serve with lamb or pork; sauté with onions, chopped tomatoes and garlic.
Kidney	Large, kidney-shaped; dark red, red or white	Red are traditionally added to chili con carne; use white in soups.	Add wholesome texture and color to salads; excellent with sweet-and-sour dressing.
Lima (butter bean)	Large, flat, kidney-shaped; white when dried	Add to soups; add with kidney beans to chili con carne.	In salads, mix with onion rings and herb dressing; bake in a mustard-honey sauce just until warmed through.

CURRIED CHICK-PEA SAUTÉ

Up until recently the only way we used chick-peas was to purée them in a garlicky hummus dip. Then we discovered that the firm, nutty flavor of the whole bean works beautifully as a side dish. Here we've curried it up as a great companion to chicken.

Preparation time: 5 minutes / Cooking time: 10 minutes

Makes: 5 servings

2 tbsp butter or vegetable oil
1 onion, finely chopped
2 garlic cloves, minced
$\frac{1}{2}$ tsp ground ginger or 1 tbsp minced fresh gingerroot
1 tsp each of ground cumin and coriander
$\frac{1}{2}$ tsp each of turmeric and cayenne pepper
19-oz (540-mL) can chick-peas
Chopped fresh parsley (optional)

1. Heat the butter or oil in a large frying pan. Add the onion, garlic and ginger. Turn heat to low. Sprinkle with the seasonings and stir frequently for about 2 minutes until onion has softened a little.

2. Add the liquid drained from the can of chick-peas and boil vigorously until reduced to about $\frac{1}{3}$ cup. Stir in the chick-peas and just heat through. Serve warm, sprinkled with parsley, or cover and refrigerate. The flavor improves with at least 1 day's refrigeration. This dish is delicious cold or hot and goes well with chicken.

PER SERVING: *163 calories, 5.7 g protein, 21.3 g carbohydrates, 6.9 g fat, 64.4 mg calcium, 3.6 mg iron, 5.7 g fiber.*

HOT 'N' TANGY BLACK BEANS

For a fast side dish with lots of dash combine a chopped red pepper, a chopped onion, 1 tablespoon chopped jalapeno pepper, $\frac{1}{2}$ teaspoon dried leaf thyme and 2 tablespoons olive oil in a 6-cup (1.5-L) microwave-safe dish.

Heat in the microwave, covered, on high for 3 minutes. Stir in 3 cups cooked black beans and 1 tablespoon lime juice. Heat, covered, on high for 2 minutes or until the beans are hot. Great with chicken. Serves 4 to 6. See photo opposite page 65.

NUTRITIONAL PROFILE
(Based on $\frac{1}{2}$ cup cooked beans)

BEAN/PEA	CALORIES	PROTEIN (g)	FIBER (g)	NUTRITIONAL BENEFITS
Broad (fava)	72	6.2	0	Rich in vitamins C and A
Chick-pea (garbanzo)	113	7	1.5	Rich in calcium and iron
Great Northern (haricot or cannellini)	111	7.5	1.5	Rich in calcium and iron
Kidney	142	8	1.1	Rich in calcium and iron
Lima (butter bean)	100	7	1.2	Rich in vitamin C and niacin

FAST HERBED BEANS

Here's a high-speed way to turn beans into a savory side dish. Terrific with grilled lamb chops.

Preparation time: 5 minutes / Cooking time: 7 minutes

Makes: 4 servings

1 tbsp butter
1 crushed garlic clove
1 large onion, chopped
19-oz (540-mL) can white or Romano beans
½ tsp dried leaf thyme
Pinch each of dried sage and cayenne pepper

1. Heat the butter in a large frying pan. Add the garlic and onion. Sauté over low heat for 5 minutes or until soft. Add the rinsed and drained beans. Sprinkle with seasonings. Stir gently over low heat until beans are warm.

PER SERVING: *118 calories, 8.2 g protein, 22 g carbohydrates, 3.3 g fat, 47.2 mg calcium, 2 mg iron, 6.8 g fiber.*

CHICK PEAS

RECYCLED BEANS
Overcooked beans can be recycled as a dip. Purée them with some garlic, adding a little sour cream to thin the mixture to a dipping consistency. Serve surrounded by red pepper strips or pita triangles.

THE SCOOP ON BEANS

Healthy beans are chock-full of incomplete protein — called incomplete because they lack some of the amino acids necessary to meet our bodies' essential protein needs — which is easily supplemented by serving with another complementary incomplete protein, such as whole wheat bread, or with a small amount of complete protein, such as ham, a slice of bacon or a sprinkling of cheese. Beans are rich sources of B vitamins and iron, calcium, magnesium, phosphorus and potassium. They contain little fat and are high in fiber to aid normal digestion.

Buying
Avoid soft, broken or wrinkled dried beans. Pick ones that are uniform in color and shape.

Many varieties of cooked beans are sold in cans, including chick-peas, lima beans and kidney beans. You just drain them and rinse before using.

Soaking
Place the beans in a sieve and rinse with cold running water until the water runs clear. Soaking gives the beans a chance to reabsorb water lost during drying. Rehydrated, they take 1 to 3 hours to cook depending on the bean. Without soaking, the beans need 1 to 2 hours more cooking and about twice the liquid called for in most recipes.

Short Soak Method
Place the beans in a large saucepan and cover with water. Bring to a boil and boil, uncovered,

CHICK-PEA AND FRESH TOMATO TOSS

Here's a quick 'n' easy way to add exotic Middle Eastern flavor to a can of chick-peas.

Preparation time: 5 minutes / Makes: 4 servings

19-oz (540-mL) can chick-peas
1 large tomato, chopped
3 whole green onions, thinly sliced
2 tbsp vegetable oil
1 tbsp lemon juice
1 tsp ground cumin
½ tsp chili powder
¼ tsp salt

1. Rinse and drain the chick-peas. Place them in a bowl. Add the tomato and onions. Whisk remaining ingredients together. Toss with the chick-pea mixture until coated. Serve right away or refrigerate for up to 2 days.

PER SERVING: 209 calories, 6.9 g protein, 25.6 g carbohydrates, 9.7 g fat, 69.3 mg calcium, 4.4 mg iron, 7.5 g fiber.

KIDNEY

LIMA

for 3 minutes. Cover the pot, remove from the heat and let stand for 1 hour. Drain and throw away the soaking water. Don't leave the beans in the hot soaking water for more than an hour as they may sour.

Long Soak Method
Cover the beans with water and leave at room temperature for 8 hours. Don't soak too long — they'll absorb too much water and become mushy. Always discard the soaking water.

Cooking
Put presoaked beans in a saucepan with enough water or other liquid to keep them covered during the cooking. (Beans double to triple in size during cooking; 2 to 3 inches of liquid over the beans should be sufficient.) Add about 1 tablespoon oil or fat to help keep the water

from boiling over, and salt for flavor. Bring to a boil, cover, reduce heat and simmer until the beans are tender — from half an hour to 3 hours. To tell whether they're done, pinch or bite beans; they should feel soft but not mushy.

Baking
Beans are usually cooked on top of the stove until almost tender, combined in a bean pot or casserole dish with liquid and seasonings and baked, covered, for 1 to 6 hours, depending on the bean. To brown the beans, remove the cover, sprinkle the beans with brown sugar and bake another half hour.

Fast Bean Dishes

A can of beans — kidney, Romano or chick-peas — sitting on your cupboard shelf means you always have the makings of a satisfying supper. Drain the beans and rinse them with cold water before using, unless otherwise noted.

Mexican-Spiced Beans 'n' Rice

Chop 1 onion, 1 celery stalk and 1 red pepper. Sauté in 1 teaspoon olive oil with 1 crushed garlic clove for 3 minutes. Add the entire contents of a 19-oz (540-mL) can of kidney beans, ¼ teaspoon dried leaf oregano and ¼ teaspoon chili powder. Stir gently until hot. Serve over rice. Serves 4.

3-Bean Salad

Mix a 19-oz (540-mL) can of kidney beans, a 19-oz (540-mL) can of Romano beans, and a 14-oz (398-mL) can of pinto beans with ½ small chopped red onion, a chopped red pepper, ¼ cup Italian salad dressing and ½ teaspoon each of ground cumin and coriander. Makes 6 cups.

Beans and Greens Toss

Whisk ⅓ cup olive oil with 2 tablespoons lemon juice, ½ teaspoon basil and ½ teaspoon granulated sugar. Toss with 1 head leafy lettuce, torn into pieces, a 14-oz (398-mL) can of drained artichoke hearts, a 19-oz (540-mL) can of chick-peas and ¼ lb (125 g) julienned salami slices. Serves 4.

Quick Protein Soup

In a saucepan, cook a chopped sweet pepper and an onion with 4 slices of chopped bacon over medium heat, stirring often, for 7 minutes. Add a 10-oz (284-mL) can of undiluted chicken broth, a 19-oz (540-mL) can of tomatoes including juice, a 19-oz (540-mL) can of Romano beans and 1 teaspoon dried leaf thyme. Simmer for 10 minutes. Makes 5 cups.

Curried Beans 'n' Lamb

Combine 1 lb (500 g) ground lamb or beef, 1 chopped sweet pepper, 1 onion, ½ teaspoon each of ground coriander, cumin and curry powder and 1 crushed garlic clove in a frying pan. Cook, stirring often, for 10 minutes. Add a 19-oz (540-mL) can of Romano beans. Serves 4.

Hot Sausages and Beans

Cut up 4 Italian sausages. Brown the sausages in a large frying pan. Stir in a 19-oz (540-mL) can of red kidney beans, a 7½-oz(213-mL) can of tomato sauce and ¼ cup red wine. Simmer mixture, uncovered, for 5 minutes, stirring often. Serves 4.

Hearty Hummus Spread

In a food processor, purée a 19-oz (540-mL) can of chick-peas with 3 tablespoons lemon juice, 2 tablespoons water, 1 tablespoon sesame oil, 2 crushed garlic cloves, ½ teaspoon ground cumin, a dash of Tabasco sauce and generous pinches of salt and pepper. Makes 1¾ cups.

Warm Cheddar Bean Dip

Mash a 14-oz (398-mL) can of pinto beans. Stir with ⅓ cup mayonnaise, 1 cup grated cheddar cheese, 1 crushed garlic clove and 1 to 2 teaspoons finely chopped jalapeno peppers. Spoon into a small baking dish. Bake at 350F until bubbling, about 20 minutes. Makes 2½ cups.

HUMMUS SPREAD

CHEERS FOR CHICKEN

Canadians are having a love affair with chicken. No wonder. It's smart, sexy and easy to get along with. In these fat-conscious times, chicken's high protein and low fat content make it a natural choice. Its subtle understated taste comes alive at dinner parties with dress-up fresh herb seasonings and sassy sauces. And what could be more comforting than the aroma of a golden bird roasting in the oven? Then there's the newest game in town — free-range chicken — which costs a little more than the cooped-up bird but since it's had an opportunity to strut its stuff it delivers much more true old-fashioned chicken flavor. Sautéed, sauced, stuffed, broiled, roasted or grilled — use our winning ways to bring this never-boring bird to your table.

CHEERS FOR CHICKEN • TRIPLE TESTED

CHICKEN EVERY DAY AND EVERY WAY

For all kinds of reasons chicken is the right choice for our times. You can do as much or as little as you want with it. Nutritionists praise it, and if you shop smartly, it's easy on your pocketbook.

For weekday budget stretchers we go for legs and thighs — hot 'n' spicy in a chicken-chili combo or flavored with intriguing tastes from the Orient. On Friday nights we like to wing it with devilishly hot three-alarm sauce. Try tucking a little garlic butter underneath the skin of the whole bird for the popular Sunday roast chicken. Whatever turns you on — legs, breasts, thighs or wings — there's an almost endless combination of sassy herbs and sauces to spice up the naturally delicate flavor of chicken. Every day and every way. No kidding!

SOUTHWEST CHICKEN

Salsa is the ketchup of the '90s. It's a fresh, fiery tomato sauce chockful of hot peppers and onions and it contains a mere 4 calories per tablespoon. Here we've used it as a fast flavor-booster for chicken breasts.

Preparation time: 10 minutes / Baking time: 45 minutes

Makes: 8 servings

8 chicken breasts, bone-in
1 cup hot salsa
½ cup white wine
3 tbsp olive or vegetable oil

1. Preheat oven to 375F. Remove the skin from the chicken and arrange pieces in a 9x13-inch pan, trying not to overlap them. In a small bowl, stir the salsa with the wine and oil. Pour evenly over the chicken.

2. Bake, uncovered, in centre of the preheated oven until the chicken feels springy to the touch, about 45 minutes. Baste the chicken at least every 15 minutes to keep it moist.

PER SERVING: *198 calories, 25.5 g protein, 2.1 g carbohydrates, 8.6 g fat, 17.8 mg calcium, 1.2 mg iron, 0 g fiber.*

8-Minute Classy Chicken Loaf

The ultimate juicy low-cal meatloaf. Juiciness comes not from fat but yogurt, and the moistness is maintained by microwaving.

Preparation time: 10 minutes / Microwave time: 8 minutes
Standing time: 5 minutes / Makes: 4 to 6 servings

1 small celery stalk, thinly sliced
1 small onion, finely chopped
1 egg
$\frac{1}{4}$ cup light sour cream or Balkan-style yogurt
1 tbsp Dijon mustard
$\frac{1}{4}$ tsp dried tarragon
$\frac{1}{8}$ tsp each of ground nutmeg and salt
$\frac{1}{8}$ tsp freshly ground white pepper
1 lb (500 g) ground chicken
$\frac{1}{2}$ cup dry bread crumbs
$\frac{1}{4}$ cup grated old cheddar cheese

1. Put the celery and onion in a bowl. Stir in the egg, sour cream, Dijon and seasonings.

2. Crumble the chicken over the egg mixture. Sprinkle with the bread crumbs. Using your hands or a fork, mix thoroughly.

3. Divide the mixture in half and shape each into an oblong loaf with rounded edges. (Rounded edges cook better than square edges.) Place the loaves, side by side, on a 10-inch microwave-safe pie plate, ensuring they do not touch one another or the sides of the plate.

4. Microwave the loaves, uncovered, on high for about 4 minutes. If the microwave does not have a turntable, rotate the plate a quarter-turn. Continue cooking, uncovered, for 4 more minutes. Remove from the microwave and sprinkle with the cheese. Cover and let stand for 5 minutes to allow the centres of the loaves to continue cooking. Chicken loaves should feel dry and firm on the sides, while the tops should feel a little softer.

PER SERVING: *182 calories, 15.7 g protein, 8.3 g carbohydrates, 9.2 g fat, 72.6 mg calcium, 1.1 mg iron, 0.6 g fiber.*

Best Chicken Stock

Place about 2 lbs (1 kg) chicken carcasses or bones in a large saucepan. Cover with 12 cups water. Add 2 chopped onions, 2 sliced carrots, a handful of celery leaves, 1 bay leaf and 1 teaspoon salt. Bring to a boil, then reduce heat and simmer, covered, about 3 hours. Stir occasionally and skim the surface. Strain the stock through a sieve and refrigerate. When cool, skim off the fat and discard. Store, covered, in the refrigerator for several days or in the freezer.

CHICKEN LOAF

LIFE-OF-THE-PARTY FAJITAS

For easy entertaining, we like to set out a platter of sizzling chicken with baskets of warm tortillas and small dishes of toppings so guests can make their own Mexican roll-ups.

Preparation time: 15 minutes / Cooking time: 10 minutes

Makes: 4 servings

TEARLESS ONIONS
Refrigerate or put onions in the freezer for a few minutes before chopping.

1 onion
1 red pepper
4 single chicken breasts, skinned and boned
1 tbsp vegetable or olive oil
1 tsp chili powder
½ tsp ground cumin
¼ tsp each of dried leaf oregano and black pepper
½ tsp salt
1 crushed garlic clove
3 drops of Tabasco sauce
1 tbsp freshly squeezed lime juice
1 avocado, sliced
1 tomato, cut into wedges
Fresh coriander sprigs
4 to 8 flour tortillas or pitas, warmed
Salsa
Guacamole

1. Slice the onion and red pepper into ¼-inch strips. Slice the chicken into ¾-inch strips.

2. Heat 2 teaspoons oil in a large frying pan set over medium heat. When the oil is hot, add the chicken. Sprinkle with the chili powder, cumin, oregano, black pepper and salt. Stir frequently until light golden and slightly firm, about 5 minutes. Place on a plate and keep warm.

3. Reduce heat to medium-low. Add remaining teaspoon of oil to the pan. Add the garlic, onion and red pepper. Stir frequently until softened, about 5 minutes. Return the chicken to the pan. Stir the Tabasco sauce into the lime juice and drizzle over the chicken and vegetables. Stir until well coated and the chicken is hot. Then, pour the contents of the pan into a large serving bowl.

4. Garnish the chicken with the avocado, tomato and fresh coriander sprigs. Serve with warm flour tortillas. Guests should spoon the chicken mixture onto the warm tortillas, then top with salsa and guacamole.

PER SERVING: *318 calories, 20.5 g protein, 26 g carbohydrates, 3.6 g fat, 15.5 mg calcium, 3 mg iron, 3.6 g fiber.*

PHOTO: *Life-of-the-Party Fajitas, see recipe at right.*

Basil Balsamic Chicken

A spritz of balsamic vinegar is all it takes to add a delicate sweet 'n' sour zing to chicken breasts.

Preparation time: 10 minutes / Cooking time: 15 minutes
Makes: 4 servings

1 tbsp butter
4 chicken breasts, skinned and boned
¼ cup chicken broth or bouillon
1 tbsp balsamic vinegar
¼ tsp dried basil

1. Melt the butter in a large frying pan set over medium heat. Add the chicken and sauté until pale golden on all sides, about 3 minutes per side.

2. Add remaining ingredients. Cover, reduce heat to low and simmer until the chicken feels springy to the touch, about 7 to 8 minutes. Turn the chicken breasts partway through simmering.

3. Remove the chicken to a platter. Increase heat to high and boil the sauce, stirring occasionally, until reduced to ¼ cup. Pour over the breasts and serve.

PER SERVING: *118 calories, 16.5 g protein, 0.3 g carbohydrates, 5.3 g fat, 10.4 mg calcium, 0.6 mg iron, 0 g fiber.*

Elegant Ginger Chicken Sauté

Preserved ginger sparked with lime gives a fast sense of elegance to this easy sauté.

Preparation time: 10 minutes / Cooking time: 35 minutes
Makes: 4 servings

4 chicken breasts, boned or bone-in
All-purpose flour
3 tbsp butter
¼ cup chicken broth
2 tbsp syrup drained from preserved ginger
1 lime, cut in half
¼ cup slivered preserved ginger
Pinch each of salt and white pepper
Sliced whole green onions

Vary Your Vinegars

For years, vinegar was either cider or white. Today's flavored vinegars range from black currant to green peppercorn or sage. Italian balsamic vinegar, aged for years in wood barrels, is superb in salad dressings with its sweet-and-sour taste and rich winey bouquet. Rice wine vinegar is a light, low-acid, faintly sweet vinegar from Japan; mix it with soy sauce for fish marinades and sauces. Used alone, tarragon vinegar is a perfect low-calorie salad dressing. Raspberry vinegar adds a delightful fruity flavor to chicken and veal.

PHOTO: *Celebration Country Chicken, see recipe on page 197.*

FIRST-CLASS BROWNING

If a recipe calls for large amounts of poultry or meat, brown it in several small batches instead of one large one. Overcrowding the pan causes the juices to flow into the pan, steaming instead of browning the pieces.

1. Skin the chicken breasts. Bone only if you wish. Lightly coat with flour, shaking off the excess. Melt the butter in a large frying pan. Add the chicken breasts and sauté over medium-high heat until golden brown on both sides, about 10 minutes.

2. Add the chicken broth to the pan along with the syrup drained from the preserved ginger and the juice squeezed from half the lime. Cover tightly and simmer for 5 to 10 minutes for boned or 15 to 20 minutes for bone-in chicken until the chicken feels springy. Turn once during this time. Remove the chicken to serving dishes and cover to keep warm.

3. Stir the slivered ginger into the sauce. Squeeze in the remainder of the lime juice and season with salt and white pepper. Turn heat to high and boil vigorously until thickened, about 2 minutes. Pour over the chicken. Garnish with sliced green onion.

PER SERVING: 229 calories, 16.9 g protein, 15.3 g carbohydrates, 11.1 g fat, 16.7 mg calcium, 1.1 mg iron, 0.1 g fiber.

SHORT-NOTICE CHICKEN SAUTÉS

Boneless, skinless chicken breasts stored in your freezer are a lifesaver. Quickly sautéed or broiled, they're a nutritious entrée: a 4-oz (125-g) breast provides 27 g of protein and about 4.5 g of fat. Here are a few easy embellishments.

Zesty Chutney
Sauté 4 breasts in 1 tablespoon butter for 4 minutes per side. Stir ¼ cup orange juice and 2 tablespoons mango chutney into the pan juices. Cover and simmer for 2 minutes.

Herbed Parmesan
Dip the chicken into beaten egg. Stir ¼ cup dry bread crumbs with 2 tablespoons grated Parmesan cheese and 1 tablespoon chopped parsley. Press onto 4 boneless, skinless chicken breasts. Sauté in 1 tablespoon butter for 4 minutes per side.

Paprika Stroganoff
Sprinkle 4 breasts with ½ teaspoon paprika and a pinch of black pepper. Sauté with ¼ cup minced onion in 1 tablespoon butter for 4 minutes per side. Then, stir in ¼ cup sour cream.

Peppery Mustard
Whisk 2 tablespoons Dijon with 1 cup sour cream and 2 teaspoons drained and rinsed green peppercorns. Spoon over sautéed chicken.

Mustard-Dill
Sauté 4 breasts in 2 tablespoons butter until golden on both sides. Add ¼ cup white wine and 2 tablespoons chopped fresh dill. Cover, simmer for 10 minutes. Remove chicken. Whisk 1 tablespoon Dijon mustard and ½ cup sour cream into the sauce.

Orange-Honey
Sauté 4 breasts in 2 tablespoons butter until golden on both sides. Add the juice of 1 orange, 1 tablespoon liquid honey and ¼ teaspoon each of ground ginger and curry powder. Cover and simmer for 10 minutes.

Roquefort
Sauté 4 breasts in 2 tablespoons butter until golden on both sides. Add ¼ cup water. Cover, simmer for 10 minutes. Remove chicken. Add ¼ cup crumbled Roquefort cheese and 2 finely chopped whole green onions. Stir over medium heat until thick.

Elegant French
Combine 2 tablespoons cognac, ½ cup table cream, ¾ teaspoon dried tarragon and a pinch of salt in a small saucepan. Boil, stirring frequently, until slightly thickened, and pour over sautéed chicken.

Cinnamon and Ginger Harvest Chicken

A glistening red currant glaze — with a heady hint of cinnamon, ginger and allspice — beautifully coats tender pieces of chicken and juicy apples. See photo on front cover.

Preparation time: 20 minutes / Cooking time: 50 minutes

Makes: 4 servings

1 tbsp vegetable oil
4 serving-size pieces of chicken
Salt and freshly ground black pepper
5 small cooking onions
1 tbsp freshly grated gingerroot
1/2 cup each of red currant jelly and chicken broth
1/2 tsp allspice
3 (1½-inch) cinnamon sticks
1 large red cooking apple

1. Heat the oil in a large frying pan set over medium heat. Sprinkle the chicken with salt and pepper and place 2 or 3 pieces in the hot pan. Cook, turning at least once, until lightly golden, about 8 to 10 minutes. Then, transfer to a plate or bowl. Repeat with the remaining chicken. (It is best to cook only a few pieces at a time as chicken will not brown properly if pan is overcrowded.) Meanwhile, cut the onions in half, then quarter.

2. Discard all but 1 teaspoon fat from the pan. Add the onions and cook, stirring often, until glistening and lightly browned, about 4 minutes. Stir ginger into the pan, then add the jelly, broth and allspice. Stir until the jelly is melted. Scrape the pan gently to lift browned bits from the bottom. Add the cinnamon sticks.

3. Arrange chicken pieces in the pan and add any juices that have accumulated. Cover and simmer over medium-low heat for about 15 minutes.

4. Meanwhile, core and slice the apple. Turn the chicken and add apple. Continue simmering, covered, until chicken is springy to the touch, about 10 more minutes.

5. With a slotted spoon, remove the chicken, apple and onions to a serving platter. Bring sauce to a boil and boil vigorously, uncovered, stirring occasionally, until thickened, about 3 to 4 minutes. Spoon over chicken. Serve with steamed brown rice or couscous tossed with sliced green onions or coriander.

PER SERVING: *518 calories, 40 g protein, 39.7 g carbohydrates, 22.1 g fat, 53 mg calcium, 2.6 mg iron, 2.9 g fiber.*

ELEGANT STUFFED CHICKEN BREASTS

Cut a pocket in the thick portion of 4 boneless, skinless chicken breasts. Finely chop 2 sun-dried tomatoes and stir into 1/4 cup chèvre along with a crushed garlic clove. Stuff into chicken breasts. Sauté, covered, in 1 tablespoon oil in a large frying pan for 12 minutes, turning once.

For a variation, try one of the following fillings:

• Grated Parmesan cheese and snipped chives

• Cold garlic butter and sliced whole green onions

• Sliced prosciutto and Swiss cheese or Dijon mustard

• Herbed cream cheese

New Chicken à la King

Chicken à la king cascading ever so correctly from puff pastry casings was one of those dishes often served at ladies' luncheons in the '40s and '50s. Today's version has a lot more comfort, less prissiness, and it's a snap to whip up with chicken breasts you've stashed in the freezer.

Preparation time: 10 minutes / Cooking time: 10 minutes
Makes: 4 servings

4 chicken breasts, skinned and boned
1 small sweet pepper, seeded
½ tbsp each of butter and vegetable oil
1 small crushed garlic clove
10-oz (284-mL) can cream of mushroom soup
¼ cup milk
¼ tsp each of dried leaf thyme and dried rosemary
Freshly ground black pepper

1. Slice the chicken into 1-inch cubes. Cut the pepper into ½-inch pieces. Combine the butter and oil in a frying pan set over medium-high heat. Add the chicken, sweet pepper and garlic. Sauté until the chicken is lightly browned, about 4 minutes.

2. Add remaining ingredients. Reduce heat to low. Cook, stirring frequently, until the sauce is smooth and hot. Serve over thick slices of toasted crusty bread.

PER SERVING: *407 calories, 36.1 g protein, 14.4 g carbohydrates, 22.4 g fat, 98.6 mg calcium, 2 mg iron, 0.5 g fiber.*

BBQ Chicken

To avoid burning chicken on the barbecue, partially precook bone-in chicken in the microwave or in the oven before grilling, or place the chicken at least 6 inches from the coals to prevent the outside from burning before the inside is cooked. If using sweet sauces, baste toward the end of grilling only — as they tend to burn.

Barbecued Cumin-Lime Chicken

Cumin and lime give Caribbean overtones to this no-work barbecued chicken. Grill zucchini and red peppers to go alongside and toss new potatoes with chives.

Preparation time: 10 minutes / Marinating time: 2 hours
Grilling time: 10 minutes / Makes: 2 to 4 servings

2 large limes
1 tbsp vegetable oil
1 large crushed garlic clove
2 tsp ground cumin
¼ tsp ground coriander
2 to 4 chicken breasts, skinned and boned

1. Two hours before cooking, combine in a shallow dish the juice and finely grated peel of the limes, the vegetable oil, garlic, cumin and coriander. Immerse the chicken breasts in the marinade and refrigerate for 2 hours, turning the chicken at least once during this time.

2. Then, preheat barbecue and place the grill several inches from the hot coals. Arrange the marinated chicken breasts on the grill and barbecue about 5 minutes per side, until the chicken feels springy to the touch. Season with salt and white pepper, if you wish.

PER SERVING: 236 calories, 17.1 g protein, 4.3 g carbohydrates, 17 g fat, 58.3 mg calcium, 3.4 mg iron, 0.01 g fiber.

CRUNCHY PECAN DRUMSTICKS

Dijon mustard adds a nippy twist to these crispy finger-lickin' legs.

Preparation time: 15 minutes / Baking time: 50 minutes

Makes: 4 servings

PECANS

8 small chicken drumsticks, thigh portion removed
2 cups pecan halves
$\frac{1}{2}$ cup fine dry bread crumbs
$\frac{1}{3}$ cup Dijon mustard
2 eggs
$\frac{1}{2}$ cup all-purpose flour

1. Preheat oven to 375F. Partially cook the drumsticks for 25 minutes in the centre of the preheated oven.

2. Meanwhile, finely chop the pecans. (Do not use a food processor or you'll end up with pecan butter.) Place the pecans and bread crumbs (do not use freshly made bread crumbs) in a shallow dish and stir with a fork until evenly blended. In another shallow dish, whisk the Dijon with the eggs. Place the flour in a third shallow dish and set aside.

3. As soon as the drumsticks are partially cooked, remove them from the oven but leave the oven temperature set at 375F. When the drumsticks are cool enough to handle, roll the meaty end of the drumstick in the flour, shaking off any excess. Then, roll it in the Dijon mixture, followed by the pecan-bread-crumb mixture. Place on waxed paper. Repeat with remaining chicken.

4. Place the coated drumsticks on a wire rack set on a foil-lined baking sheet. Bake until the pecans are toasted and the juices run clear when the chicken is pierced with a fork, about 20 to 25 more minutes. Watch the chicken closely near the end of the cooking, as the pecans can burn quickly.

PER SERVING: 649 calories, 32.4 g protein, 31.4 g carbohydrates, 45.1 g fat, 62 mg calcium, 3.6 mg iron, 4.4 g fiber.

Lickin' Good Barbecued Chicken

This homey skillet supper creates its own barbecue sauce as it simmers. Serve with big baked potatoes, sour cream and lots of green beans. Tuck in.

Preparation time: 20 minutes / Cooking time: 45 minutes

Makes: 3 to 4 servings

6 chicken legs
2 large crushed garlic cloves
$\frac{1}{2}$ cup water
$\frac{1}{4}$ cup ketchup
2 tbsp soy sauce
1 tbsp liquid honey

1. Place the drumsticks in a large nonstick frying pan. Place over medium-high heat. Sauté the chicken until lightly browned on all sides, about 10 minutes, adding a little vegetable oil to the pan, if needed.

2. Reduce heat to low. Stir the garlic into the fat in the pan, if needed. Then, add the water, ketchup and soy sauce and stir until mixed. Cover and simmer for about 30 minutes, turning the chicken about every 5 minutes, until the chicken feels springy to the touch. Remove to a platter.

3. Increase heat to medium. Gently boil the sauce, uncovered, stirring often, until the sauce is thick enough to coat the chicken, about 5 minutes. Stir in the honey. Pour the sauce over the chicken and serve.

PER SERVING: *179 calories, 21.9 g protein, 12.8 g carbohydrates, 4.2 g fat, 19.3 mg calcium, 1.4 mg iron, 0.02 g fiber.*

Runny Honey

If liquid honey crystallizes, remove the lid and place the jar in a saucepan filled with several inches of hot water and heat gently until the honey melts, or warm the jar in a microwave.

Double Chili Chicken Bake

Hot chilies and chili powder give a double punch of flavor to this quick-fix supper.

Preparation time: 10 minutes / Baking time: 1 hour, 5 minutes

Makes: 4 servings

4 chicken pieces (breasts, thighs, drumsticks)
$7\frac{1}{2}$-oz (213-mL) can tomato sauce
$\frac{1}{2}$ tsp each of chili powder and ground cumin
Salt and freshly ground black pepper
4-oz (114-mL) can green chilies, drained and chopped
1 onion, finely chopped
2 crushed garlic cloves
$\frac{1}{4}$ cup freshly grated Parmesan cheese

1. Preheat oven to 350F. Skin the chicken and place it in a casserole dish just large enough to hold the pieces in a single layer. Combine remaining ingredients, except the Parmesan cheese. Pour over the chicken. Cover loosely with foil.

2. Bake in the centre of the preheated oven for 45 minutes. Turn and baste occasionally. Sprinkle with the Parmesan and continue to bake, uncovered, for 15 to 20 minutes.

PER SERVING: 176 calories, 25.3 g protein, 8 g carbohydrates, 4.9 g fat, 128 mg calcium, 1.7 mg iron, 1.3 g fiber.

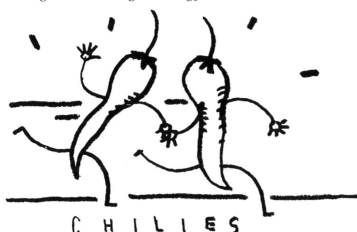

CHILIES

SWEET NUTCRACKER CHICKEN

Buy a whole roasted chicken. Cut it in pieces and lightly brush with maple syrup. Sprinkle liberally with chopped hazelnuts or pecans, chopped parsley and crumbled dried rosemary. Pop it into a 425F oven and roast until the nuts are lightly toasted, about 5 to 7 minutes.

NUTRITION KNOW-HOW

For health-conscious, time-strapped cooks, poultry is a number one entrée. Easy to prepare, high in protein, low in calories — and without skin it's low in fat and cholesterol. Here's a nutritional breakdown of popular poultry cuts and fast foods.

CUT (3½ oz/100 g, roasted)	CALORIES	PROTEIN (g)	FAT (g)
Chicken, white meat, no skin	165	31	4
Chicken, white meat, with skin	197	30	8
Chicken, dark meat, no skin	172	28	6
Turkey, white meat, no skin	157	30	3
Turkey, white meat, with skin	197	29	8
Turkey, dark meat, no skin	187	29	7
Turkey, dark meat, with skin	221	27	12
Turkey, roll, light and dark meat	149	18	7
Fast Foods			
Kentucky Fried Chicken (100 g)	303	19	17
McDonald's Chicken McNuggets (115 g)	312	18	21
Swiss Chalet 1/4 chicken (125 g)	308	35	19

LIGHT CHICKEN BURGERS

Chicken burgers are a terrific, light alternative to beef — 3 oz (85 g) of ground chicken have only 117 calories and 15 g of protein. Since broiling or grilling can dry out patties, always cook, covered, in a nonstick pan over medium heat. For a sassy low-calorie topper, consider salsa at only 4 calories per tablespoon or light sour cream at 15 calories per tablespoon.

Preparation time: 5 minutes / Cooking time: 8 minutes per batch

Makes: 8 burgers

1 egg
½ tsp Dijon mustard
½ tsp dried dillweed
¼ tsp each of salt and white pepper
2 lbs (1 kg) ground chicken or turkey
1 tsp butter or vegetable oil

1. Place the egg, Dijon and seasonings in a bowl. Stir until blended. Add the chicken. Work in with your fingers until combined. Form into 8 patties, about ½ inch thick each. Melt the butter in a large nonstick pan. Add half the patties and cook over medium heat, covered, for about 4 minutes per side. Repeat with remaining patties, using more butter, if needed.

PER SERVING: 147 calories, 18.5 g protein, 0.2 g carbohydrates, 7.4 g fat, 14.9 mg calcium, 1 mg iron, 0.02 g fiber.

LOW-CAL STAND-INS

If you're calorie counting, substitute ground chicken or turkey for beef in spaghetti sauce, shepherd's pie or tourtière.

When making meatballs or burgers with ground poultry, add extra flavor with light seasonings — fresh dill, a pinch of basil, poultry seasoning, tarragon, lemon pepper, ground cumin or coriander. A little light sour cream, salsa or Dijon mustard keeps them moist.

GARLIC CHICKEN

Garlic butter tucked under the skin seeps into the flesh of the chicken.

Preparation time: 15 minutes / Roasting time: 1¼ hours

Makes: 4 servings

2 tbsp butter
2 small crushed garlic cloves
¼ cup butter, chilled
2 whole green onions, very thinly sliced
3½-lb (1.75-kg) chicken

1. Prepare the garlic butter by placing 2 tablespoons butter and the garlic in a small frying pan. Sauté over low heat for 5 minutes. Do not let it brown. Then, pour it into a bowl. Add ¼ cup cold butter and work it in with a fork until blended. Stir in the green onions.

2. Preheat oven to 375F. To stuff the garlic butter under the chicken skin, begin with the breast side up. Fold the wings under the back of chicken. To loosen the skin from the flesh, start at the neck cavity and carefully push your fingertips between the skin and the breast meat. Move your fingertips to the thighs and loosen the skin.

3. Then, take about a tablespoon of the garlic butter and stuff it between the skin and the meat, pushing it right to the thighs. Distribute as much as possible over the thigh area. Repeat with the other thigh. Then, cover the breast area close to the thighs. Continue until all the garlic butter is used and the entire breast and most of thigh area is covered. Gently press on top of the chicken skin to evenly distribute the mixture. Skewer or sew the chicken cavity closed and tie the legs together.

4. Place the chicken breast-side up on rack in open roasting pan. Brush the skin with a little butter. Roast, uncovered, in the centre of the preheated oven for $1\frac{1}{4}$ hours or until a drumstick moves easily. Baste frequently with the pan juices.

PER SERVING: *518 calories, 47.5 g protein, 0.6 g carbohydrates, 35.1 g fat, 33.4 mg calcium, 2.3 mg iron, 0.06 g fiber.*

10-MINUTE PRESSURE COOKER CURRIED CHICKEN

Pressure cookers are making a comeback and no wonder. We were amazed at what a flavorful chicken curry we could create in just ten minutes.

Preparation time: 10 minutes / Cooking time: 15 minutes

Makes: 4 servings

1 to 2 tbsp butter
2 large onions, chopped
2 crushed garlic cloves
1 tbsp finely chopped fresh gingerroot (optional)
1 tbsp curry powder
1 tsp each of ground cumin and coriander
$\frac{1}{4}$ tsp cayenne pepper
19-oz (540-mL) can tomatoes, including juice
10-oz (284-mL) can undiluted chicken broth
6 pieces chicken, skinned
$\frac{1}{2}$ cup light sour cream

1. Melt the butter in the cooker. Add the onions, garlic and gingerroot, if using. Sprinkle with the seasonings. Sauté for 5 minutes over medium-low heat, stirring often. Stir in the tomatoes and chicken broth.

FAST ROAST CHICKEN

A whole chicken comes out fast and juicy in a microwave. The skin will not be crispy, but if you're fat conscious you'll discard it anyway.

Remove metal clips. If frozen, defrost in the microwave. Pierce skin in several places. Cover the wing tips and drumstick ends with small pieces of foil, dull-side out. Tie wings and legs close to the body with string or rubber bands. Sprinkle cavity with herbs or fill with your favorite stuffing but reduce the amount of fat and liquid to avoid sogginess. Sew cavity closed or use toothpicks.

Place breast-side down on a microwave roasting rack in an ovenproof dish. Brush skin with melted butter mixed with paprika. Cook chicken, uncovered, on high for 7 to 8 minutes per pound. Pour off pan juices as they collect. Halfway through cooking, turn breast-side up and remove foil. When cooking time is up, cover and leave 15 minutes — this time is essential.

Break up the tomatoes into small pieces. Stir in the chicken until coated. The chicken should not touch the bottom of the pan.

2. Lock the lid in place. Bring to high pressure over high heat. Adjust heat to low to medium-low to maintain high pressure and cook for 10 minutes.

3. Remove the cooker from the heat. Let the pressure drop naturally. For a thicker sauce, remove the chicken and boil the sauce, uncovered, over medium heat, stirring often, until it is as thick as you like. Stir in the sour cream and pour the sauce over the chicken.

PER SERVING: 523 calories, 61.5 g protein, 19.6 g carbohydrates, 21.8 g fat, 141 mg calcium, 4.8 mg iron, 2.9 g fiber.

THREE-ALARM WINGS

These sensational triple-hot-tasting wings must be served with a bowl of sour cream for dipping and cooling.

Preparation time: 15 minutes / Baking time: 30 minutes

Makes: 8 appetizer servings

2½ lbs (1.25 kg) chicken wings
⅔ cup chili sauce
2 tbsp vegetable oil
4 garlic cloves, finely chopped
1 tbsp liquid honey
½ to 1 tsp Tabasco sauce
¼ tsp crushed dried chilies
¼ tsp cayenne pepper

1. Remove the wing tips from the chicken wings. Cut the wings in half at the joint. In a large bowl, stir remaining ingredients together. Add the chicken pieces and stir until coated.

2. Preheat oven to 375F. Arrange the wings on a rack on a foil-lined baking sheet. The wings should not be touching. Bake in the centre of the preheated oven for 15 minutes. Turn the wings and brush with remaining marinade. Continue baking for an additional 10 to 15 minutes or until the chicken is tender.

PER SERVING: 190 calories, 12.4 g protein, 7.6 g carbohydrates, 12 g fat, 13.3 mg calcium, 0.7 mg iron, 0.03 g fiber.

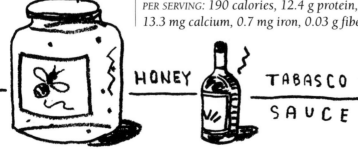

HONEY   TABASCO

SAUCE

CAESAR WINGS

Make up a batch of these great garlicky nibblers for munching on during the Grey Cup game.

Preparation time: 15 minutes / Baking time: 30 minutes

Makes: 12 servings

4 lbs (2 kg) chicken wings
2 cups bottled vinaigrette-style Caesar salad dressing
3 tbsp finely grated Parmesan cheese
4 tsp freshly ground black pepper
Pinch of salt

1. Preheat oven to 375F. Remove the wing tips from the chicken wings. Cut the wings in half at the joint.

2. In a small bowl, stir remaining ingredients together. Brush chicken pieces liberally with the marinade.

3. Arrange the wings on a rack on a foil-lined baking sheet. The wings should not be touching.

4. Bake in the centre of the preheated oven for 15 minutes, basting occasionally. Then, turn the pieces and brush with any remaining marinade. Continue baking for an additional 10 to 15 minutes or until the chicken is tender. Serve hot or cold.

PER SERVING: *529 calories, 14.1 g protein, 3.1 g carbohydrates, 51.8 g fat, 56.1 mg calcium, 1.1 mg iron, 0.3 g fiber.*

GINGER SAIGON WINGS

Whisk together ¾ cup soy sauce, ½ cup vegetable oil, ⅓ cup brown sugar, ¼ cup sesame oil, 2 tablespoons grated ginger, 4 crushed garlic cloves and 2 tablespoons dry mustard. Marinate 3 lbs (1.5 kg) wings in mixture overnight. Bake these oriental treats according to the method given in Caesar Wings. Serves 6.

CAESAR WINGS

HOT WINGS

At one time, chicken wings' only claim to fame was as part of the stock pot. Then, some hotshot bartender basted them with hot sauce and served them up with cold beer — instant hit! Here's how to coat and crisp them up at home.

• For fast, even cooking, separate wings at the joints. Remove the tips and freeze them — they make terrific chicken stock.

• For thorough marinating, place wings and marinade in a plastic bag in a bowl. Turn the bag or massage it periodically so the marinade coats all the pieces. For a fast marinade, use a bottled vinaigrette.

• When making your own brush-on bastes, add some vegetable oil to prevent burning and keep food moist. Keep the sugar content low, because it burns easily.

• For crisp skin, place the pieces on a rack set in a baking pan, instead of directly on the pan. For easy clean-ups, line the baking pan with foil or parchment paper before baking.

PARTY BIRDS

When simple roast chicken simply won't do, let our golden party birds strut their stuff.

GLAZED CORNISH HENS WITH PECAN-RICE STUFFING

There's something special about presenting guests with their own little golden birds. Plumped with a nutty rice stuffing and glazed with apple juice, honey and Dijon mustard.

Preparation time: 25 minutes / Cooking time: 20 minutes
Baking time: 45 minutes / Makes: 8 servings

8 Cornish game hens
6 cups Pecan-Rice Stuffing (recipe follows)
¼ cup butter
2 cups apple juice
1 to 3 tsp liquid honey
1 to 3 tsp Dijon mustard

1. Preheat oven to 375F. Clean the cavities of the Cornish game hens and loosely stuff them with Pecan-Rice Stuffing. Overlap the skin to cover the opening and hold in place with a small skewer. Tie the legs together.

2. Place the hens in a small roasting pan with shallow sides. Rub ½ tablespoon butter into the skin of each hen. Roast, uncovered, in the preheated oven for 45 minutes to 1 hour or until a drumstick moves easily. Baste several times with the pan juices.

THE FESTIVE BIRD

When it's your turn to host the turkey-and-all-the-trimmings dinner, don't be intimidated by the size of the bird. It's as easy as roasting a chicken. Just think of it as "the more the merrier." Here are the simple steps to a golden, moist bird.

To Buy
Plan on at least a pound per person. If you buy a fresh turkey, store it in the refrigerator and cook it within 2 days. Frozen turkeys can be stored in the freezer up to a year.

To Thaw
Don't leave turkey on the kitchen counter: bacteria thrives at room temperature. Do leave it in its original wrapping on a tray in the refrigerator. Count on 5 hours thawing per pound. For a faster way, place it in the sink and cover with cold water. Change the water occasionally. This takes a half hour per pound.

To Stuff
Remove the giblets and neck from the body and neck cavity. Rinse inside and out with cold water. Pat dry.

Spoon enough stuffing into the neck cavity

3. While the Cornish game hens are roasting, place the apple juice in a large saucepan. Boil vigorously, uncovered, until reduced to 1 cup, about 20 minutes.

4. Once the hens are roasted, remove them to a platter. Pour the pan juices into the reduced apple juice. Whisk in the honey and Dijon to taste. Serve the glaze over the Cornish game hens.

PER SERVING: 1020 calories, 78.1 g protein, 45 g carbohydrates, 59.4 g fat, 30.8 mg calcium, 2.4 mg iron, 1.5 g fiber.

PECAN-RICE STUFFING

Preparation time: 10 minutes / Cooking time: 50 minutes

Makes: 6 cups

CHICKEN

2 tbsp butter
1 tsp curry powder
2 tsp ground cumin (optional)
1½ cups long-grain rice
4 cups chicken bouillon
3 whole green onions, thinly sliced
½ cup golden raisins
½ cup coarsely chopped pecans or almonds, toasted

1. Heat the butter and seasonings in a large heavy-bottomed saucepan. Add the rice and stir over medium heat until the rice is evenly coated. Add the bouillon and bring to a boil, stirring often. Then, cover, reduce heat and simmer until most of the liquid is absorbed, about 45 minutes. Remove the saucepan from the heat and stir in the onions, raisins and nuts. Use immediately to stuff Cornish game hens, or refrigerate for several days or freeze to use later.

PER SERVING: 163 calories, 3.9 g protein, 24.6 g carbohydrates, 5.6 g fat, 16.2 mg calcium, 1.5 mg iron, 0.9 g fiber.

to make it rounded. Do not pack. Bring the neck skin up over the back, or fasten it with skewers. Fill the body cavity with stuffing. Don't pack. Sew closed, or fasten with skewers and lace butcher's twine through the skewers.

To Roast
Remove large birds from the refrigerator and leave them at room temperature for about an hour before stuffing and putting them in the oven. Preheat oven to 325F. Place the bird breast-side up on a rack in a shallow roasting pan and brush the skin with butter, margarine or vegetable oil. Cover the pan with the pan lid or foil, dull-side out.

Roast, basting often with the pan juices. Self-basting birds, however, are already injected with oils so they require less basting. To brown, remove the foil for the final hour of cooking. If browning unevenly, cover the dark areas with small pieces of foil.

Turkey is done when the juices run clear when the thigh is pierced with a skewer, or when a drumstick moves easily. Another way to test for doneness is to insert a meat thermometer into the thigh of the bird before roasting. When the temperature reads 180F, the bird is done.

TURKEY BREAST STUFFED WITH SMOKED SALMON AND GREEN ONION

A simpler and more elegant version of Chicken Kiev with a surprise of smoked salmon. When sliced it's drizzled with a white wine sauce. Accompany with asparagus or steamed cucumber and green fettuccine tossed with pesto.

Preparation time: 15 minutes / Roasting time: 50 minutes

Makes: 4 servings

3 tbsp unsalted butter, at room temperature
1 tbsp finely chopped whole green onion
½ turkey breast, about 2 lbs (1 kg)
2 oz (60 g) sliced smoked salmon
⅔ cup white wine
Salt and pepper
¼ cup whipping cream (optional)

1. Preheat oven to 325F. Stir 2 tablespoons butter with the green onion in a small bowl. Set aside. With a sharp knife, bone the turkey breast and remove the skin. You'll see an opening on the side of the breast that forms a natural pocket. Spread the inside of the pocket with the onion butter. Lay pieces of smoked salmon over the butter. Pull down the top part of the breast to meet the bottom. The opening will seal itself as the turkey breast cooks.

2. Place the turkey breast in an oven dish just large enough for the breast to fit. Spread the top of the breast with remaining tablespoon butter. Cover with a loose tent of foil. Roast in the centre of the preheated oven for 30 minutes. Remove the foil. Pour 2 tablespoons wine over the turkey. Increase the oven temperature to 375F and continue roasting for 20 more minutes, basting often, to lightly brown the turkey. Remove to a platter and cover to keep warm.

3. Pour remaining wine into the pan with the turkey drippings. Scrape the pan to remove any brown bits. Place the pan over medium heat or pour the contents into a frying pan over medium heat. Bring the wine and pan drippings to a boil and boil vigorously, uncovered and stirring often, until reduced by half. Taste and add salt and pepper as needed, and cream, if you wish.

PER SERVING: 402 calories, 49.9 g protein, 0.6 g carbohydrates, 19.7 g fat, 46.1 mg calcium, 2.3 mg iron, 0.02 g fiber.

CREATIVE WAYS WITH CRANBERRIES

Cranberry-Orange Relish
Stir grated orange peel or chopped pecans and raisins into whole-berry cranberry sauce.

Fresh Cranberry Relish
In a food processor, whirl the flesh of 1 orange with 1 cup fresh cranberries and 2 to 3 tablespoons granulated sugar.

Cranberry Cream
Mix equal amounts of cranberry sauce and sour cream.

PERFECT ROAST TURKEY

Here's the best way to treat your holiday bird.

Preparation time: 30 minutes / Roasting time: 5 to 5½ hours

Makes: 12 servings

12-lb (6-kg) turkey
8 to 10 cups stuffing
2 tbsp butter or 4 bacon strips

1. Preheat oven to 325F. Remove the giblets (heart, liver and gizzard) and neck. Wash the turkey inside and out. Pat dry with paper towels. Spoon some stuffing into the neck cavity, filling so it's nicely rounded but not packed. Bring the neck skin up over the back and fasten it with skewers or sew closed. Fill the body cavity with remaining stuffing. Don't overpack (stuffing expands during cooking). Sew closed, or fasten with skewers and lace with butcher's twine. Place the turkey breast-side up on a rack in a large roasting pan. Rub the skin with the butter or lay the bacon slices over the breast and legs.

2. Cover the roasting pan with a lid or loose tent of foil, dull-side out. Roast, covered, in the preheated oven for about 4 hours, basting frequently with the pan juices. Then, uncover and remove the bacon strips, if using. Continue roasting, uncovered, basting often for 1 to 1½ hours or until the turkey is golden brown and a drumstick moves easily. If the turkey seems to be browning unevenly, cover the dark areas with pieces of foil to prevent further browning. Remove the turkey to a platter and let it sit for 20 minutes before carving.

PER SERVING: *215 calories, 32.6 g protein, 0 g carbohydrates, 8.4 g fat, 23.9 mg calcium, 1.6 mg iron, 0 g fiber.*

FAST LOW-CAL STUFF-ITS

As a fast flavor boost, fill the turkey cavity with:

• Whole lemons, oranges or tangerines. Prick the fruit skins several times.

• Whole garlic cloves. Don't bother peeling.

• Slices of fresh gingerroot.

• Handfuls of fresh herbs — sage, rosemary or thyme. Or use 2 tablespoons of dried herbs.

• Fresh rosemary sprigs with orange wedges, or fresh sage with apple slices.

ROASTING TIMES

Agriculture Canada recommends the following roasting times.

Stuffed Turkey	Roast at 325F
8 lbs (4 kg)	4½ hours
11 lbs (5.5 kg)	5 hours
13 lbs (6.5 kg)	5¾ hours
20 lbs (10 kg)	6¾ hours

FESTIVE ROAST DUCKS WITH GALA STUFFING

Spiced rice fragrant with ginger and fennel, and chockful of pine nuts and apricots offers a winter symphony of flavors to balance the rich duck. This recipe is from Anita Hill, a great Toronto cook.

Preparation time: 40 minutes / Cooking time: 15 minutes
Roasting time: 2 hours / Makes: 6 to 8 servings

2 (4½-lb/2.25-kg) ducks
¼ cup vegetable oil
1 tsp cumin seeds
1 tsp fennel seeds
30 fenugreek seeds, about ⅛ tsp
2 onions, finely chopped
2 ½-inch pieces of fresh gingerroot, minced
7½-oz (213-mL) can tomato sauce
½ cup chopped Italian parsley
4 cups cooked rice
¼ cup raisins
¼ cup chopped dried apricots
¼ cup pine nuts
2 tsp freshly squeezed lemon juice
2 tsp granulated sugar
¼ tsp cayenne pepper
½ tsp salt (optional)
Freshly ground black pepper

1. For even cooking, bring the ducks to room temperature before roasting. Clean the cavities, saving the livers, gizzards and hearts. Dry the cavities and pat the outer skins dry. Prick the skins with a fork so the lining of fat will ooze out as it melts.

2. Preheat oven to 400F. Have all the ingredients measured before starting to cook. Finely mince the livers, gizzards and hearts and set aside. Heat the oil in a large frying pan. Add the cumin, fennel and fenugreek seeds and immediately begin stirring over medium-high heat. In less than 30 seconds the cumin seeds will begin to darken. Immediately add the onions and gingerroot. Stir-fry until the onions turn a little brown, about 3 minutes.

3. Continuing to stir-fry, scatter in the minced livers, gizzards and hearts. When they have lost their red color, add the tomato sauce and parsley. Then, stir in the cooked rice.

QUICK CRANBERRY DUCK

Buy Peking duck at an Oriental take-out shop. Cut it into serving-size pieces and warm, uncovered, in a 350F oven. Serve with cranberry sauce dressed up with candied ginger, chopped pears and mandarin orange sections.

4. Turn heat to low and stir in the raisins, apricots and nuts. Stir fairly frequently for about 5 minutes, to thoroughly blend the ingredients. Then remove the pan from the heat and stir in the lemon juice and sugar. Stir in the cayenne pepper. Taste and add salt, pepper and a little more sugar and lemon juice, if you like.

5. Loosely stuff this mixture into the ducks. (If there is any left over, it can be reheated in a casserole dish during the last half hour of roasting.) Sew the opening closed or fasten with skewers. Place the ducks in a roasting pan breast-side up.

6. Then, to brown the ducks, roast them, uncovered, in the preheated oven at 400F for 30 minutes. Drain the fat from the pan. Reduce the oven temperature to 350F and continue roasting, uncovered, for another 1½ hours to thoroughly cook the ducks. To check if the ducks are done, prick the skin. The juices should run clear yellow and a drumstick should move easily.

PER SERVING: 1007 calories, 46.5 g protein, 40.8 g carbohydrates, 72.2 g fat, 69.6 mg calcium, 8.2 mg iron, 2.8 g fiber.

**BEST-
BUY
TURKEY**

TURKEY WITH SOUTHERN RICE STUFFING

A pecan-rice stuffing and spicy butter baste give jazzy new flavor to turkey.

Preparation time: 20 minutes / Cooking time: 30 minutes
Roasting time: 3½ to 4 hours / Makes: 6 to 8 servings

1½ cups long-grain rice
3 cups chicken broth or bouillon
8- to 10-lb (4- to 5-kg) turkey
2 celery stalks, thinly sliced
1 red pepper, cored, seeded and chopped
2½-oz (75-g) pkg pecan halves
⅓ cup butter, melted
¼ cup finely chopped parsley
1 tsp each of dried leaf thyme, dry mustard and
　freshly ground black pepper
½ tsp cayenne pepper
3 tbsp butter, melted
1 tsp each of ground cumin and chili powder
¼ tsp cayenne pepper
½ cup all-purpose flour (optional)

1. Cook the rice in the chicken broth in a medium-size saucepan according to package directions.

BEST-BUY BIRDS

A whole large turkey is a better buy than a chicken. Buy a whole bird on special, then ask the butcher to cut the frozen or fresh bird into quarters. Wrap each quarter separately and freeze for at least four different meals. One breast, for example, once thawed, can be sliced into many cutlets.

Festive Fruit
Frost green and red grapes or fresh cranberries with beaten egg white. Dip or roll them in granulated sugar and dry on waxed paper. Place on the platter around the turkey with sprigs of parsley for color.

Orange Cups Nouveau
Fill hollowed-out orange cups with chopped orange sections, diced red apple and kiwi fruit.

Apple Cups
Hollow out the centres of small red and green apples and fill with chutney and raisins.

Vegetable Medley
Alternate pan-roasted potatoes, broccoli or brussels sprouts and carrots on a platter surrounding the bird.

Lemon Boats
Fill hollowed-out lemon halves with cranberry relish.

2. Meanwhile, remove the giblets (heart, liver, gizzard) and neck from the turkey. Wash the turkey inside and out. Then, pat dry with paper towels. Place the giblets in a small saucepan over medium heat. Cover with water and cook, covered, for 15 to 20 minutes. Drain the giblets well, reserving the water, if you wish, to make gravy. Then, cut the giblets into $\frac{1}{2}$-inch pieces. Set aside until ready to use.

3. Preheat oven to 325F. When the rice is cooked, turn it into a large bowl along with the giblets, celery, red pepper and pecans. Then, toss with $\frac{1}{3}$ cup melted butter, the parsley, thyme, mustard, black pepper and $\frac{1}{2}$ teaspoon cayenne pepper.

4. When ready to stuff the turkey, fill the neck cavity with the stuffing so it is nicely rounded but not packed. Bring the neck skin up over the back and fasten with skewers or sew closed. Fill the body cavity with remaining stuffing. Don't overpack (stuffing expands during cooking). Sew closed or secure with skewers and lace with butcher's twine.

5. If you have extra stuffing, place it in a casserole dish and cover or wrap in foil. Place it in the oven during last hour of roasting. Stir the stuffing in the casserole once during cooking.

6. Place the turkey breast-side up on a wire rack in a large roasting pan. In a small bowl, stir 3 tablespoons melted butter with the cumin, chili powder and $\frac{1}{4}$ teaspoon cayenne pepper. Brush the mixture over the turkey. Cover the turkey with the roasting pan lid or a loose tent of foil, dull-side out. Roast in the preheated oven for about $2\frac{1}{2}$ hours, basting frequently with the pan juices. Then, uncover and continue roasting, basting often with the pan juices, for 1 to $1\frac{1}{2}$ more hours or until the skin is golden brown and a drumstick moves easily. The turkey will take about 20 to 30 minutes per pound. If the turkey is browning unevenly, cover the dark areas with pieces of foil.

7. Remove the turkey to a platter and let stand for 20 minutes before carving. Meanwhile, prepare a gravy using the reserved giblet water, if you wish. To prepare the gravy, place the roasting pan containing the pan juices and fat over medium heat. (If the pan can't be placed on a burner, drain the juice and fat, scraping any brown bits from the pan bottom, into a frying pan.)

8. Place all the flour in the juices at 1 side of the pan. Then, gradually whisk the flour into the pan juices, scraping up any brown bits from the bottom of the roasting pan. Continue whisking the gravy over medium heat until it starts to thicken and is fairly smooth.

9. Then, gradually whisk in the reserved giblet water. Continue whisking until the gravy is thick and smooth. Taste and add salt and pepper as needed. If gravy is thicker than you'd like, continue whisking in water, 1 to 2 tablespoons at a time, until it is just thick enough to coat the turkey.

PER SERVING: *918 calories, 90.1 g protein, 42.2 g carbohydrates, 41.4 g fat, 120 mg calcium, 8.6 mg iron, 2 g fiber.*

TRADITIONAL SAGE STUFFING WITH VARIATIONS

When you're in the mood for a traditional turkey and all the fixings, this stuffing more than fits the bill.

Preparation time: 20 minutes / Baking time: 10 minutes
Cooking time: 5 minutes / Makes: 12 cups

24-oz (675-g) loaf white bread
2 tsp ground sage
1 tsp ground savory
1 tsp salt
Generous grinding of black pepper
½ cup butter
Turkey gizzard, heart and liver
3 large onions, chopped
1½ cups chopped celery, including some leaves

1. Preheat oven to 350F. Remove the crusts from the bread. Slice the bread into ⅓-inch cubes. Spread it out on baking sheets. Place the bread cubes in the preheated oven. Stir often until lightly browned, about 10 minutes. (This makes about 7 cups of bread cubes.) Place the cubes in a large bowl and toss with the seasonings.

2. Melt the butter in a large frying pan. Finely chop the gizzard, heart and liver. Add them to the butter along with the onions. Sauté until the onions are limp, about 5 minutes. Stir often. Then, add the entire contents of the pan to the bread mixture. Add the celery and toss. The dressing can be prepared the day before roasting the bird. Keep the dressing covered and refrigerated, but do not stuff the bird until ready to roast.

VARIATIONS

Stir in 1 cup chopped pecans, walnuts or toasted almonds and celery.

Stir in ½ cup chopped parsley and 1 red pepper, seeded and chopped, along with the celery.

PER SERVING: 126 calories, 4.1 g protein, 15.4 g carbohydrates, 5.2 g fat, 45.7 mg calcium, 1.3 mg iron, 1 g fiber.

S A G E

When time is short, don't tear bread for stuffing. Start with store-bought croutons or rice as we've done here.

Apple and Nut

Melt ¼ cup butter in a large saucepan. Stir in 1 chopped onion and sauté until soft. Then, stir in 1 chopped celery stalk, 2 peeled, cored and chopped apples, ½ cup chopped nuts, ½ teaspoon sage, 3 cups store-bought seasoned croutons and 1 cup apple juice. Stuff into the bird. Or place in a greased 6-cup (1.5-L) casserole dish and bake in a preheated 375F oven for 20 minutes or until lightly browned. Makes 4 cups.

Rice and Raisin

Melt ¼ cup butter in a large saucepan. Add 2 crushed garlic cloves, 2 teaspoons poultry seasoning and 1 teaspoon curry powder. Sauté until soft, about 2 minutes. Add 2 cups long-grain rice, 5 cups chicken bouillon and 1 cup golden raisins. Bring to a boil. Cover, and simmer until liquid is absorbed, about 30 minutes. Stir in 4 chopped green onions. Makes 6 cups.

FRESH FRUIT STUFFING

Apples, pears and golden raisins add natural moisture to the traditional sage and thyme stuffing, so we've been able to add a lot less fat — and since there's no sausage or bacon, it's deliciously lighter.

Preparation time: 25 minutes / Baking time: 10 minutes
Cooking time: 5 minutes / Makes: 10 cups

24-oz (675-g) loaf white bread
2 tsp each of ground sage and dried leaf thyme
1 tsp salt
½ tsp dried marjoram
½ tsp freshly ground black pepper
¼ cup butter
2 onions, finely chopped
1 tart apple, peeled and finely chopped
1 pear, peeled and coarsely chopped
4 whole green onions, thinly sliced
3 celery stalks, including leaves, chopped
⅓ cup golden raisins

1. Preheat oven to 350F. Remove the crusts from the bread. Slice the bread into ⅓-inch cubes. Spread the cubes out on baking sheets. Place the bread cubes in the preheated oven. Stir often until lightly browned, about 10 minutes. (This makes about 7 cups bread cubes.) Toss the cubes in a large bowl along with the seasonings.

2. Melt the butter in a large frying pan. Add the onions and sauté until soft, about 5 minutes. Then, pour the onions over the bread cubes and seasonings, stirring until mixed. Stir in the fruit, green onions, celery and raisins. Toss until well mixed. The stuffing can be prepared the day before roasting the bird, but keep the stuffing covered and refrigerated. Do not stuff the turkey until ready to roast.

3. If you have extra stuffing, place it in a large casserole dish or wrap it in foil. Stir ¼ cup water into the stuffing in the casserole for added moisture, then cover tightly. (Water isn't needed if the stuffing is wrapped in foil.) Place the stuffing in the oven during the last hour of roasting. Stir the stuffing in the casserole dish once during cooking.

PER SERVING: *128 calories, 3 g protein, 21.1 g carbohydrates, 3.7 g fat, 52.4 mg calcium, 1.2 mg iron, 1.5 g fiber.*

MEAT MATTERS

Compared to twenty years ago, Canadians are these days eating meat in moderation. Portions are smaller and cuts are leaner. We may not eat meat every day, but when we do there's nothing modest about the ways we're preparing it. Our cooking goes well beyond roast beef, fried pork chops or long-simmered lamb stew. Now we use faster methods and less fat. We tend to grill, barbecue and sauté. And we enhance our meat entrées with all sorts of partners — from a classy cognac and shallot sauce for a New Year's Eve tenderloin to a prime rib smothered with Dijon and peppercorns. Canadian pork takes perfectly to simmering in a winter fruit sauce or to an Italian spinach stuffing in a glorious crown roast. Whereas years ago we generally served lamb only on special occasions, our repertoire now includes everything from Grilled Salsa Chops to a French Herbed Leg of Lamb.

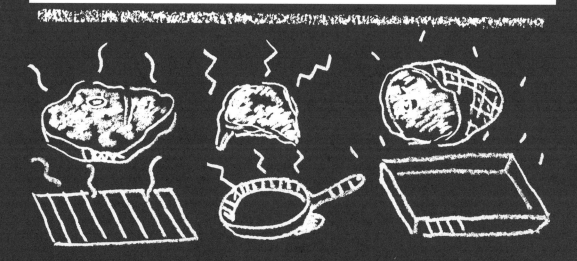

ALL-SEASON LAMB

No other meat comes close to lamb's special flavor. We crave it all year long. In summer, toss thick chops on the barbecue, grill to juicy, pink perfection and eat with your fingers. Over the festive season, pull out all the stops and roast a Dijon-crusted rack for two. And what better way to herald the coming of spring than a roasted leg of lamb stuffed with lemony rice and fresh spinach?

SPRING LAMB STUFFED WITH LEMON RICE AND SPINACH

A perfect centrepiece for Easter dinner. Highly seasoned rice, aromatic with lemon, garlic, ginger and streaked with spinach fills the centre of a spring lamb roast.

Preparation time: 30 minutes / Cooking time: 35 minutes
Roasting time: 1 hour, 20 minutes / Makes: 10 servings

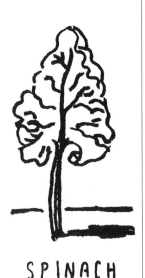

SPINACH

½ cup butter
3 onions, finely chopped
4 garlic cloves, minced
2 tbsp finely chopped fresh gingerroot
2 tsp ground cumin
1 tsp ground coriander
¼ tsp cayenne pepper
1 tsp salt
2 cups rice
5 cups chicken bouillon
Finely grated peel of 1 lemon
2 lbs (1 kg) fresh spinach or 2 (12-oz/375-g) pkgs
   frozen chopped spinach
4-lb (2-kg) boneless leg of lamb
1 cup dry white wine

1. Melt the butter in a large heavy-bottomed saucepan. Add the onions, garlic and gingerroot. Sprinkle with the seasonings. Sauté until the onions are soft. Add the rice and stir until the grains are coated with the onion mixture. Add the bouillon and lemon peel. Bring to a boil. Then, cover, reduce heat to low and simmer about 30 minutes.

2. Meanwhile, cook the spinach in boiling water until it is heated through. Drain well. Place in a kitchen cloth and wring out all the moisture. Chop the spinach. Stir it into the cooked rice.

3. When ready to roast the lamb, preheat oven to 350F. Spread the lamb fat-side down on a sheet of waxed paper. Make a lengthwise slash in the thickest portion of the meat and open it up book-fashion to achieve a fairly even thickness. Spread about 2 cups of the rice mixture over the lamb. Roll up the roast and tie it with butcher's twine.

4. Place the roast, fat-side up, on a rack in a roasting pan. Pour the wine over top. Roast, uncovered, in the preheated oven for 20 minutes per pound. Baste often. When the meat has been roasting for 45 minutes, wrap remaining rice mixture in a piece of foil or place it in a baking dish. Bake alongside the roast until hot. The meat will be rare when the internal temperature reads 140F on a meat thermometer; medium at 150F; well done at 160F. Let meat sit for 10 minutes before carving.

PER SERVING: *377 calories, 27.3 g protein, 30.4 g carbohydrates, 14.5 g fat, 126 mg calcium, 6 mg iron, 0.6 g fiber.*

DIJON-CRUSTED RACK OF LAMB

For true lamb lovers, a rack with this classic herb coating is the ultimate. Have the butcher French the bones and scrape away the fat from the bone tips.

Preparation time: 10 minutes / Cooking time: 30 minutes

Makes: 8 servings

4 racks of lamb
$\frac{1}{4}$ cup each of vegetable oil and Dijon mustard
4 crushed garlic cloves
1 tsp dried rosemary, crumbled
$\frac{1}{2}$ tsp freshly ground or cracked black pepper
$\frac{1}{2}$ cup finely chopped parsley

1. Trim excess fat from the lamb. Bring the meat to room temperature. Preheat oven to 400F. Lightly oil a baking pan large enough to hold the four racks of lamb. Stir remaining ingredients together. Spread over the meaty side of the racks.

2. To prevent the tips of the rib bones from burning, wrap the top $\frac{1}{2}$ inch with foil. Place the racks in a baking pan, coated-side up. Roast, uncovered, in the preheated oven for 25 to 30 minutes for medium-rare lamb. Remove racks to a cutting board or warmed platter. Let sit for 5 minutes before slicing into chops.

PER SERVING: *372 calories, 34.3 g protein, 1.4 g carbohydrates, 24.5 g fat, 38.6 mg calcium, 2.6 mg iron, 0.2 g fiber.*

RIBS AND RACKS

A rack is the menu name for a lamb rib roast. There are usually about 7 ribs per rack and the first 5 from the front of the rib section are the best. The meat is tender and well marbled, with a thin fat covering that bastes the meat as it roasts. Cook it simply: Rub the rack with a cut garlic clove. Spread with Dijon mustard or a light coating of olive oil. Lightly sprinkle with herbs, such as rosemary and thyme, and place it in a small baking dish with the rounded side upward and the rib tips resting on the pan. Roast, uncovered, in a 400F oven for 10 to 12 minutes per pound. Let sit for 10 minutes before carving.

Grilled Lamb Leg with Garlic and Cumin

A boneless lamb leg is much easier for a party than dealing with a bunch of chops. You simply put the marinated meat under the broiler or on the grill, turn once and it's done to medium-rare perfection in under 20 minutes. Wonderful with ratatouille and rice.

Preparation time: 15 minutes / Marinating time: 2 hours
Broiling time: 16 minutes / Makes: 8 servings

3½-lb (1.75-kg) boneless leg of lamb
½ cup vegetable oil
1 tbsp ground cumin
1 tsp ground coriander
½ tsp cayenne pepper
¼ tsp salt
½ tbsp grated fresh gingerroot
4 crushed garlic cloves

1. Trim as much fat as possible from the lamb. For grilling, the meat should be of even thickness; if there is a thick portion, slash it and open it up butterfly-fashion. In a shallow dish just large enough to hold the lamb, stir remaining ingredients together. Place the meat in the marinade. Cover and refrigerate for at least 2 hours or overnight. Turn the lamb halfway through this time.

2. Bring the meat to room temperature before grilling.

3. Preheat broiler. Place the meat, still covered with a little marinade, on a broiler rack positioned about 6 inches from the heat. Broil about 8 minutes per side, brushing with the marinade after turning.

PER SERVING: 402 calories, 40.6 g protein, 1.6 g carbohydrates, 25.1 g fat, 32.8 mg calcium, 4.2 mg iron, 0 g fiber.

Grilled Salsa Chops

This is the simplest way to embellish without overpowering delicate lamb chops. We love it with a cucumber-dill salad and baked potatoes with Roquefort, sour cream and chives.

Preparation time: 5 minutes / Marinating time: 4 hours
Grilling time: 10 minutes / Makes: 4 servings

8 fresh or frozen lamb loin chops
¾ cup hot salsa
3 tbsp vegetable oil

Curried Lamb Patties

Whisk ¼ cup sour cream with 1 egg, ½ teaspoon each of curry powder, ground cumin and coriander, and pinches of salt and cayenne pepper. Stir in ¼ cup bread crumbs and 1 lb (500 g) ground lamb. Shape into 4 patties and sauté in butter for about 7 minutes per side.

Lamb Chops with Red Wine-Tarragon Sauce

After cooking 4 lamb chops in a frying pan, remove and add ¼ cup dry red wine or port, 1 teaspoon Dijon mustard and ½ teaspoon dried tarragon to the pan. Stir over medium heat and scrape up brown bits from the bottom. Pour over chops.

1. Trim excess fat from the edges of the chops. Nick the edges to prevent curling during cooking. Place the fresh or frozen chops in a dish just large enough to hold them in a single layer.

2. Stir salsa and oil together. Pour over the chops. Cover with clear wrap. If the chops are fresh, marinate in the refrigerator for about 4 hours. Turn halfway through the marinating. If marinating frozen chops, leave them at room temperature for 2 hours, then refrigerate for 2 hours. Turn halfway through the marinating.

3. When ready to grill, preheat barbecue. Lightly grease the grill. Bring the chops to room temperature before grilling. Remove them from the marinade and brush off all sauce from the chops. Place lamb on the grill and barbecue for about 5 minutes per side for medium-rare lamb.

PER SERVING: *303 calories, 28.2 g protein, 3 g carbohydrates, 20.2 g fat, 23.6 mg calcium, 2.3 mg iron, 0 g fiber.*

FRENCH HERBED LEG OF LAMB

The white wine, garlic, rosemary and thyme tenderize and tantalize in this superb marinated lamb.

Preparation time: 10 minutes / Marinating time: overnight
Broiling time: 12 minutes / Makes: 8 servings

DRY WHITE WINE

3½-lb (1.75-kg) boneless leg of lamb
1½ cups dry white wine
¼ cup olive oil
6 crushed garlic cloves
2 tsp dried rosemary, crumbled
1 tsp dried leaf thyme
1 tsp coarsely ground black pepper
½ tsp cayenne pepper (optional)

1. Place the lamb in a shallow dish just large enough to hold it snugly.

2. Stir remaining ingredients together. Pour them over the lamb. Cover with clear wrap and refrigerate overnight. Turn the lamb at least once during this time.

3. Remove the lamb from the refrigerator at least 2 hours before cooking to bring to room temperature.

4. Preheat broiler. Place the oven rack 4 inches from the heat. Remove the lamb from the marinade and place it on a rack in a shallow baking pan. Broil for 5 to 6 minutes per side for medium-rare lamb.

PER SERVING: *276 calories, 27.3 g protein, 1.5 g carbohydrates, 14.2 g fat, 22.1 mg calcium, 2.5 mg iron, 0.06 g fiber.*

MEAT MATTERS
TRIPLE TESTED

NEW STYLE BEEF

Beef used to dominate Canadian menus and even though we're cutting back on red meat, cravings for soul-satisfying beef still overtake us. But now instead of a whopper steak that dwarfs a dinner plate, we're grilling one thick steak and slicing it into several servings. In place of huge standing ribs, we're roasting small tender eye-of-rounds and cutting them into four steaks. Comfort foods like meat loaves are back on our menus because they're so kind to our budget, but now we spice them up with lots of seasonings and cook them quickly in the microwave. And there's nothing predictable about our burgers spiked with hot chilies.

TENDER-
LOIN

NEW YEAR'S EVE TENDERLOIN WITH COGNAC AND SHALLOTS

Chef Nigil Didcock of stately Langdon Hall in Cambridge, Ontario, created this romantic recipe for two.

Preparation time: 20 minutes / Cooking time: 12 minutes
Broiling time: 3 minutes / Makes: 2 servings

2 tbsp vegetable oil
Freshly ground black pepper
2 (5-oz/150-g) filets mignons, about 1 inch thick
2 tbsp cognac
3 large shallots, very finely chopped
1 tsp crushed white peppercorns
½ cup dry red wine
¼ cup beef stock or diluted broth
4 oz (125 g) chèvre
Sprigs of rosemary (optional)

1. Preheat broiler. Then, heat the oil in a heavy-bottomed frying pan set over medium heat. Sprinkle pepper over both sides of the filets. To seal in the juices, wait until the pan is very hot before adding the filets. Sauté for 3 to 4 minutes on each side for medium-rare meat. Transfer to a platter and cover.

2. Reduce heat to low. Remove the pan from the heat and let it cool for 2 minutes. Place the pan back on the heat and add the cognac, shallots and peppercorns. Stir well, gently scraping any brown bits from the bottom of the pan. Cover and cook for 4 minutes. Pour in the wine and beef stock. Increase heat to high and bring the mixture to a boil. Add any juices that have accumulated on the meat platter. Boil, uncovered, stirring occasionally, until the sauce is reduced to about ½ cup.

3. Place a piece of chèvre on each filet and place the filets on a baking sheet. Broil 6 inches from the heat for 3 minutes or until lightly browned. Serve surrounded with the sauce on the side. Garnish with sprigs of rosemary, if you wish.

PER SERVING: *556 calories, 38.3 g protein, 4 g carbohydrates, 34.5 g fat, 99.7 mg calcium, 5 mg iron, 0.02 g fiber.*

BRANDIED EYE-OF-ROUND

When you want to pull out all the stops — and want to do it quickly — this is the essence of a special steak dinner. While an eye-of-round isn't as tender as a filet, it provides an affordable sense of elegance. It has a slightly firmer texture and is very juicy and flavorful, and it's lower in calories than chicken with skin. Serve it with spinach noodles tossed with Stilton or goat cheese, and red peppers and baby carrots seasoned with fresh dill.

Preparation time: 5 minutes / Cooking time: 5 minutes

Makes: 4 servings

1 tbsp butter
4 thinly sliced eye-of-round steaks, about 12 oz (375 g)
Freshly ground black pepper
¼ cup brandy
¼ tsp Worcestershire sauce
Pinch of salt

1. Melt the butter in a large frying pan. Do not scrimp on the butter. Place the steaks in the pan. Add a generous grinding of pepper. Cook the meat for 2 minutes over medium heat. Then, turn the steaks and add another generous grinding of pepper. Cook for 2 more minutes. Remove to a platter and cover to keep warm.

2. Add remaining ingredients to the pan. Bring to a boil, stirring to remove any brown bits from the bottom of the pan. Boil for 1 minute. Pour sauce over the steaks and serve.

PER SERVING: *176 calories, 19.9 g protein, 0.1 g carbohydrates, 6.2 g fat, 4.9 mg calcium, 1.4 mg iron, 0.02 g fiber.*

NUTRITIONAL ROUND-UP
When we first shied away from some beef favorites, we did so under the mistaken belief that all beef was fat-laced and cholesterol-laden. Not so. The most recent research reveals that beef doesn't deserve such a bum rap nutritionally. As a matter of fact, a 3-oz (85-g) lean beef burger contains only 183 calories; a 3½-oz (100-g) sirloin steak has just 185 calories; 3½ oz (100 g) of special-occasion tenderloin rings in at 196 calories.

LIGHT GRILLED FIERY STEAK

Steak on the barbie doesn't necessarily mean high-fat feasting. As a matter of fact, that little pat of butter you plunk on the baked potato can have more fat than a substantial steak. Two teaspoons of butter have 8 g of fat, while 3½ oz of round steak have about 4 g. A sirloin or slice of eye-of-round has 6.7 g. An added barbecue bonus: no oil in the cooking pan. Here we've embellished lean eye-of-round with a thin coating of hot 'n' fiery spices producing a terrific, satisfying steak at about 247 calories a serving.

Preparation time: 5 minutes / Grilling time: 8 minutes
Makes: 4 servings

1 tsp ground cumin
½ tsp chili powder
¼ tsp cayenne pepper
¼ tsp garlic powder
4 slices of eye-of-round, about 1 inch thick

1. Preheat barbecue or broiler and oil the grill or grease the broiler pan. Blend the seasonings in a small bowl. Sprinkle both sides of the meat with the seasonings, then gently press them into the meat. Place the meat on the barbecue or under the broiler and grill for 4 minutes per side for medium-rare meat. The steaks are great with baked potatoes and a Caesar salad.

PER SERVING: *247 calories, 40.1 g protein, 0.8 g carbohydrates, 8.1 g fat, 17.7 mg calcium, 3.4 mg iron, 0.1 g fiber.*

SIZZLING SESAME STIR-FRY

Sesame oil and grated orange peel elevate this three-minute stir-fry to special status. Expensive sirloin isn't necessary: just slice the round steak thinly and treat it to a quick marinade.

Preparation time: 10 minutes / Standing time: 20 minutes
Cooking time: 3 minutes / Makes: 4 servings

1 lb (500 g) round steak
2 tbsp soy sauce
2 tsp dark sesame oil
1 tsp brown sugar
¼ tsp ground ginger
Finely grated peel of 1 orange
1 tbsp vegetable oil
3 whole green onions, cut into 1-inch pieces

1. Slice the beef into ¼-inch-wide bite-size strips. Stir the soy sauce, sesame oil, sugar, ginger and orange peel together in a bowl. Stir in the beef until coated with the soy sauce mixture. Leave at room temperature for at least 20 minutes. Heat the vegetable oil in a wide frying pan over medium-high heat. Add the coated beef and green onions and stir-fry for 2 to 3 minutes or until the beef is cooked as you like.

PER SERVING: 241 calories, 30.4 g protein, 2.5 g carbohydrates, 11.5 g fat, 13 mg calcium, 3 mg iron, 0.1 g fiber.

BAKED GARLIC

As garlic roasts, it loses its harshness and becomes sweet and mellow.

Separate unskinned cloves and roast them in a small baking dish in a 375F oven for 15 to 20 minutes, or until the cloves feel soft when pricked with a fork. The length of time will depend on the size of the cloves. Cool briefly, then, squeeze the cloves out from the skins and spread them on a steak.

FAT FACTS

Here's a rundown of the calories and fat content of some of the leaner beef cuts.

Cut of Beef (3½ oz/100 g)	CALORIES	PROTEIN (g)	FAT (g)
Top round steak	163	31.5	3.9
Eye-of-round	176	31.2	6.7
Sirloin	185	29.4	6.7
Tenderloin	196	28.3	8.4
Rib-eye steak	202	29.5	8.4
Wing steak	202	27.2	9.5

PRIME RIB ROAST WITH DIJON AND PEPPERS

When I was growing up, a standing rib roast was our standard Sunday night fare. Now, thank goodness, it's making a comeback at dinner parties. It couldn't be easier. You don't have to stuff it, sauce it, turn it or babysit it. There is only one essential step for melt-in-the-mouth meat: let the roast stand, covered, on the carving board for at least 15 minutes after it comes out of the oven. If carved right away, it's so hot that precious meat juices run out onto the board.

Preparation time: 10 minutes / Roasting time: 55 minutes
Standing time: 15 minutes / Makes: 6 to 8 servings

RED BELL
PEPPERS

2½-lb (1.25-kg) standing rib roast
2 tbsp Dijon mustard
1 tsp freshly ground or cracked black pepper
2 large red peppers, cored and seeded
12 small white onions

1. If the roast has been refrigerated, bring it to room temperature before cooking. Preheat oven to 325F. In a small bowl, stir the Dijon with the pepper. Brush the mustard mixture over the fat on the meat.

2. Place the meat on a small rack set in a shallow baking pan. Slice the red peppers into 1½-inch-wide strips. Lay them evenly around the roast in the pan. Peel the white onions and place them around the roast.

3. Roast the meat, uncovered, in the centre of the preheated oven for about 50 minutes. The roast will need about 20 minutes per pound for rare meat. Then, to richly brown the meat, increase the oven temperature to 500F and continue roasting the beef for about 5 to 7 more minutes or just until evenly browned. Watch the roast carefully.

4. Remove the roast to a heated platter. Cover loosely with foil. Let the meat stand for 15 minutes before carving.

5. Meanwhile, transfer the roasted onions and peppers to a paper-towel-lined platter. Cover loosely to keep warm. Carve the beef into thin slices and serve it with the roasted onions and peppers on the side.

PER SERVING: *298 calories, 31.9 g protein, 5 g carbohydrates, 16 g fat, 22.9 mg calcium, 3.2 mg iron, 1 g fiber.*

ONE-HOUR SUNDAY ROAST

This small roast with a peppery Dijon mustard coating couldn't be easier to prepare. Serve with roasted sweet peppers and Wild Rice with a Hint of Horseradish (see page 81).

Preparation time: 15 minutes / Roasting time: 1 hour
Makes: 8 servings

3-lb (1.5 kg) eye-of-round roast, covered with a layer of fat, tied in place
3 whole garlic cloves
1 tbsp black or white peppercorns or combination of colored peppercorns, crushed
⅓ cup Dijon mustard
½ cup red wine

1. Preheat oven to 425F. Make 6 small slits, randomly, around the roast. Slice each garlic clove in half. Place one-half in each slit.

2. To crush the whole peppercorns, place them on a plastic cutting board or a firm surface that will not be penetrated by the peppercorns. Using the bottom of a flat heavy metal saucepan or mallet, firmly crush the peppercorns. They will crush quite easily. Press the pepper firmly over the entire roast.

3. Smear the Dijon over the roast, including the ends. If using a meat thermometer, insert it in the centre of the roast. Place the roast fat-side up in a small roasting pan. Place the pan in the centre of the pre-heated oven and roast, uncovered, for 15 minutes. Then, reduce heat to 375F and continue roasting for 45 minutes, until a meat thermometer reads 125F, for medium-rare meat.

4. Remove the meat from the pan and set it aside to rest 10 minutes before slicing. Immediately pour the wine into the roasting pan along with the juices. Place the pan on the stove over medium-high heat. Cook, stirring often, until slightly thickened. Pour the wine sauce through a strainer, if you wish. Spoon a little over each serving of beef.

PER SERVING: *225 calories, 36.9 g protein, 1.3 g carbohydrates, 6.7 g fat, 12 mg calcium, 2.6 mg iron, 0.1 g fiber.*

PEPPERCORN MAGIC
Green peppercorns are unripe berries, softer and less pungent than black or white peppercorns. They are usually sold in jars in brine or vinegar. They add a pleasantly piquant yet mildly sweet edge to meats and sauces. Try folding some into creamy goat cheese as a topping for steak.

SUNDAY
ROAST

BIG-BATCH FREEZER SPAGHETTI SAUCE

A great make-ahead investment that pays off in many heat 'n' serve workday dinners. You can cut calories and use ground chicken. Or, omit the meat entirely and add canned beans or cubes of an assertive cheese, such as feta or Asiago, during the last minutes of heating.

Preparation time: 15 minutes / Cooking time: 70 minutes

Makes: 6 cups

2 tbsp vegetable oil
2 lbs (1 kg) regular ground beef or chicken
4 onions, chopped
2 crushed garlic cloves
28-oz (796-mL) can tomatoes, including juice
5½-oz (156-mL) can tomato paste
1 bay leaf
1 tbsp brown sugar
1 tbsp dried leaf oregano
½ tsp each of dried leaf thyme, dried basil and salt
½ tsp Tabasco sauce
¼ tsp dried sage
Freshly ground black pepper

1. Heat the oil in a very large heavy-bottomed saucepan. Add the meat, onions and garlic. Cook over medium heat, stirring often with a fork to keep the meat separated. When the meat loses it red color, drain off the fat. Add remaining ingredients. Break up the tomatoes with a fork. Bring to a boil, stirring often. Reduce heat, cover and simmer for about 1 hour to blend the flavors. Stir frequently. Taste and add another tablespoon brown sugar if you like. Cool, then freeze in convenient quantities for later use.

2. When ready to use, thaw the sauce in a microwave oven. Or place about ¼ cup water in the bottom of a saucepan and add the frozen sauce. Cook over low heat, stirring often, until thawed and heated through. After a couple of months in the freezer, the spices start to lose their strength, so you may wish to add more spices when reheating the sauce.

PER CUP: *438 calories, 34.7 g protein, 17.7 g carbohydrates, 2.9 g fat, 76.8 mg calcium, 5 mg iron, 2.9 g fiber.*

SPAGHETTI SAUCE TOPS IT ALL

Spaghetti sauce has many uses beyond a pasta toss.

• For a healthy low-cal dinner bake a spaghetti squash, separate its strands and top with sauce.

• Mix sauce and cooked rice, stuff in sweet peppers and bake.

• Lightly spread sauce over a store-bought pizza crust. Top with grated cheese and bake.

• Add a can of kidney beans, a can of tomatoes and chili powder for a fast-fix chili.

• Spoon sauce over a split baked potato and dab with sour cream.

PHOTO: *Big-Batch Freezer Spaghetti Sauce, see recipe at right.*

Bold 'n' Spicy Texas Rib Sauce

The chili seasoning gives this incredible chunky rib sauce a distinctive "western" taste. We loved it so much the first time we made it, we wound up spooning it over burgers, cold roast beef, grilled cheddar sandwiches, even scrambled eggs.

Preparation time: 20 minutes / Cooking time: 25 minutes

Makes: 1¾ cups

2 onions
¼ cup vegetable oil
2 crushed garlic cloves
1 tbsp chili powder
1 tsp ground cumin
1 tsp celery seed (optional)
1 cup ketchup
¼ cup brown sugar
¼ cup freshly squeezed lemon juice
2 tbsp Worcestershire sauce

1. Finely chop the onions. Heat the oil in a medium-size heavy-bottomed saucepan set over medium heat. Add the onions and garlic, then sprinkle with the chili powder, cumin and celery seed, if using. Cook, stirring often, until the onions have softened, about 5 minutes.

2. Stir in the remaining ingredients. Bring the sauce to a boil. Then, reduce heat and simmer, uncovered, until the flavors mingle, about 15 to 20 minutes. Stir the mixture often, especially near the end of the cooking time.

3. The sauce can be used immediately, refrigerated or frozen. Brush over ribs, steaks or burgers near the end of their cooking time on the grill. Then, serve remaining sauce at the table for guests to add to their meat.

PER ½ CUP: *156 calories, 1.2 g protein, 21.6 g carbohydrates, 8.3 g fat, 33.1 mg calcium, 1.4 mg iron, 0.8 g fiber.*

He-Man Beef Ribs

For a meaty treat that's always a big hit at a barbecue party, ask your butcher to cut beef ribs, which are usually about 7 inches long, in half. Barbecue, turning once, for about 30 minutes. Liberally brush with Bold 'n' Spicy Texas Rib Sauce and barbecue the ribs meat-side down, and on the sides, for a total of about 10 more minutes. Terrific with corn-on-the-cob and a garlicky Caesar salad.

PHOTO: *Bold 'n' Spicy Texas Rib Sauce, see recipe at left.*

DOUBLE CHILI BURGERS

Hot chili peppers and bold seasonings give new gusto to these juicy burgers. Serve on warm tortillas with lettuce, a slice of toma-to and a great dollop of sour cream.

Preparation time: 10 minutes / Cooking time: 12 minutes

Makes: 4 burgers

4-oz (114-mL) can green chilies
1 small onion, finely chopped
1 large crushed garlic clove
2 tbsp ketchup
1 tsp chili powder
$\frac{1}{2}$ tsp ground cumin
$\frac{1}{4}$ tsp salt
$\frac{1}{4}$ tsp Worcestershire sauce
2 tbsp fine dry bread crumbs (optional)
1 lb (500 g) medium ground beef
1 tsp vegetable oil
1 tsp butter

1. Drain the chilies. Slice them in half, scrape off the seeds and fine-ly chop. Place the chilies in a large bowl along with the onion, garlic, ketchup, seasonings and Worcestershire sauce. Stir in bread crumbs to help hold the burgers together if barbecuing. Add the meat and work in with a fork or your hands until thoroughly blended. Shape the mixture into 4 patties, about 4 inches wide and $\frac{3}{4}$ inch thick.

2. Heat the oil and butter in a large frying pan over medium-low heat. Add the patties and sauté, uncovered, for 6 minutes per side for medium-rare burgers. Don't press down or prick with a fork while they're cooking or you'll lose precious juices.

PER BURGER: *283 calories, 24.9 g protein, 4.8 g carbohydrates, 18.2 g fat, 56.3 mg calcium, 2.9 mg iron, 0.4 g fiber.*

BURGER

8-Minute Italian Microwave Meatloaf

An easy route to a great moist meatloaf in record time.

Preparation time: 10 minutes / Microwave time: 8 minutes
Standing time: 4 minutes / Makes: 4 servings

2 whole green onions, thinly sliced
1 crushed garlic clove
1 egg, lightly beaten
$\frac{1}{2}$ tsp Italian seasoning
$\frac{1}{4}$ tsp each of salt and freshly ground black pepper
$\frac{1}{2}$ cup tomato sauce
$\frac{1}{4}$ cup dry bread crumbs
1 lb (500 g) lean ground beef
$\frac{1}{4}$ cup grated mozzarella cheese

1. In a bowl, stir the egg with green onions, garlic, seasonings, half the tomato sauce and bread crumbs. Work in half the meat, then remaining meat. Divide in half and shape each into an oblong loaf with rounded edges so there are no corners to overcook. Place loaves, side by side, in a 10-inch microwave-safe pie plate, ensuring they do not touch one another or the sides of the pan. Microwave, uncovered, on high for 4 minutes. Rotate the pie plate a quarter-turn. Spoon remaining tomato sauce over top. Continue microwaving, uncovered, for 4 minutes. Sprinkle with cheese. Cover and let stand 4 minutes.

PER SERVING: *313 calories, 28.5 g protein, 7.7 g carbohydrates, 18.1 g fat, 77.1 mg calcium, 3.1 mg iron, 0.8 g fiber.*

MEATLOAF MUFFINS IN MINUTES

You can cut the time it takes to bake meatloaf in a conventional oven. Spoon your favorite meatloaf mixture into muffin cups or miniature foil pans and they'll be ready in about 15 minutes.

GREAT CANADIAN GROUNDS

There's a lot more than ground beef to choose from these days. Here's how the popular ground meat choices stack up.

3 oz/85 g	CALORIES	PROTEIN (g)	FAT (g)
Chicken	117	15.3	6.8
Turkey	121	14.8	6.4
Veal	122	16.5	5.8
Lean beef	183	15.9	12.8
Pork	190	14.5	14.5
Medium beef	225	15	17.6
Lamb	240	14.1	19.9
Regular beef	264	14.1	22.6

LUXURIOUS VEAL

In this age of lighter dining, veal's delicate flavor makes it an appreciated alternative to richer meats. Because it's young and often milk-fed beef, it costs more than most meats, but with a little ingenuity, you can turn a small amount of veal into a generous entrée for many. We've included lots of budget-stretching ways, from gingery scaloppine to juicy burgers.

VEAL AND CREAMY CHÈVRE BURGER

For an upscale patty, special enough to be served by candlelight, stir ¾ cup crumbled goat cheese with 1 egg, ½ teaspoon dried rosemary and ¼ teaspoon salt. Work in 1 lb (500 g) ground veal and ¼ cup bread crumbs. Shape into 4 patties and barbecue for about 5 minutes per side. Accompany with red pepper relish and an artichoke or avocado salad.

10-MINUTE VEAL MARSALA

Earthy mushrooms and marsala enhance delicately flavored veal in our fast version of this Italian classic.

Preparation time: 10 minutes / Cooking time: 10 minutes
Makes: 4 servings

½ lb (250 g) fresh mushrooms
2 tbsp butter
1 lb (500 g) thinly sliced veal scaloppine or cutlets
Salt and freshly ground black pepper
⅓ cup marsala

1. Clean and slice the mushrooms and set aside. Melt 1 tablespoon butter in a large frying pan. Add about half the veal and cook over medium heat for no more than 2 minutes per side. Remove the veal to a platter and cover to keep warm. Repeat with remaining butter and veal. Then, sprinkle the veal generously with salt and pepper.

2. Add the mushrooms to the fat remaining in the pan and stir-fry just until the mushrooms are heated through, about 2 minutes.

3. Pour the marsala over the mushrooms. Sprinkle generously with more salt and pepper. Stir-fry for about 1 minute only. If overcooked, the mushrooms may water out. Pour the mushroom mixture over the veal and serve immediately.

PER SERVING: *251 calories, 28.8 g protein, 4.6 g carbohydrates, 10.6 g fat, 13.3 mg calcium, 2 mg iron, 0.01 g fiber.*

GINGERY VEAL PICCATA

Simply prepared scaloppine is sauced with a sexy trio: the elegant heat of ginger, tart lemon and garden-fresh green scallions.

Preparation time: 15 minutes / Cooking time: 7 minutes

Makes: 8 servings

2 eggs
1 tbsp water
½ cup all-purpose flour
Pinch of salt and freshly ground black pepper
8 veal scaloppine, about 2 lbs (1 kg)
¼ cup olive oil
1 tbsp butter
2 tbsp finely grated fresh gingerroot
8 thin whole green onions
Freshly squeezed lemon juice
1 lemon, cut into wedges

GINGER

1. In a shallow dish, whisk the eggs and water together. Measure the flour, salt and pepper into another shallow dish. Set both dishes aside until ready to use.

2. Place some veal scaloppine between 2 sheets of waxed paper and pound until very thin. Repeat with remaining veal. Dip 1 scaloppine in the egg mixture, then dip it in the flour mixture. Shake off the excess flour. If not evenly coated, dip the scaloppine in the egg mixture and then the flour mixture again. Set the coated scaloppine aside on waxed paper until ready to cook. Repeat with remaining scaloppine.

3. Heat half the oil in a large wide frying pan over medium-high heat. Add 2 to 3 pieces of scaloppine. Do not overcrowd the pan. Cook for about 1 minute per side. Do not overcook. Remove to a platter and cover to keep warm. Repeat with remaining scaloppine.

4. Meanwhile, in another large frying pan, melt the butter over medium-low heat. Add the gingerroot and whole green onions and sauté for 3 to 5 minutes or until the green onions are soft. Arrange the gingerroot and green onions over the veal on the platter. Squeeze lemon juice over the veal and garnish with lemon wedges. Serve immediately.

PER SERVING: *277 calories, 29.8 g protein, 6.2 g carbohydrates, 14.1 g fat, 17.3 mg calcium, 1.5 mg iron, 0.3 g fiber.*

TENDER VEAL CHOPS WITH ANCHOVY SAUCE

Anchovies add an assertive flavor and distinctive taste to this white wine sauce. Serve with springtime asparagus and a mild mushroom risotto.

Preparation time: 20 minutes / Cooking time: 55 minutes

Makes: 4 to 6 servings

ANCHOVY
PASTE

4 to 6 veal chops, about $\frac{3}{4}$ inch thick
1 tbsp each of butter and vegetable oil
2 medium-size onions
1 cup chicken bouillon or stock
$\frac{1}{2}$ cup dry white wine
1 tbsp anchovy paste
2 crushed garlic cloves
$\frac{1}{2}$ tsp dried leaf oregano
Freshly ground black pepper
$\frac{1}{4}$ cup pimentos (optional)
$\frac{1}{2}$ cup pitted black olives

1. Slash the edges of the chops in several places to prevent curling during cooking. Heat the butter and oil in a large heavy-bottomed saucepan. Add as many chops as will fit comfortably in the pan. Sauté over medium heat until the chops are golden on both sides, about 5 minutes per side. Remove to a platter and set aside. Repeat with remaining chops.

2. Cut the onions into quarters and sauté in remaining fat in the pan until soft and golden, about 5 minutes. Remove with a slotted spoon and scatter them over the chops. Drain the fat from the pan and add the bouillon, wine, anchovy paste, garlic, oregano and pepper. Bring to a boil. Return the chops and onions to pan along with any juices that may have collected on the platter. Cover tightly and simmer for 30 minutes or until the chops are almost fork-tender. Turn the chops once halfway through cooking.

3. Meanwhile, cut the pimentos, if using, into thin strips and slice the olives in half. Scatter over the veal after it has cooked for 30 minutes. Then, spoon the pan juices over top. Cover and continue to simmer for another 10 minutes or until the chops are tender.

4. Remove the chops to a heated deep platter and cover to keep warm. Boil the sauce vigorously until thickened, about 5 minutes. Stir in lots of freshly ground black pepper and pour the sauce over the chops.

PER SERVING: 206 calories, 20.2 g protein, 3.3 g carbohydrates, 11.2 g fat, 37.7 mg calcium, 1 mg iron, 0.7 g fiber.

PUSATERI'S SENSATIONAL VEAL TENDERLOIN

When you feel like splurging, think veal tenderloin — the ultimate prime cut. Stylishly stuff it with porcini mushrooms and fontina cheese and simmer in white wine. A family favorite of the Pusateris, owners of a gourmet supermarket in North Toronto.

Preparation time: 20 minutes / Standing time: 30 minutes
Cooking time: 20 minutes / Makes: 4 servings

100-g pkg dried porcini mushrooms
1 cup grated fontina or mozzarella cheese, about 3 oz (85 g)
1 oz (30 g) schinkenspeck* or smoked prosciutto, finely chopped
2 tbsp finely chopped Italian parsley
1 tbsp melted butter
1¼ lbs (625 g) veal tenderloin
1 tbsp each of butter and olive oil
2 garlic cloves, peeled and slightly crushed
½ cup dry white wine
½ cup veal stock or undiluted canned chicken broth

1. Rinse the dried mushrooms under cold running water to remove any grit. Then, place them in a dish. Cover with ¾ cup warm water and let sit at room temperature for 30 minutes. Meanwhile, grate fontina and place in a dish. Stir in schinkenspeck, parsley and melted butter.

2. Slit the tenderloin horizontally almost all the way through. Open the tenderloin and place it between 2 sheets of waxed paper. Pound it until it's about ½ inch thick. Spread the cheese mixture over the tenderloin, leaving a ½-inch border. Wrap the meat around the filling. Then, tie the tenderloin securely with butcher's twine.

3. Heat butter and olive oil in a large wide saucepan. Add the garlic, then the veal, and cook over medium heat, turning often, until lightly browned. Add the wine and broth. Cover and cook over medium-low heat for 15 minutes, turning the veal partway through the cooking. Remove to a platter and let stand for 10 minutes before cutting.

4. Meanwhile, add the mushrooms and their liquid to the wine mixture remaining in pan and boil gently, uncovered, until the liquid is reduced to about ½ cup, about 5 minutes. Slice the meat into 1½-inch pieces and place it on heated dinner plates. Pour the sauce over top.

*Schinkenspeck is a smoked meat sold in specialty food stores.

PER SERVING: *554 calories, 32.6 g protein, 54.8 g carbohydrates, 23.8 g fat, 143 mg calcium, 2.2 mg iron, 0.1 g fiber.*

CLASSY VEAL SAUTÉS
Dress up sautéed veal chops or scaloppine with one of these combos.

Rosemary Hazelnuts
Sauté ½ cup coarsely chopped hazelnuts sprinkled with 2 teaspoons dried rosemary, ¼ teaspoon pepper and a pinch of salt in 1½ tablespoons butter for 4 minutes. Sprinkle over 4 cooked scaloppine or chops.

Lemony Olives
After sautéeing 4 veal chops or scaloppine, melt 1 tablespoon butter in the pan. Then, add ¼ cup each of sliced black olives, stuffed green olives, chopped parsley, white wine and 1 tablespoon freshly squeezed lemon juice. Stir until warm, then pour over the veal.

P O R K
————
C H O P

LEAN CANADIAN PORK

Since Canadian pork is the leanest in the world, it's prized on the international market. These days nutritionists are comparing it favorably to chicken. Pork tenderloin, for example, has less fat than chicken with the skin on. A 4-oz (125-g) chop rings in at 168 calories and comes chock-ful of 20 g of protein. It's so lean, in fact, that it has to be cooked carefully as it can quickly dry out. Our new ways with what's been touted as "the other white meat" range from nutritious flash-in-the-pan chops, to sassy sausage suppers and finger lickin' fiery ribs.

PORK CHOP AND WINTER FRUIT MEDLEY

Keep a package of dried fruit in the cupboard, some orange juice and chops in the freezer, and with very little effort you can turn out this wholesome skillet supper.

Preparation time: 15 minutes / Cooking time: 1½ hours

Makes: 4 servings

4 pork chops, at least 1 inch thick
1 tbsp vegetable oil
2 cups orange juice
¼ tsp allspice
Generous pinch of salt
Freshly ground black pepper
½ tsp Worcestershire sauce
8-oz (250-g) pkg dried mixed fruit, about 1½ cups
1½ tsp cornstarch

1. Trim the fat from the chops and nick the edges in several places to keep them from curling during cooking. Heat the oil in a large frying pan that has a tight-fitting lid. Add the chops and cook over medium-high heat until golden brown on both sides. Drain off the fat.

2. Add 1 cup orange juice, seasonings and Worcestershire sauce to the frying pan. Cover and simmer over low heat for 45 minutes. Turn the chops. Add remaining orange juice and scatter the dried fruit around the chops, making sure the fruit is covered with the liquid. Taste the sauce and add more seasonings, if you like. Cover tightly and continue simmering for 25 to 30 minutes, until the chops and fruit are tender. Stir occasionally. Remove the chops to a platter. Surround with the cooked fruit.

3. Blend the cornstarch with a couple of tablespoons of cold water until smooth. Stir into the sauce in the frying pan and boil, stirring constantly until thickened, about 3 minutes. Pour the sauce over the chops and fruit and serve with steamed rice.

Per serving: 512 calories, 31.4 g protein, 56 g carbohydrates, 19.3 g fat, 40.2 mg calcium, 1.9 mg iron, 1 g fiber.

PORK TENDERLOIN WITH BRANDY-DIJON SAUCE

Begin a Friday night dinner for two with smoked salmon. Serve artichokes, carrots and new potatoes with the pork and wind down with a ripe pear, cambozola cheese and candied ginger coated with dark chocolate.

Preparation time: 10 minutes / Cooking time: 25 minutes

Makes: 2 servings

Freshly ground black pepper
1 pork tenderloin, about ¾ lb (375 g)
1 tsp butter
3 tbsp brandy or cognac
½ cup table cream
1 tbsp Dijon mustard
Generous pinches of dried leaf thyme, dried marjoram
  and rosemary
Salt (optional)

1. Coarsely grind enough black peppercorns to measure ¼ teaspoon. Press the pepper into the outer surface of the meat. Heat the butter in a frying pan just large enough to hold the meat. Add the meat and sauté over medium heat until lightly and evenly browned, about 8 minutes.

2. Reduce heat to low. Pour the brandy over the meat. Add remaining ingredients to the pan. Whisk until blended. Cover and cook over low heat, turning frequently, for 10 to 15 minutes, until the meat feels springy. Remove the meat from the pan and let it rest for a couple of minutes. Meanwhile, taste the sauce and add more seasonings and salt, if needed. Boil gently, uncovered and stirring often, until the sauce is thick enough to coat the pork. Slice the pork into ½-inch pieces and pour the sauce over top.

PER SERVING: *412 calories, 39.7 g protein, 2.8 g carbohydrates, 20.2 g fat, 73.2 mg calcium, 2.2 mg iron, 0.02 g fiber.*

PORK CHOPS PRONTO

Brown 4 to 6 pork chops and finish off with one of our quick sauces.

Homey Mushroom
Add a 10-oz (284-mL) can of condensed cream of mushroom soup and ¼ teaspoon poultry seasoning. Cover and simmer until chops are tender.

Hot Italian
Add 14-oz (398-mL) store-bought spaghetti sauce, ½ teaspoon crushed dried chilies and 1 tablespoon brown sugar. Cover and simmer until chops are tender.

Spiced Apple
Add 1 cup apple juice, 2 tablespoons brown sugar, ¼ teaspoon cinnamon and a pinch each of ground nutmeg and black pepper. Cover and simmer until chops are tender. Remove the chops. Boil the sauce until it's thick enough to coat the meat.

Tarragon-Wine
Add ½ cup white wine, ½ teaspoon dried tarragon, and a pinch each of salt and pepper. Cover and simmer until the chops are tender. Remove the chops. Boil the sauce until it's thick enough to coat the meat.

Pork Tenderloin en Croûte

As elegant and tender as Beef Wellington, this pastry-wrapped tenderloin takes a fraction of the time to make. Begin dinner with Fast 'n' Flavorful Squash Soup (see page 21), then serve with asparagus and Baked Cognac Carrots (see page 65).

Preparation time: 20 minutes / Baking time: 45 minutes

Makes: 4 servings

2 pork tenderloins, about ¾ lb (350 g) each
14-oz (411-g) pkg frozen puff pastry, thawed
¼ lb (125 g) Westphalian or smoked ham, very thinly sliced
Dijon mustard
1 egg
1 tbsp water

1. Preheat oven to 350F. To produce a tenderloin of even thickness, fold the slim end of the loins toward the centre, making a strip about 6 inches long.

2. Cut a ½-inch strip from the dough to use later for decoration. Cut remaining dough in half and place one portion on a very lightly floured surface. Roll into a 9-inch square.

3. Trim the fat from the ham. Overlap 3 or 4 slices down the centre of the pastry, leaving a 1-inch pastry border at each end. Place the folded loin in the centre of the ham slices. Lightly and evenly spread the loin with Dijon.

4. Bring the long sides of the pastry together and fold over. Fold in the ends to form a triangle then fold over the pork. Pinch-seal all folded pastry edges to the underlying pastry wrap.

5. Place the roll, seam-side down, on a lightly greased baking sheet with shallow sides. Repeat with the second loin. Make a small decorative hole in the top of each roll for steam to escape. Roll out thinly the pastry cut from the ends, then cut it into leaf or petal shapes. Brush the rolls with 1 egg beaten with 1 tablespoon of water. Don't drip down the side of the cutout areas as the moisture will prevent the pastry from rising. Dip the leaves in the egg mixture. Press them into the top around cutout circle.

6. Bake in the centre of the preheated oven for about 45 minutes until golden brown. Serve immediately.

PER SERVING: *716 calories, 49.4 g protein, 36.1 g carbohydrates, 40.5 g fat, 19.1 mg calcium, 2.5 mg iron, 0 g fiber.*

BEAUTIFUL BAKED HAM

Snip through the centre of the rind with scissors and peel off. Score the fat in a diamond pattern. Place the ham, uncovered, on a rack in a preheated 325F oven. Bake ready-to-serve whole hams with the bone in 10 to 12 minutes per pound; half hams need 20 minutes per pound. A meat thermometer should reach 130F. Baste with glaze during the last hour of baking and/or serve a sauce with the sliced ham.

H A M

CROWN ROAST OF PORK WITH ITALIAN-SPINACH STUFFING

Our tender spinach and Italian sausage stuffing, a far cry from the predictable bread-crumb mixture, adds a crowning glory to this special-occasion roast.

Preparation time: 30 minutes / Cooking time: 15 minutes
Roasting time: 3½ hours / Makes: 8 to 12 servings

8-lb (4-kg) crown roast of pork*
½ lb (250 g) Italian sausage
2 (12-oz/375-g) pkgs frozen spinach
2 onions, coarsely chopped
2 crushed garlic cloves
1 egg
Salt and freshly ground black pepper (optional)
Freshly grated nutmeg (optional)
Vegetable oil

1. Bring the roast to room temperature. Remove the sausage from its casing. Cook in a frying pan, about 10 minutes, working from time to time with a fork to keep the meat separated. Meanwhile, heat the frozen spinach according to package directions, just until warmed through. Place the drained spinach in a kitchen cloth and wring out all the moisture. It will measure about 2 cups.

2. As soon as the sausage is cooked, remove it from the pan with a slotted spoon, draining off as much fat as possible. Add the sausage to the spinach. Add the onions to the fat remaining in the pan and cook until soft, about 5 minutes, then stir into the spinach mixture. Finely chop the entire mixture and then stir in the garlic and slightly beaten egg. Or place the spinach mixture, along with the chopped garlic and egg, in a food processor fitted with a metal blade, and whirl, using an on-and-off motion, until the mixture is coarsely chopped and well mixed. Taste and add salt, pepper and nutmeg, if needed. You can prepare this stuffing as far as 2 days ahead and refrigerate, covered. It's not necessary to bring it to room temperature before stuffing. But don't stuff the roast until just before you place it in the oven.

3. Preheat oven to 325F. Fill the centre of the pork crown with the stuffing, mounding it slightly in the centre. Wrap any extra stuffing in foil to bake alongside the roast during the last hour of cooking. Lay a round of foil, just slightly larger than the top of the crown, over the bones protruding from the meat. Pinch the foil edges around the bones to protect them and hold the foil in place. Place the stuffed crown in a shallow roasting pan. Roast in the preheated oven for 25 minutes per

---

GLITZY HAM GLAZES

Ham is easy to bake and needs only a quick glaze to dress it up for a buffet party or gargantuan family gathering.

Orange Glaze
Stir a 6-oz (178-mL) can of frozen orange juice concentrate with ½ cup brown sugar and 1 tablespoon regular prepared mustard.

Old-Fashioned Glaze
Stir 2 cups brown sugar with 2 tablespoons all-purpose flour, 2 tablespoons corn syrup, 2 teaspoons dry mustard and 3 tablespoons white vinegar.

Maple Glaze
Stir ¼ cup Dijon mustard with ¼ cup maple syrup and ½ teaspoon dried leaf thyme.

Marmalade Glaze
Heat ½ cup orange marmalade with 2 tablespoons brown sugar, 2 teaspoons Dijon mustard and ¾ teaspoon ground ginger until blended.

No matter what the dish, sausages provide an instant hit of satisfying flavor. Here are quick ways to serve them up.

Scalloped Supper
Turn your favorite scalloped potato recipe into a complete dinner by adding layers of crumbled cooked sausage along with the onion layers.

Beer and Chili Baste
Brown 1 lb (500 g) sausages and drain off the fat. Add ½ cup beer, ¼ cup chili sauce, 2 tablespoons brown sugar and 2 teaspoons regular prepared mustard. Cover and simmer until cooked through. Serves 3 to 4.

Italian Pasta Sauce
Slice ½ lb (250 g) sweet or hot Italian sausage into ½-inch pieces. Brown in 1 tablespoon oil. Drain the fat. Stir in 1 cup spaghetti sauce, 2 chopped tomatoes and ⅛ teaspoon cayenne pepper. Cover and simmer for 5 minutes, stirring often. Makes 3 cups.

pound or until a meat thermometer registers 175F. An 8-lb roast will take about 3½ hours.

4. Using a wide lifter underneath the centre of the roast to ensure that the stuffing doesn't stick to the bottom of the pan, place the roast on a platter. Let it rest for 10 minutes before slicing. Hold the top of one of the ribs and use a sharp knife to cut down through each rib.

*Ask your butcher to prepare a crown roast of pork ready for stuffing. Order the roast according to the number of guests you are serving — allow at least 2 ribs per person.

PER SERVING: *428 calories, 47.5 g protein, 3.6 g carbohydrates, 23.7 g fat, 72.5 mg calcium, 2.5 mg iron, 0.2 g fiber.*

FINGER LICKIN' RIBS

We like to keep a jar of our favorite fast rib baste in the fridge. Although we created it for ribs, we soon discovered it's just as terrific on chicken, grilled steaks and salmon, or as the finishing touch for a stir-fry.

Preparation time: 15 minutes / Cooking time: 1¼ hours
Barbecuing time: 10 minutes / Makes: 8 to 10 servings

6 lbs (3 kg) back spareribs
1 cup ketchup
⅓ cup soy sauce
⅓ cup liquid honey
4 large crushed garlic cloves
2 tbsp Worcestershire sauce
¼ to ½ tsp cayenne pepper

1. Cut the ribs into 8 to 10 portions. Place them in a heavy saucepan. Cover with water and boil gently, covered, for 1 to 1¼ hours or until tender. Drain. If not using immediately, cover and refrigerate.

2. To make the sauce, stir the remaining ingredients together. Coat the ribs with the sauce and place them on a preheated greased grill over hot coals. Barbecue, turning often and basting with sauce, until hot and glazed, about 8 to 10 minutes.

PER SERVING: *1022 calories, 70.2 g protein, 17.4 g carbohydrates, 72.6 g fat, 124.2 mg calcium, 5 mg iron, 0 g fiber.*

NEW WAVE FISH

Calorie-conscious Canadians are eating lighter than ever, which means more and more of us are turning to fish. Whether it's fresh, frozen, whole or filleted, fish is one of the speediest high-protein entrées you can prepare. A sole fillet, for example, needs no more than a mere flip in and out of the frying pan. You can broil a whole school of halibut steaks to meaty, moist perfection in under ten minutes. A stuffed salmon bakes in twenty minutes. In addition to the recipes — which include lots of ten-minute quickies — we also provide a buy-and-cook fish chart so you'll never again find yourself at the fish counter wondering what Boston bluefish or turbot tastes like, or how to cook swordfish or tuna.

A Fine Kettle of Fish

Fish goes a long way toward providing energy in your diet. If every calorie counts, stick to low-fat fish, such as sole or haddock, and poach, bake or microwave it with a sprinkling of fresh herbs. A 3½-oz (100-g) sole fillet, for example, reels in 15 g of protein — more than one-third of a woman's daily requirement. Here's a nutritional breakdown and a guide to flavor and best cooking methods for many of the fish you'll find at your local market.

3½ oz/100 g Fish	Calories	Protein (g)	Fat (g)	Flavor, Texture & Embellishments
Boston Bluefish	95	20	0.9	A cross between cod and haddock. Dry and firm. Very versatile.
Cod (Scrod)	78	18	0.3	Mild. Firm and milky white. Adapts to all cooking methods.
Grouper	87	19	0.5	Sweet. Lean and firm. Skin before cooking. Tastes great broiled, and in chowders.
Haddock	79	18	0.1	Flavorful but delicate. Lean. Perfect for elegant sauces.
Halibut	100	21	1.2	Extremely flavorful. Fine, milky white. Good poached in milk.
Mackerel	191	19	12.2	Rich and soft. Excellent smoked. Cook with tomatoes, wine or Dijon mustard.
Pickerel	84	19	0.5	Wonderfully sweet. Firm. Ideal for steaming or baking whole.
Rainbow Trout	195	22	11.4	Delicate, moist and soft. Great for pan-frying or baking.
Red Snapper	93	20	0.9	Excellent full flavor. Large fish can be coarse. Good stuffed and baked.
Salmon	217	23	13.4	Firm. Pink to red in color. Needs few fixings.
Shark	195	17.4	13.4	Mild; can be sweet, coarse and meaty. Good broiled, with wine or soy sauces.
Skate	98	22	0.7	Delicate, sweet and firm. Taste like scallops. Sauté in butter.
Sole	68	15	0.5	Delicate and lean — don't deep fry.
Swordfish	118	19	4.0	Similar to shark. Rich. Firm yet tender. Good with seasoned butter, soy sauce.
Tuna	145	25	4.1	White meat is finest. Firm and moist. Particularly good pan-fried and broiled.
Turbot	193	14.8	14.4	Mild, delicate. Fine and firm. Excellent with mild creamy sauces.

FOOLPROOF FISH COOKERY

Canada's Department of Fisheries and Oceans developed this easy, foolproof method for timing the cooking of fish. It is recognized around the world as the most accurate method for achieving perfectly moist fish.

• Measure the fish at its thickest point and cook ten minutes per inch of thickness.

To Bake
• Allow 10 minutes' baking time per inch of thickness. A rainbow trout may need 10 minutes, while a stuffed salmon takes about 30.

• Frozen fish need not be thawed — simply double the baking time to 20 minutes per inch. If fish is wrapped in foil, increase the total baking time by 10 minutes.

To Broil
• Because of the intense heat, broiling must be done carefully to prevent the fish from drying out. For whole fish, leave head and tail intact to cut down on the loss of natural juices. Steaks and fillets should be at least an inch thick. Lean fish needs frequent basting.

• Always preheat broiler. To prevent sticking, oil the pan or rack, or cover it with oiled foil. Adjust the oven rack so that the top of the fish is 4 to 6 inches from the broiler. (The thicker the fish, the farther away it should be, so the outside won't overcook before the inner flesh is done.) Broil 10 minutes per inch of thickness, lowering the rack if the fish browns too fast.

To Poach
• Wrap a whole cleaned small fish in cheesecloth to prevent it from falling apart, leaving some cloth at both ends to act as handles. Fish steaks don't require wrapping. Use a shallow pan large enough to hold the fish. A roasting pan with a roasting rack works well. Larger fish are best done in a poacher, an oblong pan fitted with a metal rack. Lower the fish into the poacher or pan, then add enough liquid to cover. Use tepid water, white wine and fish stock, or court bouillon. Season with fresh or dried herbs such as dill or tarragon, several whole white or black peppercorns, sliced onion and lemon. Set the pan over two burners, if necessary, and heat until the water begins to simmer. Cover the pan, reduce heat and simmer 10 minutes per inch of thickness, counting from the time the water starts to simmer. The fish is done when a skewer inserted into the thick flesh behind the gills meets little resistance. If serving cold, cool the fish in broth in the refrigerator before unwrapping.

To Sauté
• Place a little vegetable oil, or half oil and half butter in a frying pan — just enough to thinly coat the bottom. Place the pan over medium heat until a cube of bread dropped into the fat begins to brown. Coat the fish lightly with flour. Don't put too many pieces in the pan at one time. Sauté over medium heat until one side is lightly browned. Turn only once and repeat on the other side.

To Barbecue

• Invest in a hinged fold-over rack for barbecuing fish fillets and steaks. A well-greased rack holds the delicate fish flesh together and means you don't have to risk breaking a fillet or steak when you turn it. Oil the barbecue grill as well as the hinged rack.

• Whole fish too large to fit into a rack can be loosely wrapped in oiled chicken wire and grilled the same way.

• Or you can use foil. Season and wrap each fish piece in a sheet of well-greased heavy foil large enough to seal with a double fold. Place the packages over the grill on low heat, turning frequently with tongs.

To Microwave
• A pound of fish can be microwaved in 5 minutes. Place fresh or thawed fish in a single layer in a microwave-safe dish. Cover with plastic wrap, and turn back a small edge or pierce the wrap to allow steam to escape. One pound of fillets needs 3 to 5 minutes on high, while a 3-lb fish requires about 10 minutes. Always use the minimum cooking and standing time, then check to see if the flesh flakes easily when lifted in the centre with a fork.

NEW WAVE FISH · TRIPLE TESTED

SALMON SUPREME

Whether it's a glorious red B.C. coho or a delicate pink Atlantic species, Canadian salmon is our all-time favorite fish. Besides its marvelous color, unique flavor and texture, recent research tells us that salmon flesh is rich in fatty acids that lower cholesterol. Healthy, delicious and truly Canadian. No wonder we love it.

TARRAGON SALMON STEAKS WITH DIJON

A fast and foolproof microwave method for salmon steaks splashed with white wine and topped with a Dijon and green onion sauce. See photo opposite page 161.

Preparation time: 10 minutes / Microwave time: 10 minutes

Makes: 4 servings

4 salmon steaks, about ¾ inch thick
Salt and white pepper
2 tbsp white wine
1 tbsp butter
1 whole green onion, thinly sliced
1 tbsp all-purpose flour
1 tsp Dijon mustard
½ tsp dried tarragon
Milk

1. Place the steaks on a microwave-safe pie plate. Sprinkle with a pinch of salt and white pepper. Drizzle with wine. Cover with waxed paper. Microwave on high until fish flakes easily, about 6 minutes. Remove the steaks to a platter and cover.

2. Pour the liquid from the plate into a measuring cup and save. Place the butter and green onion on the plate. Microwave, uncovered, on high for 1 minute. Stir in the flour, Dijon and tarragon and microwave, uncovered, on high for 1 minute.

3. Add enough milk to the reserved liquid to make ⅔ cup. Gradually stir into the onion mixture. Microwave, uncovered, on high for 2 minutes. Stir. Pour the sauce over the steaks.

PER SERVING: *185 calories, 22.4 g protein, 2.6 g carbohydrates, 8.4 g fat, 41.3 mg calcium, 1.2 mg iron, 0.09 g fiber.*

FLAVORED FISH BUTTERS

Top hot fish steaks with a pat of cold, flavored butter for a burst of rich flavor.

• Mix equal amounts of pesto and butter. Refrigerate.

• Stir 2 tablespoons of finely chopped fresh dill and 1 teaspoon finely grated lemon peel into ¼ cup room-temperature butter. Refrigerate.

• Sauté 2 crushed garlic cloves in ¼ cup butter for 5 minutes. Stir in 1 teaspoon dried tarragon and ¼ teaspoon white pepper. Refrigerate.

SALMON TERIYAKI

Salmon takes beautifully to our freshly made teriyaki sauce and fast broiling. Position the steaks at least six inches from the element, and the teriyaki will form a thin, glazed crust — a delightful contrast to the moist fish.

Preparation time: 5 minutes / Broiling time: 10 minutes
Makes: 4 servings

2 tbsp soy sauce
2 tbsp dry sherry
1 tbsp brown sugar
1 tsp finely grated fresh gingerroot
1 crushed garlic clove
4 salmon steaks, about 1 inch thick

1. Preheat broiler. Stir the soy sauce with the sherry, sugar, gingerroot and garlic. Place the salmon steaks on a lightly greased broiler rack set in a shallow pan. Generously brush the top of the steaks with the soy mixture.

2. Broil the steaks 6 inches from the broiler for 5 minutes. Turn salmon and generously brush with the soy mixture. Continue to broil for 4 to 5 more minutes or until salmon flakes easily with a fork. Any remaining soy mixture can be covered and stored in the refrigerator.

PER SERVING: *211 calories, 29 g protein, 5 g carbohydrates, 6.8 g fat, 23.5 mg calcium, 1.6 mg iron, 0 g fiber.*

SALMON

START WITH A CAN OF SALMON

A can of salmon in the cupboard means you can have a light supper ready almost in the time it takes to open the tin. Canned salmon packs a high-protein, low-calorie punch: half a can has 20 g of protein and about 150 calories. Use a drained 7½-oz (213-g) can in these quickies.

Salsa Salmon
Purée salmon with 4 oz (125 g) cream cheese and 2 tablespoons salsa until smooth. Use as a spread for open-faced sandwiches, crackers or rye bread squares.

Hot Southern Salmon
Drain a 4-oz (114-mL) can of green chilies and remove seeds. Place the chilies in a blender with the salmon and its juice and 4 oz (125 g) cream cheese. Whirl until smooth. Great as a sandwich spread or healthy dip with nachos.

Salmon Patties
Stir a can of salmon with ½ cup bread crumbs, ¼ cup sliced whole green onion, 1 egg, 1 teaspoon lemon juice and some black pepper. Form into 6 patties. Fry on both sides in a little oil until golden.

ROYAL SALMON DUXELLE IN PUFF PASTRY

Serve these golden party packages on a special occasion — New Year's Eve perhaps.

Preparation time: 20 minutes / Cooking time: 40 minutes

Makes: 2 servings

$\frac{1}{2}$ lb (250 g) fresh mushrooms
$\frac{1}{4}$ cup butter
$\frac{1}{4}$ tsp each of salt and dried dillweed
Pinch of white pepper
$\frac{1}{4}$ lb (125 g) puff pastry
2 (3-oz/90-g) pieces of boned salmon
1 egg yolk
2 tbsp milk
$\frac{1}{4}$ cup clarified butter
$\frac{1}{2}$ tsp dried dillweed

1. Preheat oven to 400F. Chop the mushrooms very fine, about a $\frac{1}{4}$-inch dice. Melt the butter in a large wide frying pan. Add the mushrooms, salt, $\frac{1}{4}$ teaspoon dillweed and white pepper. Cook over medium heat, uncovered, stirring occasionally, until all the liquid has evaporated, about 20 minutes.

2. Roll out half of the pastry to an $8\frac{1}{2}$-inch square. Spoon a quarter of the mushroom mixture into the centre of the pastry. Place 1 salmon piece over the mushrooms and top with another quarter of the mushroom mixture. Bring the two longest sides of the pastry together and seal, then bring remaining ends over top and seal. Repeat the process with remaining fish. Turn both pieces seam-side down on a baking sheet with shallow sides. Using a pastry cutter, cut out a small hole in the centre of each puff pastry package, then brush the pastry with a mixture of egg yolk and milk.

3. Bake in the preheated oven for 20 minutes or until golden brown. Remove from the oven and leave on the pan for a couple of minutes. Then, remove to dinner plates. Meanwhile, heat the clarified butter and dill together and pour a little through the opening of each puff pastry package. Serve the remainder separately to pour over the fish.

PER SERVING: *851 calories, 19.2 g protein, 27.4 g carbohydrates, 74.9 g fat, 62.2 mg calcium, 3.5 mg iron, 0 g fiber.*

CREAMY PARTY LEMON STEAKS

Melt 2 tablespoons butter in a frying pan. Add 4 salmon steaks. Sauté 4 minutes per side over medium heat. Set aside. Stir $\frac{1}{4}$ cup whipping cream, 1 teaspoon grated lemon peel, 2 tablespoons chopped fresh dill, and salt and pepper into the pan. Stir until thickened, about 2 minutes. Spoon the sauce over the steaks.

GRILLED SALMON WITH SMOKED SALMON CRÈME FRAÎCHE

Vancouver chef Rebecca Dawson invented this sublime smoked salmon crème fraîche which she spoons over broiled salmon steaks. For a dramatic first course it's also wonderful dabbed over a thin bundle of warm asparagus, swirled in the centre of a bowl of leek soup or tossed with spinach fettuccine.

Preparation time: 10 minutes / Standing time: 4 hours
Refrigeration time: 8 hours / Barbecuing time: 8 minutes
Makes: 4 servings

1 cup (250-mL container) whipping cream
2 tbsp sour cream
1 tbsp freshly squeezed lemon juice
1½ oz (50 g) thinly sliced smoked salmon
4 salmon steaks about ¾ inch thick
Juice of 1 lemon
1 tbsp clarified butter
Chive flowers (optional)

1. Prepare smoked salmon crème fraîche by placing the whipping cream, sour cream and 1 tablespoon lemon juice in a large jar. Leave at room temperature for 4 hours. Then, slice the smoked salmon into small julienne strips and stir into the cream mixture. Cover and refrigerate for at least 8 hours to thicken and allow the flavors to develop.

2. When ready to cook the salmon steaks, grease the grill and preheat barbecue to medium-high. Bone and skin the salmon, so each steak is in 2 pieces.

3. Place 2 pieces of salmon on each skewer to form an S-shape. Brush the salmon with lemon juice, then clarified butter.

4. Place the skewers on the grill about 3 inches from the hot coals. Grill for about 4 minutes per side. Do not overcook.

5. Remove the skewers from the fish and serve the salmon with cold smoked salmon crème fraîche on the side. Garnish with chive flowers, if you wish.

PER SERVING: 444 calories, 28 g protein, 3.9 g carbohydrates, 35.2 g fat, 70.7 mg calcium, 1.3 mg iron, 0.06 g fiber.

CHIVE
FLOWERS

SALMON WITH DILLED SOUR CREAM

Want a quick and satisfying way to cook salmon steaks tonight? Try this twelve-minute version with a coating of dilled sour cream.

Preparation time: 5 minutes / Baking time: 15 minutes

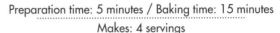

Makes: 4 servings

4 salmon steaks, about 1 inch thick
½ cup sour cream
2 tbsp melted butter
½ tsp dried dillweed
Pinch of freshly ground white pepper

1. Preheat oven to 450F. Place the salmon steaks in a shallow baking dish. Stir remaining ingredients together in a bowl. Spread over top of the steaks.

2. Bake, uncovered, in the centre of the preheated oven for 12 to 15 minutes or until the cream is piping hot.

PER SERVING *294 calories, 29.5 g protein, 1.3 g carbohydrates, 18.5 g fat, 54.7 mg calcium, 1.4 mg iron, 0 g fiber.*

D I L L -
W E E D

FAST SALMON STEAK SUPPERS

Here's a catch of easy ways to bring salmon steaks to the table. We used one-inch-thick steaks for each recipe.

En Papillote
Preheat oven to 450F. Place each salmon steak on a piece of heavy foil. Sprinkle each with ⅛ teaspoon dried dillweed and a pinch of white pepper. Drizzle each with 1 tablespoon white wine. Seal foil well. Bake for 15 to 20 minutes.

Dijon Cream
Preheat oven to 425F. Place 4 salmon steaks on a baking sheet and bake, uncovered, for 5 minutes. Stir ½ cup sour cream with 1 teaspoon Dijon mustard and ½ teaspoon dried dillweed. Spread over the steaks. Continue baking, uncovered, for 5 minutes.

Barbecued Spicy Cajun
Stir 1 teaspoon chili powder with 1 teaspoon ground cumin and ¼ teaspoon each of cayenne pepper and garlic powder. Brush both sides of 6 steaks with vegetable oil and generously sprinkle with seasonings. Barbecue or broil 5 minutes per side.

Lemon and Fresh Herbs
Place 4 steaks, ¼ cup white wine and 1 tablespoon lemon juice in a medium-size frying pan. Cook, covered, over medium-low heat for 5 minutes. Turn and sprinkle with ½ cup fresh dill or basil. Cover and continue cooking for 3 to 5 minutes.

Easy Oriental
Whisk 3 tablespoons teriyaki sauce with 1 tablespoon vegetable oil, 1 tablespoon Dijon mustard, ¼ teaspoon ground ginger and 1 crushed garlic clove. Place 4 to 6 salmon steaks on a broiler pan or barbecue grill. Brush with the sauce. Broil for 5 minutes. Turn and brush with more sauce. Broil for 5 more minutes.

Capers and White Wine
Melt 1 tablespoon butter in a medium-size frying pan. Add 4 salmon steaks, ½ cup white wine and 1 tablespoon drained capers. Cover and cook over medium-low heat for 5 minutes per side. Remove the steaks to dinner plates. Boil the sauce, uncovered, until reduced to ⅓ cup. Pour over the steaks.

HEALTHY STEAKS

Most fish steaks, including swordfish, halibut, haddock, tuna or salmon, can be used interchangeably in a recipe, so ask your fish monger for the freshest catch of the day. Buy them one inch thick and they'll broil, bake, steam or barbecue perfectly — in ten minutes. Remember, these are the fastest low-fat "steaks" you can cook.

HALIBUT STEAKS WITH WHITE WINE ANCHOVY SAUCE

Tender yet firm-fleshed, mild yet sweet — we can't go on enough about fresh halibut. Here's our favorite way to prepare it with a white wine anchovy sauce that doesn't override its delicate taste.

Preparation time: 2 minutes / Cooking time: 12 minutes

Makes: 4 servings

1 tbsp each of butter and olive oil
4 halibut steaks, about 6 oz (180 g) each
¼ cup all-purpose flour
1 cup dry white wine
1 tbsp anchovy paste or 3 anchovy fillets, finely chopped
Freshly ground white pepper
¼ cup finely chopped fresh dill
½ lemon (optional)

1. Heat the butter and oil in a large wide frying pan set over medium-high heat. Meanwhile, lightly coat the halibut with flour. Add the fish to the pan and cook over medium-high heat for about 2 minutes per side.

2. Immediately pour the wine over the fish. Add the anchovy paste to the wine mixture along with some pepper. Whisk until evenly blended.

3. Adjust heat so the wine boils gently, and cook the halibut steaks for about 2 to 3 more minutes per side or until fish flakes with a fork. Remove the fish to dinner plates. Increase heat to high and boil the wine mixture, uncovered, until slightly thickened, about 2 minutes. Pour over the fish. Sprinkle the fish with dill and give it a squeeze of lemon juice.

PER SERVING: *334 calories, 40.9 g protein, 6.4 g carbohydrates, 10.9 g fat, 116 mg calcium, 2.6 mg iron, 0.2 g fiber.*

GRILLED FISH STEAKS WITH LEMON-CAPER SAUCE

An easy steak barbecue that works well with the best buy at the fish counter. Keep in mind that freshness makes a whopping difference to taste.

Preparation time: 5 minutes / Barbecuing time: 10 minutes
Cooking time: 6 minutes / Makes: 4 servings

4 swordfish or other steaks, about 1 inch thick
½ cup butter
2 crushed garlic cloves
3 whole green onions, thinly sliced
2 tbsp freshly squeezed lemon juice
2 tbsp well-drained capers
Generous grinding of black pepper

1. To barbecue, preheat barbecue and grease the grill well. Bring the swordfish to room temperature before grilling. Place the fish steaks on the greased grill, about 4 inches from the hot coals. Barbecue for 4 to 5 minutes per side, brushing occasionally with oil.

2. To broil, preheat broiler. Place the oven rack about 5 inches from the broiler. Lightly oil the fish and place it on a broiler pan. Broil for 4 to 5 minutes per side or until fish flakes easily with a fork.

3. Meanwhile, in a small frying pan, melt the butter over medium heat. Add the garlic and sauté for 3 to 4 minutes or until the garlic is soft. Stir in the green onions and sauté for 1 to 2 minutes or until heated through. Then, stir in the lemon juice and capers. Taste and add a generous grinding of pepper.

4. Remove the fish from the barbecue or oven and place it on a platter. Drizzle with warm lemon-caper sauce.

PER SERVING: *326 calories, 36 g protein, 1.6 g carbohydrates, 18.7 g fat, 17.1 mg calcium, 1.6 mg iron, 0.1 g fiber.*

LEMON

Swordfish with Cajun Butter

A sprinkling of earthy but mild seasonings stands up perfectly to the meaty texture of swordfish.

Preparation time: 5 minutes

Baking time: 12 minutes *or* Microwave time: 7 minutes / Makes: 4 servings

3 tbsp butter
$\frac{1}{2}$ tsp dried leaf oregano
$\frac{1}{2}$ tsp dried leaf thyme
$\frac{1}{8}$ tsp dry mustard
$\frac{1}{8}$ tsp cayenne pepper
Pinch of salt
4 swordfish or tuna steaks, about 6 oz (180 g) each

1. Preheat oven to 400F. Melt butter in a small saucepan over medium heat. Stir in the oregano, thyme, dry mustard, cayenne pepper and salt.

2. Butter a baking dish just large enough to hold steaks in a single layer. Drizzle fish with melted butter mixture. Bake in centre of the preheated oven 10 to 12 minutes, until swordfish flakes easily with a fork.

3. To microwave, prepare butter mixture by placing the butter and seasonings in a small microwave-safe dish. Microwave, uncovered, on high for 30 seconds or until the butter is melted. Stir until blended. Place the swordfish steaks, thin ends toward centre, in a 10-inch microwave-safe pie plate. Drizzle the fish with the melted butter mixture. Microwave, uncovered, on high for 5 to 7 minutes, just until fish flakes with a fork.

PER SERVING: 295 calories, 35.7 g protein, 0.2 g carbohydrates, 15.8 g fat, 14.5 mg calcium, 1.6 mg iron, 0 g fiber.

Fast Ways with Fish Steaks

Easy dress-ups that won't overpower the delicate fish flavor. Use halibut, salmon, tuna — whichever you prefer.

Dilled Cream
Broil 4 fish steaks for 5 minutes. Spread with $\frac{2}{3}$ cup sour cream blended with $\frac{1}{2}$ teaspoon each of dried dillweed and coarsely ground black pepper. Broil for 3 more minutes.

Lime Ginger
Sauté 4 fish steaks in 2 tablespoons vegetable oil over medium heat for 5 minutes. Turn. Drizzle with 3 tablespoons lime juice blended with 1 tablespoon finely chopped candied ginger. Sauté for 5 more minutes.

Smooth Mango
Sauté 4 fish steaks in 2 tablespoons butter over medium heat for 4 minutes per side. Blend $\frac{1}{2}$ cup plain yogurt with 2 tablespoons mango chutney and a pinch of black pepper. Spoon over the fish.

Pesto Butter
Sauté 4 fish steaks in 2 tablespoons butter for 5 minutes per side. Blend 2 tablespoons pesto with 1 tablespoon butter. Dab on the fish.

Fiery Oriental
Stir 1 tablespoon sesame oil with 2 teaspoons soy sauce and $\frac{1}{4}$ teaspoon cayenne pepper. Brush on both sides of 4 fish steaks. Broil or barbecue for 3 minutes per side.

TUNA WITH OLIVE SALSA

Top tuna or halibut steaks with this robust caper, black olive and red pepper mix.

Preparation time: 15 minutes / Standing time: 1 hour
Broiling time: 8 minutes *or* Microwave time: 5½ minutes

Makes: 4 servings

⅔ cup olive oil
⅓ cup finely chopped Italian parsley
1 small red pepper, cored and diced
4 whole green onions, thinly sliced
¼ cup freshly squeezed lemon juice
2 tbsp capers, drained
2 tbsp finely chopped pitted black olives
1 tbsp dried leaf oregano
2 tbsp olive oil
4 to 6 tuna or halibut steaks, about ¾ inch thick
Freshly ground black pepper

1. In a medium-size bowl, stir ⅔ cup olive oil with the parsley, red pepper, onions, lemon juice, capers, olives and oregano. It's preferable to let the mixture stand at room temperature for at least an hour to allow the flavors to blend. The salsa can be covered and refrigerated for up to 3 to 4 days. Bring to room temperature before serving.

2. To cook the fish, preheat broiler. Lightly brush a shallow baking sheet with olive oil. Brush both sides of the fish with remaining olive oil and sprinkle with pepper. Place on a prepared baking sheet and broil 4 inches from the preheated broiler for 2 to 4 minutes per side. Serve immediately, topped with salsa.

3. To microwave, prepare salsa following the above directions. Lightly brush both sides of the fish with olive oil and sprinkle with pepper. Place the fish, thin ends toward centre, in a spokelike fashion in a 10-inch microwave-safe pie plate. Microwave, covered, on high for 4½ to 5½ minutes, until fish flakes with a fork. Top with salsa.

PER SERVING: 630 calories, 48 g protein, 3.5 g carbohydrates, 46.8 g fat, 40.3 mg calcium, 3 mg iron, 0.7 g fiber.

FAST FISH FILLETS

Fish fillets are generally thin and delicate, so they require minimal cooking and fussing. They're also economical, so when frozen fillets go on special, stock up.

HADDOCK WITH SCALLIONS AND FRESH BASIL

Another flavorful, fast fish dinner. Despite the fact that it comes with a creamy sauce, it's low in calories: light sour cream has only fifteen per tablespoon. Skip the butter to cut calories even further.

Preparation time: 5 minutes / Cooking time: 10 minutes

Makes: 4 servings

1 lb (500 g) haddock or mild-flavored fillets, such as
    whitefish or sea bass
1/3 cup dry white wine
Salt and white pepper
1 tbsp butter (optional)
1/2 cup regular or light sour cream
2 whole green onions, sliced
2 tbsp finely chopped fresh basil or 1/2 tsp dried basil

1. Cut the fish into serving-size pieces. Place the fish in a large frying pan and pour the wine over top. Sprinkle the fish with salt and white pepper. Dot with butter, if you like. To poach the fish, cover and bring the wine to a simmer. Simmer for about 5 to 10 minutes, depending on the thickness of the fish, until it flakes easily.

2. Remove the fish to a warm platter and cover to keep warm. Turn heat to high and boil the pan juices until reduced to 2 to 3 tablespoons. Stir in the sour cream, green onions and basil. Add salt and pepper to taste. Pour over the fish and serve immediately.

PER SERVING: *197 calories, 24.2 g protein, 1.6 g carbohydrates, 8.5 g fat, 51.8 mg calcium, 0.5 mg iron, 0.06 g fiber.*

RATATOUILLE-STYLE FISH FILLETS

Instead of stewing the vegetables for hours, we've lightly sautéed them to maintain an al dente texture and garden-fresh taste. A lively contrast to mild-flavored fish fillets.

Preparation time: 10 minutes / Cooking time: 20 minutes

Makes: 4 servings

PARTY LEMON WRAPS

For a classy way to avoid squeezing out the seeds as well as the juice when you serve lemon halves with fish, wrap them in small squares of cheesecloth tied with a pretty bow.

1 lb (500 g) fresh or frozen fish fillets, such as haddock or turbot
3 tbsp olive or vegetable oil
3 garlic cloves, peeled and halved
Salt and freshly ground black pepper
3 ripe tomatoes, coarsely chopped
2 small zucchini, thinly sliced
Generous pinch of dried basil

1. If using frozen fillets, thaw just until they can be separated. Heat 2 tablespoons oil in a large frying pan. Add the garlic halves, then the fish fillets. Sauté over medium heat until lightly browned on both sides. This will take about 5 minutes per side for fresh fillets or 10 minutes per side for partially thawed fillets. Add more oil, if needed. Remove the fillets to a dish. Leave the garlic in the pan. Sprinkle the fillets with salt and pepper and cover to keep warm.

2. Add another tablespoon of oil to pan. Turn heat to high. Add the tomatoes and zucchini. Sprinkle with basil, salt and pepper. Stir-fry for 1 to 2 minutes over high heat to just warm the vegetables. Spread over fillets.

PER SERVING: *234 calories, 22.4 g protein, 7.9 g carbohydrates, 12.8 g fat, 28 mg calcium, 1.1 mg iron, 1.5 g fiber.*

FROZEN FISH TRICKS

Creamy Caper
Place a 1-lb (500-g) block of frozen mild-flavored fish in heavy foil. Spread the top of the fish with a mixture of 1/3 cup sour cream, 1/2 teaspoon dried dillweed and 1 tablespoon drained capers. Wrap in foil. Bake at 450F for 35 minutes. Serves 2.

Chunky Chowder
Bring a package of leek soup mix, 3 cups water and 1/2 teaspoon dried tarragon to a boil. Add 1 lb (500 g) mild-flavored fish fillets, cut into bite-size pieces. Add 2 diced potatoes. Cover and simmer for 25 minutes. Serves 2 to 3.

Racy Ragout Stew
Pour a 28-oz (796-mL) can of tomatoes including juice into a saucepan and heat with 2 chopped onions, 1/2 teaspoon dried basil, 1/4 teaspoon dried leaf thyme, a pinch of garlic powder, salt and pepper. Add a 1-lb (500-g) block of frozen fish, cut into bite-size pieces. Cover and simmer for 20 minutes. Serves 2.

Seafood Bisque
Bring a 10-oz (284-mL) can of condensed cream of shrimp or lobster bisque and 2 cups milk to a boil. Add 1 lb (500 g) frozen fish fillets, cut into 8 pieces. Simmer, covered, for 20 minutes. Add 3 chopped whole green onions and 1/2 cup sour cream.

LIGHT SOLE STROGANOFF

A soothing Stroganoff that's comfortingly creamy yet low in calories. Serve with asparagus and rice or parslied potatoes.

Preparation time: 10 minutes / Cooking time: 10 minutes

Makes: 3 servings

1 tbsp butter
¼ lb (125 g) sliced fresh mushrooms
2 whole green onions, sliced into 1-inch pieces
½ tbsp chopped shallots
1 lb (500 g) sole fillets
2 tbsp dry white wine
⅓ cup sour cream
Generous pinches each of saffron, salt and white pepper

1. Melt ½ tablespoon butter in a large frying pan. Add the mushrooms and green onions and sauté for 2 minutes, stirring often. Turn onto paper towels.

2. Melt another ½ tablespoon butter in the pan. Add the shallots and sole. Sauté over medium heat for 3 minutes per side. Remove to a platter and cover.

3. Add the wine, sour cream and seasonings to the pan. Stir until hot. Add the mushrooms and green onions and stir gently for 1 minute, just until warm. Pour over the fish and serve immediately.

PER SERVING: 242 calories, 29.6 g protein, 3.7 g carbohydrates, 11.1 g fat, 58 mg calcium, 1.1 mg iron, 0.6 g fiber.

CREAMY CUMIN FILLETS

Add an intriguing southern touch to fast-cooking fish fillets.

Preparation time: 5 minutes / Cooking time: 12 minutes

Makes: 4 servings

1 tbsp butter
1 lb (500 g) mild-flavored fish fillets, such as sole, turbot,
    bass or tile fish
Salt and white pepper
1 tsp ground cumin
½ tsp ground coriander
1 cup sour cream
Pinches of paprika (optional)

FILLETS IN A FLASH

Orange-Basil
Melt 2 tablespoons butter in a frying pan. Add 1 lb (500 g) fillets, juice and peel of 2 oranges, ½ teaspoon dried basil, salt and pepper. Sauté about 3 minutes per side.

Lemony Yogurt
Sauté thawed fillets in butter. Serve with a sauce of ½ cup plain yogurt, grated peel of 1 lemon and 1 teaspoon honey.

Tarragon Bake
Bake 1 lb (500 g) fish fillets in a single layer in a baking dish at 450F for 5 minutes. Drain off liquid. Spread with a mixture of ½ cup sour cream, 2 teaspoons Dijon mustard and ½ teaspoon dried tarragon. Sprinkle with ¼ cup freshly grated Parmesan cheese. Bake, uncovered, for 5 minutes.

1. Melt the butter in a large wide frying pan. Add as many pieces of fish as will fit comfortably in the pan. Sprinkle with salt and pepper. Sauté over medium heat for about 2 minutes per side. Repeat with remaining fish.

2. Return all the fish to the pan. Stir the cumin and coriander into the sour cream. Spread over the fillets. Sprinkle with paprika, if you like. Cover and simmer until the sauce is warm and the fish will flake easily, about 2 to 3 minutes.

PER SERVING: 254 calories, 22.9 g protein, 3.2 g carbohydrates, 16.5 g fat, 96.9 mg calcium, 1.1 mg iron, 0 g fiber.

NEW-STYLE SOLE AMANDINE

Delicate sole fillets are enriched with a Dijon-honey-wine sauce, then topped with crunchy sautéed almonds.

Preparation time: 5 minutes / Cooking time: 12 to 20 minutes

Makes: 2 servings

1 tbsp each of butter and vegetable oil
¼ cup slivered almonds
12 oz (375 g) fresh or frozen sole fillets
½ cup dry white wine
¼ tsp dried dillweed
Pinch each of salt and white pepper
1 tsp Dijon mustard
½ tsp liquid honey

1. Heat 1½ teaspoons each of butter and oil in a large frying pan over medium-high heat. Add the almonds and stir-fry just until golden brown. Remove with a slotted spoon and set aside.

2. Add about half the fish to the hot butter-oil mixture. Cook for about 2 minutes per side over medium-high heat for fresh fish, or 4 minutes per side over medium heat for frozen fish. Remove to a platter and cover. Add remaining butter and oil and repeat with remaining sole.

3. Add remaining ingredients to the pan. Turn heat to high. Whisk until blended and boil until reduced to about ¼ cup sauce. Stir any juices from the fish back into the pan. Then, pour the sauce over the fish. Sprinkle with almonds.

PER SERVING: 405 calories, 36.5 g protein, 5 g carbohydrates, 22.3 g fat, 73.5 mg calcium, 1.3 mg iron, 1.3 g fiber.

WHOLE FISH BAKES

We are always surprised that people are intimidated by the prospect of cooking a whole fish. It couldn't be easier or faster — most whole fish bake in less than a half hour. Any of these elegant dishes would make a swimmingly successful entrée for your next soirée.

ROYAL SESAME SALMON

This recipe, like the little black dress or grey suit in your wardrobe, is a must-have. A fast brush and sprinkle is all that's needed to dress up this salmon for the poshest of parties. Wonderful served with pasta and asparagus.

Preparation time: 15 minutes / Baking time: 20 minutes

Makes: 8 servings

5½-lb (2.5-kg) whole salmon, cleaned, head and skin removed
2 tbsp sesame, peanut or vegetable oil
2 tbsp soy or teriyaki sauce
2 tbsp sesame seeds

1. Preheat oven to 425F. Line a large baking sheet with foil. Lightly brush the foil with a little vegetable oil. Measure the fish at its thickest part to determine length of baking time.

2. Rinse salmon under cold water and pat dry. Place it on the baking sheet. In a small bowl whisk together 2 tablespoons oil and soy sauce. Brush salmon generously, inside and out, with the oil-soy sauce mixture. Then, sprinkle half of the sesame seeds in the cavity and over top.

3. Bake the salmon, uncovered, in the centre of the preheated oven until fish flakes easily with a fork at its thickest point. Fish is baked 10 minutes for every inch of thickness. If your salmon is 2 inches thick, bake for 20 minutes.

PER SERVING: *329 calories, 45.3 g protein, 0.5 g carbohydrates, 15 g fat, 30.5 mg calcium, 2.3 mg iron, 0 g fiber.*

DILLED WHITE WINE AND SHALLOT SAUCE
Pour this easy elegant sauce over any baked or barbecued fish. Combine ½ cup white wine, 2 tablespoons each of finely chopped shallots and butter, ¼ cup finely chopped fresh dill and a generous pinch of white pepper in a saucepan. Gently boil, uncovered, until reduced by half, about 5 minutes. Pour over skinned whole baked fish or steaks.

SALMON

BARBECUED WHOLE SALMON

This is the easiest entrée to barbecue for a party. Provide a selection of sauces — your favorites from the Superb Salmon Sauces below.

Preparation time: 5 minutes / Grilling time: 25 to 45 minutes

Makes: 8 servings

6-lb (3-kg) whole salmon, cleaned
Freshly ground white pepper
Small bunch fresh dill (optional)
Lemon slices (optional)
Vegetable oil

1. Preheat barbecue. Sprinkle the cavity of the salmon with white pepper. Fill it with sprigs of fresh dill, if you wish, or thin slices of lemon. Brush the outside of the salmon with vegetable oil.

2. Measure the salmon at its thickest part. A 6-lb (3-kg) whole salmon will measure about 2½ to 3 inches thick. Grill 10 to 15 minutes for each inch of thickness.

3. Place the salmon in a greased fish basket and sit it about 4 inches above the hot coals. If you do not have a basket, place the fish on a greased grill about 4 inches above the hot coals.

4. Keep the barbecue lid closed or cover the fish with a loose tent of heavy foil. Barbecue for 15 to 20 minutes on each side, turning only once halfway through grilling. Place a dab of dilled butter on each serving.

PER SERVING: *367 calories, 53.5 g protein, 0.1 g carbohydrates, 15.4 g fat, 34.5 mg calcium, 2.6 mg iron, 0 g fiber.*

SUPERB SALMON SAUCES

When serving a whole salmon, hot or cold, it's always nice to provide at least one sauce. Here are some easy stir-togethers.

• Stir 2 teaspoons finely grated lemon peel and 1 teaspoon each of honey and Dijon mustard into 1 cup light sour cream or yogurt. Then, stir in chopped fresh chives, dill or basil.

• Coarsely grate half an English cucumber. Squeeze out the moisture. Stir with 2 tablespoons chopped fresh dill and 1 crushed garlic clove into ½ cup plain yogurt.

• Stir 3 tablespoons melted butter with 2 tablespoons freshly squeezed lemon juice, 1 tablespoon capers and 2 tablespoons snipped chives.

• Blend 1 teaspoon ground cumin and ½ teaspoon ground coriander into 1 cup sour cream. Then, stir in as much chopped fresh coriander as you like.

• Stir ¼ cup chopped fresh dill and 1 tablespoon Dijon or honey mustard into 1 cup plain yogurt.

• Stir ¼ teaspoon dried dillweed into ½ cup sour cream.

PASTA PASSION

In recent years pasta has pushed its way into the limelight. It has become a Canadian staple. Not that we didn't serve up pasta dishes before, we just didn't venture much beyond spaghetti and meatballs or macaroni and cheese. Today we are really using our noodles. We dress them up with smoked salmon; we toss them with exotic Thai sauces; we bake them into robust party casseroles; we use them to stretch everything from a can of tuna to a pound of ground; we translate culinary classics — like bouillabaisse — into fresh new pasta entrées. We still love the good old favorites but we've made them faster and feistier and we've come up with smart calorie-cutting tricks — ground chicken instead of beef and light sour cream as a skinny stand-in for whipping cream. Our passion for pasta knows no limits. Bravo pasta!

PASTA PASSION · TRIPLE TESTED

PRIMO PARTY PASTAS

When you want to impress without hours of fussing, nothing parties better than pasta. Among our favorites is Fresh Bouillabaisse Party Pasta. Don't be intimidated by our Creamy Smoked Salmon and Dijon Pasta. It sounds and looks like a million dollars, but won't break the bank. For a cream splurge, nothing compares with classic Noodles Alfredo, the best combination of butter, cream and Parmesan ever created. Or add a hit of heat to subtle veal tenderloin with a side dish of Pecan and Hot Chili Pasta. All of our primo pastas are elegantly dressed for black-tie entertaining.

SUMMER BASIL AND TOMATO SAUCE

When fresh basil and garden tomatoes are at their peak, make up this sauce. Freeze it and you'll have the fresh taste of summer for months to come.

Preparation time: 20 minutes / Cooking time: 30 minutes

Makes: 5 cups

SUMMER VEGETABLE SAUCE

Heat 2½ cups Summer Basil and Tomato Sauce with 1 sliced zucchini, 1 cup snow peas, 2 thinly sliced carrots and 3 sliced whole green onions. Toss with cooked penne pasta and sprinkle liberally with grated Parmesan cheese.

3 lbs (1.5 kg) ripe tomatoes, about 10
¼ cup olive oil
2 onions, coarsely chopped
2 garlic cloves, thinly sliced
½ tsp freshly ground black pepper
¼ tsp salt
⅛ to ¼ tsp dried chili flakes
¼ cup chopped fresh basil

1. Bring a large pot of water to a boil. Place tomatoes in boiling water for 40 seconds. Drain and immerse in ice-cold water. Peel off skins.

2. Heat oil in a large saucepan set over medium-low heat. Add the onions and garlic. Cook, stirring often, until soft, about 5 minutes. Meanwhile, coarsely chop the tomatoes. Stir into onions along with the seasonings. Bring to a boil. Then, reduce heat and simmer, uncovered, for 15 minutes, stirring often. Stir in basil. Taste and add more seasonings, if needed. Continue simmering for 5 minutes. Use as a pasta sauce or on chicken. The sauce can be refrigerated for 2 to 3 days or frozen.

PER CUP: 174 calories, 3.1 g protein, 17.3 g carbohydrates, 11.9 g fat, 28 mg calcium, 1.5 mg iron, 4.5 g fiber.

PHOTO: Summer Vegetable Sauce, see recipe above.

FRESH BOUILLABAISSE PARTY PASTA

Saffron bouillabaisse is flavor-rich with fresh seafood and satiny penne to trap the tender morsels of succulent shrimp. Bouillabaisse alone will seem wanting ever after. Make the sauce well ahead of the party, reheat it and add the seafood just before serving. Feel free to add other seafood, bay scallops or calamari, for example. Crusty bread is essential for sopping up the last of the sauce.

Preparation time: 30 minutes / Cooking time: 20 minutes

Makes: 6 to 8 servings

1 to 2 tbsp olive oil
3 small leeks
28-oz (796-mL) can plum tomatoes, including juice
3 crushed garlic cloves
$\frac{1}{2}$ bay leaf, finely crushed
1 tsp saffron
$\frac{1}{4}$ tsp each of ground thyme and dried marjoram
$\frac{1}{2}$ tsp salt
Freshly ground white or black pepper
1 to 2 tsp granulated sugar
1 lb (500 g) firm-fleshed fillets, such as halibut
1 lb or 450-g pkg fettuccine, spaghetti or penne
$\frac{1}{2}$ lb (250 g) whole shrimp
12 mussels, scrubbed and bearded (optional)

1. Heat the oil in a large saucepan. Trim and clean the leeks, then thinly slice. Add them to the oil and sauté for about 5 minutes. Then, add the tomatoes along with their juice, the garlic, crushed bay leaf, saffron, remaining seasonings and 1 teaspoon sugar. Taste and add more sugar, if needed. Break the tomatoes into bite-size pieces and bring to a boil.

2. Cut the fish into bite-size pieces. Add it to the boiling tomato mixture. Cover, reduce heat and simmer for 8 minutes for fresh or 20 minutes for frozen fish.

3. Meanwhile, bring a large pot of salted water to a full rolling boil. Add the pasta and boil, uncovered, stirring occasionally, until cooked al dente, about 8 to 10 minutes. Then, drain but do not rinse.

4. To avoid overcooking the seafood, wait until the pasta is almost finished cooking, then stir the shrimp into the tomato sauce. Place the mussels on top, if using. Cover tightly and simmer until the mussels are open, about 3 to 4 minutes. Toss the sauce with the drained pasta and serve with garlic bread.

PER SERVING: 376 calories, 26.1 g protein, 56.8 g carbohydrates, 4.7 g fat, 104 mg calcium, 5.1 mg iron, 1.7 g fiber.

USING YOUR NOODLE
A whole cup of cooked spaghetti contains only about 160 calories. If you're watching your weight, avoid creamy sauces: stick to vegetables, chicken, light sour cream and lean-meat tosses instead.

Pasta has virtually no sodium or cholesterol, so it's ideal for people on restricted diets.

HOW MUCH IS ENOUGH?
Nutritionists suggest 2 oz (60 g) of pasta as a first course or side dish, and 4 oz (125 g) as a main course. One lb or a 450-g package of dried pasta yields about 4 servings.

PHOTO: Tarragon Salmon Steaks with Dijon, see recipe on page 144.

THE ULTIMATE BRUNCH PASTA

Spaghetti alla carbonara is a quintessential weekend brunch entertainer: the flavor is satisfying bacon and eggs tied together with cream and Parmesan. It's definitely worth the indulgence, although you can cut down on calories by using half-and-half cream. In the spring, add barely-cooked, pencil-thin spears of asparagus and sprinkle with green onion.

Preparation time: 20 minutes / Cooking time: 20 minutes

Makes: 4 to 6 servings

3 eggs
½ cup freshly grated Parmesan cheese
10 slices bacon
1 cup (250-mL container) whipping cream or ¾ cup half-and-half cream
2 cloves garlic, minced
¼ tsp dried crushed chilies or generous pinch of cayenne pepper
1 lb or 450-g pkg spaghetti
Freshly ground white or black pepper (optional)

1. To cook the spaghetti, bring a large pot of salted water to a full rolling boil. Meanwhile, prepare remaining ingredients. Whisk the eggs together. Stir in the grated cheese and set aside.

2. Cut the bacon, crosswise, into ½-inch strips. Place it in a large saucepan (not a frying pan) over medium-high heat and cook until crisp. Pour off half the bacon fat. Add the cream, garlic and chilies to the bacon and fat remaining in the pan. Then, cover and reduce heat to low to keep the sauce warm and develop the flavors while the pasta is cooking. If making ahead, however, refrigerate this sauce and the egg mixture.

3. Add the spaghetti to the boiling water and boil, uncovered, stirring occasionally, until cooked al dente, about 8 to 10 minutes. Then, quickly drain but do not rinse. Immediately add the spaghetti to the pan containing the hot bacon sauce and toss to coat the pasta. Stir in the egg mixture. Continue tossing over medium heat for 2 to 3 minutes, until most of the liquid is absorbed. Add freshly ground pepper, if you wish.

PER SERVING: *599 calories, 21 g protein, 62.2 g carbohydrates, 29.5 g fat, 144 mg calcium, 3.5 mg iron, 0.03 g fiber.*

PRIMO NOODLES ALFREDO

If you're concerned about fat, don't even glance at this recipe. But when you want to indulge, nothing matches these butter-and-cream-bathed noodles. Use fresh fettuccine, the best unsalted butter and Parmigiano-Reggiano.

Preparation time: 10 minutes / Cooking time: 10 minutes

Makes: 6 to 8 servings

1 lb or 450-g pkg fettuccine
$\frac{1}{3}$ cup unsalted butter, cut into cubes
1 cup (250-mL container) whipping cream
$1\frac{1}{2}$ cups freshly grated Parmesan cheese
Freshly ground black or white pepper

1. To cook the pasta, bring a large pot of salted water to a full rolling boil. Add the pasta and boil, uncovered, stirring occasionally, until cooked al dente, about 8 to 10 minutes. Drain well but do not rinse. Return the pasta to the cooking pot. Add the butter cubes and toss them until partially melted.

2. Add the cream and Parmesan cheese. Stir over medium-low heat until all the noodles are evenly coated with the sauce and the cheese is melted, about 2 minutes. Sprinkle with lots of freshly ground pepper.

PER SERVING: *482 calories, 15 g protein, 42.4 g carbohydrates, 25.6 g fat, 213 mg calcium, 2 mg iron, 0 g fiber.*

NOODLES ALFREDO DRESS-UPS

We wouldn't dare mess with the basic ingredients in Noodles Alfredo but these extras are particularly complementary.

• Add a sprinkling of chopped fresh basil, chopped chives or a garnish of garlic- and basil-scented tomatoes.

• Toss with sautéed red pepper strips, sliced asparagus and a tablespoon of chopped canned jalapeno peppers.

PASTA PERFECT

The key to cooking pasta properly is lots of water. For every pound, use 20 cups (5 L) of water. Never use less than 12 cups (3 L), no matter how little you cook, and don't cook more than 2 lbs (1 kg) at a time. Add up to 1 tablespoon salt, depending on the quantity of sauce and amount of pasta that will be added. A teaspoon of oil helps keep pasta separated, but it can make noodles slippery and prevent a cream sauce from clinging. Keep the heat on high. When the water reaches a full rolling boil, add the pasta all at once. Immediately stir with a wooden spoon to separate the noodles. To submerge long, brittle pasta, such as spaghetti, press down gently on the portion above the water until the strands are completely submerged. Always keep the water boiling rapidly. Don't cover. Stir often.

Timing
Frequent testing is the only way to avoid overcooking. "Al dente" is the term frequently used to describe perfectly cooked pasta. It means "firm to the bite" — neither too hard nor too soft, firm but tender. Once the water returns to the boil, fresh pasta needs only a couple of minutes. Dried pasta takes 6 to 12 minutes; taste after 6 minutes. Remember, after draining pasta continues cooking.

Draining
Use a colander, tossing the pasta several times to shake off the water. Do not rinse. If you want the pasta to absorb a little sauce, an asset with a thin cream sauce, return the pasta to the cooking pan. Add the hot sauce and toss it with the pasta over medium heat for a minute or two. Or turn the drained pasta into a large serving bowl, add the hot sauce, butter, oil or cheese and toss.

CREAMY SMOKED SALMON AND DIJON PASTA

When you want an impressive recipe that's not a lot of work, serve this one hot or cold. Light sour cream has about one-tenth the calories of whipping cream, and never seems too rich or filling. A wonderful taste combination with roast chicken, turkey or veal.

Preparation time: 15 minutes / Cooking time: 10 minutes

Makes: 4 to 8 servings

4 cups broad egg or shell noodles
1 tbsp butter or oil
2 tbsp finely chopped shallots or 1 large crushed garlic clove
8 oz (250 g) smoked salmon
4 whole green onions
1 cup (250-mL container) regular or light sour cream
1 tbsp Dijon mustard
Freshly ground white pepper

1. To cook the pasta, bring a large pot of salted water to a full rolling boil. Add the pasta and boil, uncovered, stirring occasionally, until cooked al dente, about 8 to 10 minutes. Drain but do not rinse.

2. Meanwhile, heat the butter in a large frying pan. Add the shallots and sauté for about 5 minutes. Meanwhile, cut the salmon into thin bite-size pieces and slice the green onions; set aside. Then, whisk the sour cream, Dijon and pepper into the sautéed shallots. Remove from the heat and immediately stir into the drained cooked pasta. Add the salmon and green onions and toss. Serve hot or as a cold pasta salad. The flavor becomes fuller with a day's refrigeration. If it's not creamy enough after being chilled, simply stir in more sour cream.

PER SERVING: *191 calories, 8.5 g protein, 13.3 g carbohydrates, 16.5 g fat, 46.9 mg calcium, 1 mg iron, 0.05 g fiber.*

FRESH BASIL AND MASCARPONE LINGUINE

Place 6 oz (180 g) mascarpone cheese in a large bowl. Add 2 chopped tomatoes, ¼ cup chopped fresh basil and 2 tablespoons olive oil. Toss with 1 lb (450 g) hot cooked linguine. Wonderful with grilled lamb or veal tenderloin.

SHELL NOODLES

PECAN AND HOT CHILI PASTA

Crunchy sautéed pecans and pasta glistening with a light coating of hot garlic oil make this an unusual accompaniment for chicken, tuna steaks or pork tenderloin. Make extra chili-and-garlic oil and store it in the refrigerator to use for sautéeing fish and seafood, steaks and chips, or drizzle over sliced tomatoes.

Preparation time: 10 minutes / Cooking time: 10 minutes

Makes: 3 servings

8 oz or $\frac{1}{2}$ 450-g pkg fettuccine or spaghetti
$\frac{1}{4}$ tsp crushed dried chilies
1 large garlic clove, minced
$\frac{1}{4}$ cup good-quality olive oil
$\frac{1}{2}$ cup pecan halves
$\frac{1}{2}$ cup freshly grated Parmesan cheese

1. To cook the pasta, bring a large pot of salted water to a full rolling boil.

2. Meanwhile, combine the chilies, garlic and olive oil in a small saucepan. Place over low heat and barely simmer, uncovered, for 10 minutes. Stir often. Do not let the garlic brown.

3. When the water comes to a boil, add the pasta and cook, uncovered, stirring occasionally, until al dente, about 8 to 10 minutes.

4. When the pasta is almost finished cooking, spoon 2 tablespoons olive oil only from the saucepan containing the simmering oil, chilies and garlic into a large wide frying pan over medium-high heat. Immediately add the nuts and stir-fry for 1 to 2 minutes until nuts are piping hot. Immediately remove from the heat.

5. Then, drain the pasta, shaking off all the water. Do not rinse. Return the pasta to the cooking pot. Pour the olive oil with the chilies and garlic over top. Add the nut mixture and the Parmesan cheese. Stir until all the pasta is coated.

PER SERVING: *685 calories, 20 g protein, 71 g carbohydrates, 36.4 g fat, 185 mg calcium, 3.8 mg iron, 1.2 g fiber.*

FREEZING PASTA
You can never cook too much pasta. Freeze extra in plastic bags. Thaw it in the microwave or put it in boiling water until it separates. For a fast meal, microwave frozen cooked pasta with store-bought spaghetti sauce, stirring often. Add frozen pasta to simmering soups, sauces and stews.

Fresh Dill
Use 1 cup fresh dill sprigs and ½ cup Italian parsley in place of fresh basil. Toss with pasta. Serve with fish or chicken.

Dried Basil
Use 1½ cups Italian parsley and 1½ teaspoons dried basil in place of fresh basil.

Pesto Butter
Stir pesto with an equal amount of room-temperature butter. Place a large dollop on grilled steak or salmon.

Creamy Dip
Mix pesto with an equal amount of sour cream.

Hot Pesto Potatoes
Toss 2 lbs (1 kg) hot new potatoes with ½ cup pesto and 2 tablespoons butter.

Tomato and Pasta
Prepare pesto and toss it with 1 lb (450 g) cooked fettuccine and 2 cups cherry tomatoes or 4 ripe tomatoes, peeled, seeded and chopped. Serve hot or cold.

Zesty Sandwiches
Spread pesto on cream cheese, grilled cheese, salmon or roast beef sandwiches.

PERFECT PESTO SAUCE

Pesto is to Italian cuisine what cream sauce is to French cooking. Delicious and addictive, it's made with fresh basil, olive oil, Parmesan cheese and garlic. Traditionally, it's tossed with pasta or dotted on focaccia or pizza — but don't stop there. Here's a foolproof recipe plus some suggested ways to enliven pasta, meat, potatoes and sandwiches.

Preparation time: 5 minutes / Makes: 2 cups

3 large garlic cloves
¼ cup toasted pine nuts
¼ tsp salt
Freshly ground black pepper
1½ cups lightly packed fresh basil leaves
¾ cup good-quality olive oil
1 cup freshly grated Parmesan cheese

1. Place the garlic, pine nuts, salt and pepper in a food processor fitted with a metal blade and whirl until ground. Add basil and purée.

2. With the machine running, pour the olive oil through the feed tube in a thin even stream. Stir in the cheese. Store the sauce in a sealed jar in the refrigerator for up to 1 week or freeze.

PER TABLESPOON: *65 calories, 1.7 g protein, 0.5 g carbohydrates, 6.6 g fat, 33.9 mg calcium, 0.1 mg iron, 0 g fiber.*

FETTUCCINE WITH HAZELNUT AND ORANGE CREAM

A satiny cream sauce with a hint of orange peel and hot pepper, generously sprinkled with toasted hazelnuts, makes this pasta exciting enough for an elegant menu. Serve it with asparagus and a simple roast chicken sprinkled with rosemary and tarragon.

Preparation time: 15 minutes / Baking time: 5 minutes
Cooking time: 10 minutes / Makes: 3 servings

½ cup hazelnuts
8 oz or ½ 450-g pkg fettuccine or spaghetti
½ cup whipping cream
1 tbsp butter
Finely grated peel of ½ orange
¼ cup grated mozzarella, fontina or Parmesan cheese
Salt and cayenne pepper

1. Preheat oven to 325F. Coarsely chop the nuts. Spread them out on a large baking sheet. Place the nuts in the oven and toast them for 5 minutes while the pasta and sauce are cooking. Stir often.

2. Meanwhile, bring a large pot of salted water to a full rolling boil. Add the pasta and boil, uncovered, stirring occasionally, until cooked al dente, about 8 to 10 minutes.

3. Then, place the cream and butter in a small saucepan over medium heat. Grate the orange peel into the cream. As soon as the cream is warm to the touch, stir in the grated cheese. Stir just until the cheese is melted. Add a pinch of salt and cayenne pepper to taste. Remove from the heat and cover to keep warm.

4. As soon as the pasta is cooked, drain well but do not rinse. Place the pasta in a bowl. Add the cream mixture and nuts. Toss and serve.

PER SERVING: 647 calories, 16.9 g protein, 71.2 g carbohydrates, 33.6 g fat, 142 mg calcium, 4 mg iron, 1.6 g fiber.

FRESH TOMATO AND CHÈVRE PENNE

We love the contrast of chopped, ripe red tomatoes, fresh basil and green onions with hot pasta. Since only the pasta is heated, this is short-order cooking at its best.

Preparation time: 15 minutes / Cooking time: 10 minutes

Makes: 4 servings

1 lb or 450-g pkg penne
5 oz (140 g) chèvre
3 whole green onions, thinly sliced, or $\frac{1}{4}$ cup snipped chives
2 tomatoes
$\frac{1}{4}$ cup chopped fresh basil or 1 tsp dried basil
$\frac{1}{4}$ cup olive oil or vegetable oil
1 crushed garlic clove
Pinch of salt
$\frac{1}{2}$ tsp freshly ground black pepper
$\frac{1}{4}$ cup freshly grated Parmesan cheese

1. Bring a large pot of salted water to a full rolling boil. Add the pasta and cook, uncovered, stirring occasionally, until al dente, about 8 to 10 minutes.

2. Meanwhile, crumble the chèvre into a large bowl. Add the thinly sliced green onions. Then, coarsely chop the tomatoes and add them to the cheese mixture. Add remaining ingredients and stir well until evenly mixed.

CANADIAN CHÈVRE

Most cheese lovers adore the assertive, tangy flavor of goat cheese. Canadian producers are churning out creamy herbed feta, Colby and farmer-style, to name a few. You can cube it and marinate it in the refrigerator with oil and fresh herbs, use it as a feisty cocktail spread on crusty bread, slather it over hot burgers and grilled lamb chops, or sprinkle it on pizza.

Spanish Olive

Sauté 2 crushed garlic cloves and ⅓ cup chopped stuffed green olives in 3 tablespoons olive oil for 5 minutes, stirring often.

Blue Cheese

Heat ¼ cup half-and-half cream with 2 sliced green onions. Stir in ⅓ cup crumbled blue or Stilton cheese. Toss with cheese tortellini.

Caesar

Toss tortellini with ⅓ cup bottled creamy Caesar salad dressing, 2 tablespoons grated Parmesan cheese and 1 diced tomato.

Creamy Mexican

Heat ¼ cup hot salsa with ⅓ cup sour cream until just warm. Great with cheese tortellini and steak or chicken.

3. When the pasta is cooked, drain well but do not rinse. Immediately pour the pasta into a large bowl and toss with the tomato-and-cheese mixture. Serve hot or at room temperature.

PER SERVING: *689 calories, 24.6 g protein, 91 g carbohydrates, 24.9 g fat, 143 mg calcium, 5.4 mg iron, 1 g fiber.*

IL POSTO'S LINGUINE WITH GORGONZOLA

When we first tried this pasta at the posh Il Posto restaurant in Toronto's Yorkville area, it was so good we were sure it had to be complicated. In fact, it couldn't be easier.

Preparation time: 5 minutes / Cooking time: 10 minutes

Makes: 3 to 4 servings

1 lb or 450-g pkg linguine or spaghetti, preferably fresh
6 to 8 oz (180 to 250 g) Gorgonzola cheese
⅔ cup whipping cream
Freshly grated nutmeg
Freshly ground black pepper
Freshly grated Parmesan cheese

1. Bring a large pot of salted water to a full rolling boil. Add the pasta and cook, uncovered, stirring occasionally, until al dente, about 3 minutes for fresh pasta, or about 8 to 10 minutes for dried.

2. Meanwhile, cut the Gorgonzola cheese into small cubes. Pour the cream into a medium-size heavy-bottomed frying pan. Add a grating of nutmeg and pepper. Place the pan over medium heat. As soon as it is hot to the touch, add the cubes of Gorgonzola. Reduce heat to low and stir frequently until the Gorgonzola and whipping cream are fairly well blended.

3. As soon as pasta is cooked, drain but do not rinse. Toss it with the cheese mixture. Generously sprinkle with the Parmesan cheese and serve.

PER SERVING: *789 calories, 30.5 g protein, 92.2 g carbohydrates, 32.4 g fat, 392 mg calcium, 4.6 mg iron, 0.01 g fiber.*

MAIN EVENT PASTAS

There's no question about it. Pasta is the comfort food of the '90s. In recent years we've tarted it up with fussy sauces and trendy toppings, but now we are turning our attention to those homey casseroles that were the mainstay of family suppers twenty years ago. Macaroni and cheese tops the list. Our deluxe baked version comes flecked with jalapeno peppers and a fresh salsa topper. We've included lots of Italian favorites: a terrific classic Sicilian spaghetti sauce and a spicy hot sausage lasagna. On a lighter note, try Light Creamy Chicken Fettuccine or Tuna Casserole '90s Style.

LIGHT CREAMY CHICKEN FETTUCCINE

This is guilt-free pasta indulgence. We've used ground chicken for top-quality protein and light sour cream to produce a very satiny coating. Yet another plus — the sauce can be made in half the time it takes to boil the pasta.

Preparation time: 10 minutes / Cooking time: 13 minutes

Makes: 4 to 5 servings

8 oz or $\frac{1}{2}$ 450-g pkg fettuccine
1 tbsp butter
1 lb (500 g) ground chicken or turkey
1 cup (250-mL container) light sour cream
4 whole green onions, thinly sliced
$\frac{1}{2}$ tsp poultry seasoning
$\frac{1}{4}$ tsp freshly grated nutmeg
$\frac{1}{2}$ cup freshly grated Parmesan cheese

1. Bring a large pot of salted water to a rolling boil. Add the pasta and boil, stirring often, until al dente, about 8 minutes.

2. Meanwhile, melt the butter in a large frying pan set over medium heat. Crumble the chicken into the pan. Cook, stirring often, until the chicken is no longer pink, about 3 minutes.

3. Add the sour cream, green onions and seasonings and stir until hot. When the pasta is cooked, drain well but do not rinse. Toss with the sauce and sprinkle with Parmesan cheese.

PER SERVING: *420 calories, 27.8 g protein, 43.5 g carbohydrates, 14.5 g fat, 212 mg calcium, 2.7 mg iron, 0.1 g fiber.*

FETTUCCINE
NOODLES

LOW-CAL ZESTY LASAGNA

At 326 calories a serving, this robust lasagna is a steal. Use ground chicken in place of beef to cut calories even more, or omit both and add a chopped green pepper or sliced mushrooms instead for a terrific vegetarian version.

Preparation time: 30 minutes / Cooking time: 20 minutes
Baking time: 1 hour / Makes: 8 servings

MORE WAYS THAN ONE TO CAN A TOMATO

Canned tomatoes sold in supermarkets now come in many forms. Check the label to see whether they are whole, diced, crushed or stewed. These different styles vary greatly in texture and thickness and some have added seasonings and peppers.

½ lb (250 g) lean ground beef or chicken
3 onions, chopped
2 crushed garlic cloves
5½-oz (156-mL) can tomato paste
28-oz (796-mL) can crushed tomatoes
1 tsp each of dried leaf oregano and dried basil
½ tsp dried leaf thyme
Generous pinch of cayenne pepper
2 zucchini
1 lb (500 g) low-fat ricotta or 1% cottage cheese
2 tbsp freshly grated Parmesan cheese
1 egg
8 to 12 oven-ready lasagna noodles
¾ cup grated, partly skim-milk mozzarella cheese,
    about 4 oz (125 g)

1. Preheat oven to 350F. Crumble the beef into a large frying pan. Set the pan over medium heat. Add the onions and garlic. Cook, stirring often, until the beef is well browned and the onions are soft, about 10 minutes. Then, stir in the tomato paste, crushed tomatoes and seasonings. Cover and bring to a boil. Then, reduce heat and simmer, covered, while preparing remainder of lasagna.

2. Grate zucchini in a food processor or use the large side of a grater. Place in a bowl and stir in the ricotta, Parmesan cheese and egg.

3. To assemble the lasagna, spread one-third of the meat sauce, about 1¾ cups, over the bottom of a 9x13-inch baking pan. Spoon half the ricotta mixture over top, then cover with half of the noodles.

4. Make a second layer in same manner. Then, top the noodles with remaining meat sauce and sprinkle with the mozzarella cheese. Bake, uncovered, in the centre of the preheated oven until bubbling and golden, about 1 hour. When refrigerated, the lasagna keeps well for 2 days; frozen it will keep well for several months. Lasagna can also be frozen in individual servings for quick reheating in the microwave.

PER SERVING: 326 calories, 22.9 g protein, 31.7 g carbohydrates, 12.4 g fat, 348 mg calcium, 3.2 mg iron, 2 g fiber.

PAD THAI

No wonder this is Thailand's national noodle dish. Once you've tried it, you'll crave it for life.

Preparation time: 20 minutes / Cooking time: 6 minutes

Makes: 6 to 8 servings

8 oz or 250-g pkg rice vermicelli noodles
2 tbsp granulated sugar
$\frac{1}{2}$ cup fish sauce
$\frac{1}{2}$ cup ketchup
2 tbsp steak sauce
2 tbsp vegetable or peanut oil
8 garlic cloves, finely chopped
4 boneless, skinless chicken breasts, cut into $\frac{1}{2}$-inch pieces
8 oz (250 g) coarsely chopped fresh or frozen shrimp
$\frac{1}{2}$ tsp dried red chili peppers
2 eggs, beaten
2 cups bean sprouts
6 whole green onions, finely chopped
1 cup chopped fresh coriander
$\frac{1}{4}$ cup roasted peanuts, coarsely chopped
2 limes

1. Place the noodles in a large bowl of hot water. Soak at room temperature for about 5 minutes to soften. As soon as the noodles are tender, drain in a large colander and set aside.

2. Meanwhile, in a small bowl, stir the sugar with the fish sauce, ketchup and steak sauce. Prepare the garlic, chicken and shrimp. Heat the oil in a large wok or wide heavy-bottomed saucepan over medium-high heat. Add the garlic, chicken, shrimp and chili peppers. Stir-fry for 2 to 3 minutes, until the shrimp turn pink. If the mixture begins to stick, add another tablespoon of oil or $\frac{1}{4}$ cup water. Stir in the fish sauce mixture and stir for 2 minutes. Add the beaten eggs and stir for 1 minute. Immediately add the drained noodles and stir over medium heat until evenly coated.

3. Stir in the bean sprouts, green onions and $\frac{1}{2}$ cup chopped coriander and continue stirring until the mixture is heated through. Turn onto a serving dish and sprinkle with peanuts and the remaining chopped coriander. Surround the platter of noodles with thinly sliced limes for squeezing over the noodles.

PER SERVING: 324 calories, 14 g protein, 53 g carbohydrates, 5.4 g fat, 95.8 mg calcium, 2.6 mg iron, 0.5 g fiber.

ORIENTAL NOODLES

Rice vermicelli noodles or rice sticks are thick, brittle noodles that are folded and sold in bundles. They become crisp when deep-fried. They must be softened in hot water before using in other dishes.

Also known as cellophane noodles because of their transparency, bean thread noodles are made from mung beans. They must be softened in hot water before using.

FISH SAUCE

Fish sauce is a thick, translucent brown sauce made from fish or shrimp. It's sold in large bottles at most ethnic markets and is as important to Thai cuisine as soy sauce is to Chinese and Japanese cooking.

SPEEDY ITALIAN SAUSAGE LASAGNA

This is a full-flavored lasagna that is ready in record time, but tastes like you spent hours on it.

Preparation time: 15 minutes / Cooking time: 20 minutes
Baking time: 45 minutes / Makes: 8 servings

SPEEDY
ITALIAN
SAUSAGE

2 tbsp vegetable oil
2 lbs (1 kg) hot or sweet Italian sausage, casings removed
28-oz (796-mL) can meatless spaghetti sauce
2 crushed garlic cloves
12 lasagna noodles, preferably not oven-ready
1 lb (500 g) ricotta, drained if necessary
2 eggs
½ lb (250 g) mozzarella cheese, grated

1. In a large heavy-bottomed saucepan, heat the oil over medium heat. Cook the sausage, breaking it up with a fork, until no longer pink. Drain off the fat. Stir in the spaghetti sauce and garlic and bring to a boil. Cover and reduce heat. Simmer for 15 minutes, stirring occasionally.

FAST PAY-OFFS WITH STORE-BOUGHT SPAGHETTI SAUCE

Always keep a jar or can of spaghetti sauce in your cupboard for a runner's start to a fast dinner. Use a 14-oz (398-mL) jar or can, or about 2 cups of meatless sauce for each of these recipes.

Spanish Burgers
Heat spaghetti sauce with ½ cup sliced stuffed green olives and 2 crushed garlic cloves. Pour over pork chops or burgers.

Greek Bake
Cover the bottom of a small baking dish with a ½-inch layer of feta cheese. Top with spaghetti sauce mixed with a pinch of dried leaf oregano, dried basil and garlic powder. Cover and bake in a 450F oven until the cheese is hot, about 7 minutes. Serve with crusty bread.

Liver and Onions
Sauté 2 sliced onions in 2 tablespoons butter until soft. Stir in ½ lb (250 g) chicken livers. Add spaghetti sauce, ¼ teaspoon each of dried leaf thyme and dried sage. Simmer, covered, for 5 minutes and serve on rice.

Herbed Chowder
Heat spaghetti sauce with a 10-oz (284-mL) can of cream of potato soup. Add 1 lb (500 g) frozen fish fillets cut into bite-size pieces and ½ teaspoon dried dillweed. Cover and simmer until fish flakes easily with a fork.

Creamy Cheese Sauce
Heat spaghetti sauce. Cut a 4-oz (125-g) pkg of cream cheese into cubes. Stir into the sauce until fairly smooth. Serve over chicken, turkey or fish.

Quick Curry
Heat spaghetti sauce with 1 tablespoon curry powder. Whisk in ½ cup sour cream. Add 2 cups bite-size pieces of cooked chicken, beef or pork and heat through.

Hot Beef
Stir spaghetti sauce with 2 teaspoons horseradish. Pour over browned burgers and simmer, covered, until the meat is done.

Italian Eggs
Heat spaghetti sauce in a small frying pan. Break 4 to 6 eggs into the hot sauce. Add a light sprinkling of cheddar cheese. Cover and simmer until the eggs are poached.

2. Meanwhile, to cook the noodles, bring a large pot of salted water to a full rolling boil. Add the noodles and boil, uncovered, stirring occasionally, until al dente, about 10 minutes. Drain but do not rinse, and lay flat on clean kitchen cloths.

3. If not using smooth ricotta, place the cheese and eggs in a food processor fitted with a metal blade and whirl until fairly smooth. If the ricotta is already smooth, just beat the eggs and stir them into the ricotta in a bowl.

4. To assemble, spread 1 cup meat sauce in a 9x13-inch baking dish. Cover with a layer of noodles, half of the ricotta mixture, one-third of the remaining meat sauce and one-third of the mozzarella. Repeat the layers, ending with noodles, meat sauce and mozzarella. (Recipe can be prepared to this point, covered and refrigerated or frozen. Thaw in the refrigerator before proceeding or defrost in the microwave. Remove from the refrigerator 30 minutes before cooking.) Bake, uncovered, in a 350F oven for 30 to 45 minutes or until bubbly around the edges.

PER SERVING: 886 calories, 52.7 g protein, 42.4 g carbohydrates, 55.5 g fat, 619 mg calcium, 4 mg iron, 0 g fiber.

QUICK FIX PASTA SAUCES

Alfredo
Bring ½ cup whipping cream and ¼ cup butter to a simmer. Pour into a bowl. Toss with 8 oz (250 g) fettuccine, ½ cup grated Parmesan cheese, salt and cayenne pepper.

Fresh Tomato
Seed and chop 3 tomatoes. Add ¼ cup olive oil, 1 garlic clove, ½ teaspoon dried basil and a pinch of dried leaf oregano. Toss with 8 oz (250 g) spaghetti, ¼ cup grated Parmesan cheese and black pepper.

Italian Sausage
Cut 4 Italian sausages into bite-size pieces. Brown in 1 tablespoon oil. Add a 28-oz (796-mL) can of tomatoes and ½ teaspoon dried basil. Break the tomatoes into pieces. Boil, uncovered, until thick. Toss with 1 lb (450 g) pasta.

Bacon 'n' Tomato
Cut 4 slices of bacon into 1-inch pieces and cook until crisp. Add ¼ cup olive oil, 4 chopped tomatoes, 2 chopped whole green onions, 1 crushed garlic clove, 1 teaspoon dried basil, salt and pepper. Toss with 8 oz (250 g) pasta.

Old-Fashioned
Sauté ½ lb (250 g) ground beef in 1 tablespoon oil until the meat loses its red color. Add 14 oz (398 mL) store-bought spaghetti sauce, ½ teaspoon each of dried basil and dried leaf oregano and a pinch of garlic powder. Simmer, covered, for 5 minutes. Toss with 8 oz (250 g) spaghetti and grated Parmesan cheese.

Triple Cheese
Heat 1 cup table cream with 2 tablespoons butter. Add 1 cup grated Swiss cheese, 1 cup grated fontina cheese, ½ cup crumbled blue cheese. Stir until melted. Toss with 1 lb (450 g) spaghetti.

Garlic and Parsley
Simmer ¼ cup olive oil with 2 crushed garlic cloves for 5 minutes. Add 8 oz (250 g) finely chopped parsley. Toss with ½ lb (250 g) pasta and freshly ground black pepper. Serve with chicken.

Low-Cal
Over low heat, cook 1 cup sour cream, a 7½-oz (213-g) can of salmon or 6½-oz (184-g) can of tuna and 4 sliced whole green onions. Toss with 4 cups cooked noodles.

TERRIFIC LIGHT TUNA TETRAZZINI

This is a quick-to-make weekday standby. Chances are you'll have most of the ingredients on hand and you can pull it together in a flash. There's no time-consuming butter-and-flour thickener and light sour cream keeps the calories down.

Preparation time: 10 minutes / Cooking time: 10 minutes
Baking time: 25 minutes / Makes: 6 servings

4 oz (125 g) spaghetti
1 cup frozen peas
1 cup (250-mL container) light sour cream
½ tsp regular prepared mustard
2 tbsp sherry (optional)
1 cup grated mozzarella cheese or ⅓ cup freshly grated
    Parmesan cheese
6½-oz (184-g) can water-packed tuna, drained
White pepper (optional)

1. Preheat oven to 375F. Bring a large pot of salted water to a full rolling boil. Add the spaghetti and boil, uncovered, stirring occasionally, until cooked al dente, about 8 to 10 minutes. Then, drain but do not rinse. Meanwhile, rinse the peas under running water to remove the ice crystals. Drain well and set aside.

2. In a large bowl, blend the sour cream with the mustard and sherry, if using. Add the drained cooked spaghetti and stir until coated. Then, stir in ½ cup mozzarella or ¼ cup Parmesan cheese. Add the tuna and peas. Stir just until evenly distributed. Taste and add more mustard or some white pepper, if you wish.

3. Turn the tuna mixture into a deep-dish pie plate. Sprinkle with remaining cheese. Bake in the centre of the preheated oven until hot, about 25 minutes.

PER SERVING: 253 calories, 20.4 g protein, 26.6 g carbohydrates, 7.1 g fat, 179 mg calcium, 1.5 mg iron, 1 g fiber.

HEART-SMART TUNA AND SALMON

Nutritionists have recently given us yet another reason to open a can of tuna or salmon: these — and other fatty fish such as sardines, herring and halibut — contain a high percentage of Omega-3 fatty acids, which experts say protect us against heart disease and reduce the risk of blood clotting. When eaten regularly, they can be more effective than polyunsaturated vegetable oils in lowering the risk of heart disease.

FRANK'S BASIC SPAGHETTI SAUCE

Thank God for Frank and the Avenue Food Market. He and his family have been delivering groceries to our test kitchen for years. Here is Frank's family's Sicilian recipe for a good basic sauce. "We like to taste the meat," he says, "not a blaze of spices."

Preparation time: 20 minutes / Cooking time: 1½ hours

Makes: 11 cups

3 medium-size onions
3 carrots
3 celery stalks with leaves
¼ cup olive oil
1 lb (500 g) each of ground beef, pork and veal
1 cup dry red wine
3 to 5 tbsp tomato paste
2 (28-oz/796-mL) cans diced tomatoes,
    including juice, or 7 cups peeled and chopped
    fresh tomatoes, about 12 to 14 medium-size
½ tsp salt
1 tsp freshly ground black pepper
¼ tsp freshly grated nutmeg

1. Coarsely chop the onions, carrots and celery. Heat the oil in a large, wide deep saucepan set over medium heat. Add the vegetables and cook, stirring frequently, for about 10 minutes, until the mixture is golden.

2. Add the meat to the vegetable mixture and continue cooking, crumbling the meat with a fork. Stir often, cooking until meat is no longer red, about 7 minutes.

3. Add the wine and 3 tablespoons tomato paste, and turn heat to medium-high. If using fresh tomatoes, add 2 more tablespoons tomato paste. Cook, stirring often, for about 4 minutes. Then, add the canned tomatoes with their juice. Add the seasonings. Increase heat to high and bring the sauce to a boil. Then, reduce heat to low and simmer, partially covered, stirring occasionally, for a minimum of 1 hour. Add more salt and pepper, if needed. Serve over pasta.

VARIATION

Flavor-Booster
If you prefer a more highly seasoned sauce, add 2 teaspoons dried basil and 1 teaspoon dried leaf oregano before simmering.

PER ½ CUP: *158 calories, 14 g protein, 5.9 g carbohydrates, 8 g fat, 31.8 mg calcium, 1.5 mg iron, 1.3 g fiber.*

VIRGIN OILS

Olive oil labelled "extra virgin" comes from the first pressing of the first harvested olives. This expensive oil is sweet, fruity and light — excellent for salads. The second pressing is called "virgin" oil and produces a slightly harsher flavor. Any additional pressings after that produce an increasingly inferior semblance of the original extra virgin olive oil.

JALAPENO "MACARONI" AND CHEESE WITH FRESH SALSA TOPPER

This is one of the best macaroni-and-cheese bakes we've ever made. There's lots of nippy cheddar cheese sauce flecked with hot peppers. A tomato salsa topper adds a snazzy new flavor.

Preparation time: 15 minutes / Cooking time: 10 minutes

Baking time: 45 minutes *or* Microwave time: 8 minutes / Makes: 6 servings

5 cups rotini or fusilli

CHEESE SAUCE

3 tbsp butter

¼ cup all-purpose flour

1 tsp dry mustard

3 cups homogenized milk

3 cups grated old cheddar cheese, about ¾ lb (375 g)

1 tbsp seeded and finely chopped fresh or canned jalapeno pepper

SALSA

2 large ripe tomatoes, peeled and seeded

2 tbsp finely chopped coriander or Italian parsley

2 tsp white vinegar, lemon or lime juice

1 large crushed garlic clove

½ tsp each of dried leaf oregano and ground cumin

Pinch of salt

1. Preheat oven to 350F. Bring a large pot of salted water to a full rolling boil. Add the pasta and boil, uncovered, stirring occasionally, until nearly cooked al dente, about 7 to 8 minutes. Drain well but do not rinse. Set aside. Lightly grease a 12-cup (3-L) casserole dish.

2. Meanwhile, melt the butter in a medium-size saucepan over medium heat. Stir in the flour and mustard. Do not let the flour brown. Gradually whisk in the milk. Continue stirring gently over medium heat until the sauce thickens, about 6 minutes.

3. Remove the pan from the heat and stir in 2½ cups cheddar cheese and the jalapeno pepper. Stir until the cheese is completely melted. Taste and add more jalapeno, if you wish.

4. Pour the cheese sauce over the pasta and toss to evenly coat. Then, turn the mixture into the prepared baking dish. Sprinkle with remaining ½ cup cheese. (If making ahead, casserole can be refrigerated at this point for up to a day before serving.) Bake in the centre of the preheated oven for 40 to 45 minutes or until the sauce is bubbly around the edges and the pasta is heated through.

5. Meanwhile, chop the tomatoes. Set aside with the coriander in a medium-size bowl. Stir in the vinegar, garlic and seasonings.

6. Remove the baked pasta from the oven. Spoon some of the tomato mixture along the centre of the pasta. Serve remaining tomato mixture with each serving. The baked casserole will keep well, covered, in the refrigerator for several days or can be frozen.

7. To microwave, cook the pasta following above directions. Meanwhile, in a 12-cup (3-L) microwave-safe casserole dish, microwave the butter, uncovered, on high for 1 minute or until melted. Whisk in the flour and mustard to make a smooth paste. Then, whisk in the milk. Microwave, uncovered, on high for 2 to 4 minutes, whisking every minute. Stir in the cheese and jalapeno pepper. Microwave, uncovered, until the cheese is completely melted, about 1 minute. Turn the well-drained hot pasta into the hot cheese sauce. Microwave, uncovered, on high 1 to 2 minutes or until piping hot. Meanwhile, chop the tomatoes and stir them with the coriander, vinegar, garlic and seasonings. Spoon some of the tomato mixture along the centre of the hot pasta. Serve remaining tomato mixture with each serving.

PER SERVING: 627 calories, 28.7 g protein, 60.2 g carbohydrates, 30.4 g fat, 625 mg calcium, 3.7 mg iron, 1.2 g fiber.

IMPERIAL MACARONI BAKE

A container of all-Canadian MacLaren's Imperial Cold Pack Cheddar Cheese is the secret ingredient in this old-fashioned bake topped off with buttery golden bread crumbs.

Preparation time: 20 minutes / Cooking time: 10 minutes
Baking time: 30 minutes / Makes: 6 servings

3 cups elbow macaroni
¼ cup butter
¼ cup all-purpose flour
3 cups milk
1 tsp Dijon mustard
½ tsp salt
½ tsp white pepper
Pinch of freshly grated nutmeg
½-lb (250-g) container MacLaren's Imperial Cold Pack
    Cheddar Cheese
¼ cup butter, melted
½ cup coarse dry bread crumbs

MACARONI

1. Preheat oven to 350F. Lightly grease a 10-cup (2.5-L) baking dish and set aside. Bring a large pot of salted water to a full rolling boil. Add the macaroni and boil, uncovered, stirring occasionally, until cooked al dente, about 8 to 10 minutes.

2. Meanwhile, melt ¼ cup butter in a heavy-bottomed saucepan set over medium-low heat. Stir in the flour until blended. Cook for about 2 minutes, stirring often. Gradually whisk in the milk, Dijon, salt, pepper and nutmeg. Increase heat to medium. Stir the sauce until it comes to a boil and has thickened. Remove from the heat. Stir in spoonfuls of the cheese until blended. Cover, remove from the heat and set aside.

3. Make the topping by combining remaining ¼ cup melted butter and the bread crumbs. Set aside. As soon as the macaroni is cooked, drain but do not rinse. Stir the pasta into the cheese sauce until evenly mixed. Turn into the prepared baking dish. Sprinkle with the bread crumb topping.

4. Bake in the centre of the preheated oven for 30 minutes or until the sauce around the sides of the dish is bubbly and topping is golden. Let sit for 5 minutes before serving.

PER SERVING: 622 calories, 23.2 g protein, 58.1 g carbohydrates, 32.9 g fat, 472 mg calcium, 3 mg iron, 0.3 g fiber.

A HIT OF MUSTARD

Mustard heightens cheddar's flavor. Spread a little Dijon on the bread when you're making a grilled cheese sandwich, or add a generous pinch of dry or prepared mustard to cheese sauces.

PLANNED PASTA LEFTOVERS

The next time you cook pasta, make a little extra and keep it in a plastic bag in the refrigerator for up to a week, or freeze.

Apple-Roquefort Salad
Stir 2 cups cooked penne with ½ cup diced unpeeled apple, ¼ cup toasted chopped walnuts, 2 tablespoons blue cheese salad dressing and a pinch of pepper. Makes 3 cups.

Creamy Salmon Salad
Stir 3 cups cooked penne with a 7½-oz (213-g) can of drained salmon, ⅓ cup sour cream, 1 sliced whole green onion and black pepper to taste. Makes 4 cups.

Mozzarella Salad
Toss 2 cups cooked fusilli with ½ cup diced mozzarella cheese, ¼ cup diced tomato, 3 tablespoons Italian salad dressing and black pepper to taste. Makes 3 cups.

Steak Side Dish
Heat 1½ tablespoons oil over medium-high heat. Add 3 cups cooked penne, ½ cup diced red pepper, 1 cup small broccoli spears, ½ teaspoon dried basil and a pinch of salt and pepper. Stir-fry until hot. Pasta is great served alongside grilled steak. Makes 4 cups.

Cheddar-Tomato Soup
Combine 1 cup cooked small shell pasta with a 10-oz (284-mL) can of tomato soup, 1¼ cups milk, 1 cup grated old cheddar cheese and 1 teaspoon dried basil. Heat, stirring often, until hot. Makes 3½ cups.

Stir-Fried Oriental Pasta
Heat 1½ tablespoons oil over medium-high heat. Add 2 cups cooked fusilli with 1 tablespoon each of soy and oyster sauce and ¼ teaspoon Tabasco sauce. Stir-fry until hot. Great with chicken. Makes 3 cups.

TUNA CASSEROLE '90s STYLE

The tuna casserole of the '50s — a can of tuna, a can of mushroom soup mixed with noodles and a can of peas, all topped with potato chips — was the ultimate comfort food for some of us. Today's method is even easier. You don't have to cook the noodles. Stir the ingredients together in a casserole dish, tuck it into the oven and it's ready by the time you've changed out of your office duds. It's a meal in itself at only 164 calories a serving.

Preparation time: 15 minutes / Baking time: 40 minutes
Makes: 4 to 6 servings

10-oz (284-mL) can cream of mushroom soup
2 tbsp white wine (optional)
$\frac{1}{2}$ cup milk
$\frac{1}{2}$ tsp dried dillweed
Freshly ground black pepper
$\frac{1}{4}$ lb (125 g) medium-size fresh mushrooms
$\frac{1}{2}$ cup frozen peas
$6\frac{1}{2}$-oz (184-g) can solid tuna, packed in water
1 cup medium-size egg noodles, uncooked
$\frac{1}{4}$ cup crushed crackers

1. Preheat oven to 350F. Pour the soup into an 8-cup (2-L) casserole dish. Add the wine, if using, milk, dillweed and a generous grinding of black pepper. Whisk vigorously until fairly smooth. Then, quarter the mushrooms and stir them into the soup mixture along with the peas.

2. Drain the tuna and break it up with a fork. Add to the soup mixture along with the noodles and stir until evenly distributed. Sprinkle with the cracker crumbs.

3. Bake in the centre of the preheated oven for about 40 minutes, until bubbly and noodles are soft.

PER SERVING: *164 calories, 12.9 g protein, 15.7 g carbohydrates, 5.4 g fat, 46.9 mg calcium, 1.3 mg iron, 0.8 g fiber.*

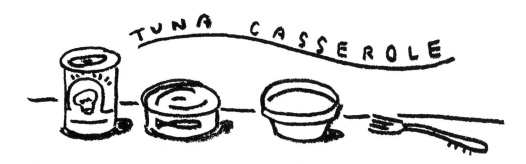

ONE-POT MACARONI AND CHEESE

The fastest goofproof route to a comforting cheesy classic.

Preparation time: 5 minutes / Cooking time: 14 minutes

Makes: 4 servings

3 cups 2% milk
2 tbsp butter
¼ tsp dried chilies
2 cups elbow macaroni or rotini
8 oz or 225-g pkg cheddar cheese, grated, about 2 cups

1. Pour the milk into a large saucepan. Add the butter and chilies. Bring to a boil over medium heat. Then, stir in the macaroni. Cover and reduce heat to low.

2. Simmer, covered, stirring often, for 12 minutes or just until the macaroni is done as you like. Remove from the heat. Immediately stir in the grated cheese. Continue stirring until the cheese is melted, about 2 minutes, returning to the heat, if necessary. Serve in a large pasta bowl.

PER SERVING: *586 calories, 27.5 g protein, 53.4 g carbohydrates, 28.9 g fat, 641 mg calcium, 2.7 mg iron, 0.04 g fiber.*

CRAFTY DINNERS: ZIPPED-UP IDEAS FOR A PACKAGE OF MACARONI AND CHEESE

Franks A Lot!
Cook macaroni and 4 wieners in boiling salted water. Toss the hot drained macaroni with ¼ cup butter, cheese sauce mix, 1 teaspoon each of regular prepared mustard and pickle relish. Slice the wieners and add. Stir until well mixed.

Florentine Supper
Cook a package of frozen spinach, squeeze out the moisture and finely chop. Sauté in a large frying pan with 3 crushed garlic cloves and ⅓ cup butter. Stir in hot cooked macaroni and cheese sauce mix.

Hot Tomato Surprise
Coarsely chop 2 or 3 tomatoes. Toss hot cooked macaroni with ¼ cup butter, cheese sauce mix, ¼ teaspoon crushed dried chilies and generous pinches of dried leaf oregano, dried basil and garlic powder. Stir in the tomatoes and serve.

Macaroni and Beef Dinner
Sauté ½ lb (250 g) ground beef in a large frying pan, stirring with a fork to separate. When lightly browned, stir in hot cooked macaroni, cheese sauce mix, a 19-oz (540-mL) can of drained tomatoes, 2 tablespoons ketchup and ½ teaspoon crumbled Italian seasoning.

Dilled Delight
Add ¼ cup each of sour cream and butter to hot cooked macaroni. Stir in cheese sauce mix, ¼ to ½ teaspoon dried dillweed and white pepper. Serve with fish.

Herbed Seafood
Stir a 6½-oz (184-g) can of drained tuna or a 7½-oz (213-g) can of salmon with hot cooked macaroni, 2 tablespoons butter, cheese sauce mix and ¼ to ½ teaspoon dried tarragon.

Easy Mac Salad
Stir hot cooked macaroni with cheese sauce mix, ⅔ cup mayonnaise, 1 teaspoon regular prepared mustard and black pepper. Add 2 stalks chopped celery. Serve right away or refrigerate and serve as a cold salad.

ONE DISH SUPERSTARS

I especially enjoyed putting these recipes together because they are the kind I love to work on and they bring back memories of easy-going good times with close friends. My definition of a perfect Sunday afternoon involves slicing and dicing some big-batch dishes, constantly tasting with a big wooden spoon, adding a soupçon of wine here, a handful of herbs there. These simmering pots and aromatic oven casseroles make no complicated demands. Most of them can be prepared ahead of time. In fact, their intense flavors blend and improve with an overnight stay in the refrigerator. For that matter, some often go straight into the freezer to be served later as instant party entrées or workday suppers. Nouvelle cuisine it's not. These dinners-in-a-dish are easy on technique and heavy on down-to-earth satisfaction.

ONE DISH SUPERSTARS · TRIPLE TESTED

EASY ENTERTAINERS

The entertaining entrées in this section combine the best of all worlds — luxury, comfort and ease. There's good reason why classics like coq au vin and beef bourguignonne have remained among our favorite dishes. The rich and full-bodied flavors that come from the long slow simmering of quality ingredients simply can't be matched. Standbys we usually consider family fare are given sophisticated makeovers: chicken pot pie is simmered in a tarragon cream with a golden phyllo crust. Make-ahead party dishes, like sassy moussaka or a robust ratatouille bake — where no baby-sitting or lots of extra go-withs are needed — allow you to enjoy the party too. Here's a cache of wonderful, homey-flavored entrées, all with elegant party twists. Enjoy and don't be surprised if your guests ask for the recipes!

FRESH DILL AND SMOKED SALMON LASAGNA

We had never thought of lasagna as elegant until we tried this version from Pauline Wayne, a great cook and mustard entrepreneur. It's a luscious combination of sublime cream sauce and extravagant smoked salmon. We love to serve it as the centrepiece of a formal brunch with a spinach salad.

Preparation time: 20 minutes / Cooking time: 20 minutes
Baking time: 55 minutes / Makes: 12 servings

6 to 8 lasagna noodles, preferably not oven-ready
1 tbsp olive oil

SAUCE
¼ cup butter
¼ cup finely chopped shallots
¼ cup all-purpose flour
2 cups chicken stock, or 10-oz (284-mL) can undiluted chicken broth and ¾ cup water
¼ cup half-and-half cream
2 tbsp dry sherry or white Dubonnet apéritif
Pinch of cayenne pepper
1 egg yolk, slightly beaten

FREEZER HERBS
Herbs can be frozen for later use. Tie in small bundles and swish in cold water to remove any grit. Drain on paper towels or a kitchen cloth and dry thoroughly. Spread on a tray to freeze. Blanching is not necessary. Once herbs are frozen, pack in airtight containers and return to freezer until ready to use.

FILLING

2 cups well-drained ricotta
2 eggs
¼ cup chopped fresh dill
Juice and finely grated peel of ½ lemon
¾ lb (375 g) sliced smoked salmon
2 (6-oz/170-g) pkgs mozzarella cheese slices
1 cup freshly grated Parmesan cheese
Fresh chopped dill

LASAGNA

1. Check the lasagna package to make sure the noodles need pre-cooking. Bring a large pot of salted water to a full rolling boil. Add the noodles and boil, uncovered, stirring occasionally, until cooked al dente, about 10 minutes. Drain pasta well, but do not rinse. Gently toss with the oil to prevent sticking. Carefully spread out on waxed paper.

2. To make the sauce, melt the butter in a medium-size saucepan. Add the shallots and sauté until soft, about 1 to 2 minutes. Then, add the flour and stir constantly over medium heat until the flour bubbles. Gradually whisk in the chicken stock (or 1 can undiluted chicken broth and ¾ cup water), followed by the cream. Stir in the sherry and cayenne pepper. Stir continuously until the mixture thickens, about 6 to 8 minutes. Taste and add more sherry and salt, if needed. (But remember, the smoked salmon and filling are salty.) Remove the sauce from the heat and whisk in the egg yolk. Cover and set aside until ready to use.

3. For filling, place the ricotta, eggs, dill, lemon juice and peel in a food processor fitted with a metal blade. Whirl, using an on-and-off motion, until blended. Turn the ricotta mixture into a bowl and set aside.

4. Just before assembling, preheat oven to 350F. Spread the bottom of a 9x13-inch baking dish with about ¼ cup sauce. Place 3 noodles lengthwise on top of the sauce. Spread half the ricotta mixture over the noodles, followed by half the smoked salmon slices and half the mozzarella slices. Pour 1 cup sauce over the cheese and spread evenly.

5. Add 3 more noodles and repeat layering, ending with remaining sauce. Sprinkle with the Parmesan cheese.

6. Place the dish with the lasagna on a baking sheet, to catch any spills, and bake in the centre of the preheated oven for 45 to 55 minutes. Remove from the oven and let stand for about 10 minutes before cutting. Liberally sprinkle with fresh dill just before serving. If baked a day ahead the flavor improves with overnight refrigeration. Freeze any leftovers and reheat in the microwave.

PER SERVING: *379 calories, 26.5 g protein, 20.5 g carbohydrates, 20.6 g fat, 413 mg calcium, 1.9 mg iron, 0.07 g fiber.*

Vin Blanc Coq au Vin

A lighter, fresher-tasting coq au vin, with white wine, green onions and shiitake mushrooms instead of the traditional heavier red wine sauce — all with a pared-down cooking time.

Preparation time: 25 minutes / Cooking time: 1¼ hours

Makes: 5 to 6 servings

4-lb (2-kg) chicken
1 tbsp vegetable oil
2 carrots
1 onion
½ lb (250 g) white, shiitake or oyster mushrooms
2 crushed garlic cloves
3 tbsp flour
2 cups good-quality dry white wine
1 tsp dried leaf thyme
½ tsp freshly ground black pepper
¼ tsp salt
1 bay leaf
3 whole green onions, thinly sliced

1. Cut the chicken into 10 pieces. Reserve the back and neck for stock or discard. Heat the vegetable oil in a wide saucepan set over medium heat. When the oil is hot, brown the chicken in several batches. Do not overcrowd the pan. When the chicken pieces are golden on both sides, transfer them to a bowl. Remove most of the fat from the pan and reserve. Reduce heat to medium-low.

2. Meanwhile, slice the carrots and onion into ½-inch pieces. Cut the mushrooms into ¼- to ½-inch-thick slices, depending on the variety.

3. Add the carrots and onion to the pan. Stir to coat with the fat remaining in the pan. Add the mushrooms and garlic and cook, stirring often, for 3 minutes or until the onion begins to soften. Then, add the vegetables to the browned chicken.

4. Add the reserved fat (about 1½ tablespoons) to the pan. Add the flour and stir constantly, scraping the bottom of the pan gently. Stir until the flour is golden, about 2 minutes. Then, gradually whisk in the wine. Add the browned chicken, vegetables, seasonings and bay leaf. Bring to a boil. Then, reduce heat and simmer gently for 1 hour, stirring occasionally, until the chicken is cooked through. Just before serving, sprinkle with green onions. The stew will keep well, covered and refrigerated, for at least 2 days. It also freezes well.

PER SERVING: *436 calories, 38.1 g protein, 9.8 g carbohydrates, 21 g fat, 46.5 mg calcium, 3.3 mg iron, 0.4 g fiber.*

COQ
AU
VIN

RIGATONI 'N' ITALIAN SAUSAGE PARTY BAKE

As this casserole bakes, the cubes of mozzarella slowly melt into the robust meat sauce. When we serve this at parties, we're often asked for the recipe.

Preparation time: 30 minutes / Cooking time: 30 minutes
Baking time: 30 minutes / Makes: 8 to 10 servings

2 lbs (1 kg) sweet Italian sausage
¼ cup olive oil
2 onions, chopped
1 red and 1 green pepper, cut into ½-inch pieces
2 stalks celery, coarsely chopped
28-oz (796-mL) can plum tomatoes, coarsely chopped
2 tbsp tomato paste
½ cup chopped fresh basil
1½ tsp crushed dried chilies
1½ tsp fennel seeds
1 lb (500 g) rigatoni
1½ lbs (750 g) mozzarella cheese, cut into ½-inch cubes
1 cup freshly grated Parmesan cheese

1. Prick the sausage in several places. Heat the oil in a large deep frying pan or saucepan. Add the sausage and cook until evenly browned. Remove the sausage from the pan. Add the onions to the fat remaining in the pan and sauté for 5 minutes.

2. Meanwhile, cut the sausage into ½-inch pieces. Return the sausage to the pan. Cook for about 5 minutes, stirring often. Add the peppers and celery and sauté for 1 or 2 minutes. Drain off excess fat. Drain the juice from the tomatoes and add it to the pan. Coarsely chop the tomatoes and add them along with the tomato paste and seasonings. Bring the sauce to a boil, stirring until well mixed. Then remove the pan from the heat.

3. To cook the pasta, bring a large pot of salted water to a full rolling boil. Add the pasta and boil, stirring occasionally, until cooked al dente, about 8 to 10 minutes.

4. Preheat oven to 375F. Once the pasta is cooked, drain but do not rinse. Stir it into the sauce along with the mozzarella cheese. Pour the mixture into a very large casserole dish. Sprinkle with the Parmesan cheese. Bake 25 to 30 minutes or until golden.

PER SERVING: *828 calories, 50.4 g protein, 49.7 g carbohydrates, 47.1 g fat, 649 mg calcium, 4.4 mg iron, 1.4 g fiber.*

BRING HOME THE BASIL

Fragrant basil is the most popular fresh herb we use. You can grow small pots on a windowsill year-round, to snip and sprinkle over pasta, salads, sauces or sliced tomatoes to give a refreshing, sweet clovelike taste. If you grow it in the garden, harvest it on a warm morning after the dew has evaporated. Snip the leaves and pack 12 to 15 together in small freezer bags. They'll keep well in the freezer for at least three months for use in cooked sauces, soups or stews.

• Use inexpensive,
well-marbled cuts of
meat. Good choices:
round, rump or
stewing beef. Trim off
the fat.

• Flour meat cubes
before browning. It
prevents the surface
from drying out and
enhances the meat's
flavor.

• When browning the
meat in hot oil, don't
put too many cubes in
the frying pan at the
same time. Turn the
cubes frequently and
remove them as soon
as they're brown.

• Most stews need to
cook for 2½ hours to
sufficiently tenderize
the meat. Vegetables
such as onions,
carrots and parsnips
can be cooked that
long, adding aromatic
flavor to the stew. But
potatoes and zucchini
should be added near
the end so they are
just fork-tender when
the meat is done.
Small cubes of potato
need 15 minutes;
zucchini just enough
to heat through, 2 to 3
minutes. For texture
and color, add a little
extra chopped pepper
or celery near the end
of cooking.

SUPERB BEEF BOURGUIGNONNE

Make this hearty French classic at least a day before the party so the rich wine, cognac and earthy seasonings have a chance to mingle and mellow. We used tender leeks instead of the usual pearl onions because they add a subtle elegance, and there's no time-consuming peeling. Use a good robust wine in the sauce and drink an even better one with this burgundy dish.

Preparation time: 30 minutes / Cooking time: 2½ hours

Makes: 8 servings

⅓ cup all-purpose flour
½ tsp each of salt, freshly ground black pepper and paprika
3 lbs (1.5 kg) cubed stewing beef
2 tbsp vegetable oil
2 leeks
2 onions
1 tbsp butter
2 large crushed garlic cloves
¼ cup chopped parsley
¼ cup cognac or brandy
2 to 2½ cups red burgundy wine
1 cup beef broth or bouillon
1½ tsp dried marjoram
½ tsp freshly ground black pepper
¼ tsp salt

1. Mix the flour with the salt, pepper and paprika in a medium-size bowl or plastic bag. Add one-third of the beef and coat evenly with the flour mixture. Heat the oil in a large wide saucepan set over medium heat. When the oil is hot, shake the excess flour from the meat and place the meat in the hot oil. Cook, turning occasionally, until the beef is well browned on all sides. Transfer to a plate. Coat and brown the beef in 2 more batches, adding more oil, if necessary. Save any remaining flour mixture.

2. Discard the dark green ends of the leeks. Trim the roots and slice the leeks in half lengthwise. Rinse well under cold running water. Coarsely chop the leeks and the onions.

3. Reduce heat to low, remove the saucepan from the heat and add the butter to the pan. Add the cut vegetables, crushed garlic and chopped parsley. Stir well and return the saucepan to low heat. Cook, stirring frequently, until the onions start to soften, about 5 minutes. Sprinkle with any remaining flour mixture and stir until evenly coated, gently scraping the bottom of saucepan as you stir to lift off any brown bits.

4. Place the meat back in the pan. Pour cognac over top and immediately ignite. Flambé for a few seconds, then stir in 2 cups wine. Stir in remaining ingredients. Cover and bring to a boil. Then, reduce heat to low and simmer gently, stirring often, until the meat is fork-tender, about 2 to 2½ hours.

5. Just before serving, taste the stew. If you would prefer a stronger wine taste, add another ¼ to ½ cup red wine. Then, continue simmering for about 2 more minutes. The stew keeps well, covered and refrigerated, for at least 2 days. In fact, the taste benefits from a day's refrigeration. It also freezes well. Adding a little wine after reheating will always perk up the flavor.

PER SERVING: 487 calories, 44.5 g protein, 11.7 g carbohydrates, 17.3 g fat, 48 mg calcium, 5.5 mg iron, 1.2 g fiber.

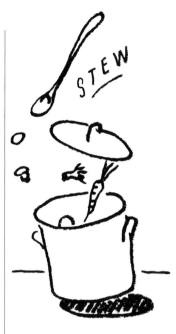

SMOKED SALMON STRATA

This is one of our all-time favorite Sunday brunch recipes. You can whip it up in no time — even after a late, late party. Put it in the refrigerator overnight then straight into the oven and it produces a creamy mélange of eggs, melted Swiss cheese and smoked salmon in every bite.

Preparation time: 20 minutes / Refrigeration time: overnight
Baking time: 35 to 45 minutes / Makes: 10 servings

1 loaf sliced white bread or dark rye
½-lb (250-g) pkg smoked salmon, thinly sliced
1 lb (500 g) Swiss cheese, grated, about 4 cups
3 cups homogenized milk
8 eggs
¼ cup finely chopped fresh dill or 1 tsp dried dillweed
Freshly ground black or white pepper
Sour cream (optional)

1. The day before serving, lightly butter a shallow 9x13-inch casserole dish. Snugly line the bottom of the casserole with a single layer of sliced bread. (Don't remove the crusts.) If necessary, cut the bread to fit the pan so the bottom of the dish is completely covered.

2. Sprinkle half the salmon on top of the bread. Sprinkle half the cheese over top. Cover with a second layer of bread. Cover with remaining salmon. Then, sprinkle remaining cheese evenly over top.

3. In a medium-size bowl, whisk the milk with the eggs, dill and a pinch of pepper. Pour the mixture evenly over the entire surface of the salmon-cheese mixture. Cover the casserole tightly with clear wrap and refrigerate overnight or for at least 8 hours.

SMOKED SALMON BARGAINS

Most fish markets sell packages of small pieces of smoked salmon, usually left over after cutting the large sides, which are priced much lower than perfectly sliced smoked salmon. They work beautifully in recipes calling for chopped smoked salmon. The less expensive chunks of smoked salmon are perfect for pâtés, spreads, dips or salads.

4. Just before baking, preheat oven to 350F. Remove the casserole from the refrigerator and place in the preheated oven. Bake, uncovered, for 35 to 45 minutes or until the top is golden brown and the centre feels set when touched. Let cool for 10 minutes on a wire rack before serving. Sprinkle with a little fresh dill. Cut into rectangles. Serve with a dab of sour cream on the side, if you like, and a green salad.

PER SERVING: *439 calories, 30 g protein, 27.9 g carbohydrates, 22.4 g fat, 650 mg calcium, 2.3 mg iron, 1.2 g fiber.*

HOT 'N' SASSY MOUSSAKA

In our version of this Greek-style lasagna, earthy eggplant replaces noodles and spicy sausage jazzes up the taste. It's a terrific make-ahead buffet supper for the chalet or a Friday night nosh.

Preparation time: 45 minutes / Standing time: 2 hours
Cooking time: 30 minutes / Baking time: 30 minutes
Makes: 10 servings

E G G -
PLANT

2 medium-size eggplants
Salt
2 lbs (1 kg) sweet or spicy Italian sausage
2 onions, chopped
28-oz (796-mL) can tomatoes, including juice
$\frac{1}{2}$ tsp dried leaf oregano
Freshly ground black pepper
$\frac{1}{3}$ cup finely chopped parsley
$\frac{1}{3}$ cup unsalted butter
$\frac{1}{3}$ cup all-purpose flour
2 cups homogenized milk
1 cup (250-mL container) table cream
Freshly grated nutmeg
Pinches of cinnamon, salt and pepper
1 cup freshly grated Parmesan cheese
$\frac{1}{4}$ cup vegetable oil

1. Peel eggplants and cut lengthwise into $\frac{1}{4}$-inch slices. Sprinkle with salt. Layer in a large dish or colander. Cover with waxed paper and weigh down with heavy cans. Let stand at room temperature for at least 2 hours.

2. Meanwhile, remove sausages from casings and place in a large saucepan along with the onions. Lightly brown, crumbling the meat with a fork. Drain off the fat and stir in the tomatoes along with their juice, oregano and pepper. Break tomatoes into bite-size pieces. Bring mixture to a boil. Then, boil gently, uncovered, stirring frequently, until all but 1 cup of the juice has evaporated, at least 20 minutes. Add salt and pepper as needed. Stir in the parsley and set aside.

3. Meanwhile, prepare the cream sauce by melting the butter in a medium-size saucepan. Blend in the flour. Stir over medium heat until bubbly. Whisk in the milk and cream. Add the nutmeg and pinches of cinnamon, salt and pepper. Continue stirring often until smooth, about 7 minutes. Stir in $\frac{1}{2}$ cup Parmesan cheese until melted. Remove from the heat. Taste and add more seasonings if needed. Cover and set aside.

4. Drain the eggplant slices. Rinse them under cold running water. Dry well with paper towels. Heat the oil in a large frying pan. Add the eggplant slices. Sauté until lightly browned on all sides. Remove them to paper towels when done and pat dry.

5. Then, preheat oven to 350F. Cover the bottom of a 9x13-inch casserole dish with a layer of eggplant. Top with half the meat mixture in an even layer. Add another layer of eggplant and remaining meat. Top with a final layer of eggplant. Cover with the cream sauce. Sprinkle with remaining cheese. If serving right away, bake in the centre of preheated oven for 25 to 30 minutes. Let stand 10 minutes before cutting.

6. When preparing ahead, simply cover the unbaked casserole and refrigerate for up to 2 days before baking. Once the casserole is baked, it can be refrigerated for several days or frozen. Thaw completely before reheating in a 350F oven for 30 minutes.

PER SERVING: 599 calories, 28.5 g protein, 17.9 g carbohydrates, 46.3 g fat, 279 mg calcium, 2.8 mg iron, 1.1 g fiber.

THE CASE FOR SALTING EGGPLANT

• Salting extracts the bitterness that is in most eggplants, and after salting eggplant will absorb less fat when sautéeing.

• Slice eggplant and sprinkle all cut surfaces with salt. Place in a colander to drain for at least 30 minutes, then pat with paper towels.

GOLDEN RATATOUILLE BAKE

This is our favorite vegetarian entrée — a carnival of herbed vegetables topped with a layer of light cheese and a golden crust.

Preparation time: 30 minutes / Cooking time: 20 minutes
Baking time: 30 minutes / Makes: 6 to 8 servings

RATATOUILLE
1 small eggplant
$\frac{1}{4}$ cup olive oil or butter
2 onions, finely chopped
$7\frac{1}{2}$-oz (213-mL) can tomato sauce
3 crushed garlic cloves
1 to 2 tbsp granulated sugar
1 tsp ground coriander
1 tsp dried basil
$\frac{1}{4}$ tsp ground thyme
$\frac{1}{4}$ tsp salt
Freshly ground black pepper

28-oz (796-mL) can plum tomatoes, undrained
2 thin zucchini
1 green pepper
Small bunch parsley
1 cup grated mozzarella cheese

TOPPING
1 lb (500-mL container) creamed cottage cheese
4 eggs
$\frac{1}{4}$ cup all-purpose flour
1 large crushed garlic clove
$\frac{1}{2}$ tsp dried basil
Generous pinch of ground thyme
1 cup grated mozzarella cheese

1. To make the ratatouille, peel the eggplant and cut it into $\frac{1}{2}$-inch cubes. Heat the oil in a large heavy-bottomed saucepan. Add the onions and sauté until soft, about 5 minutes. Add the eggplant and stir occasionally for 3 to 4 minutes.

2. Add the tomato sauce, garlic, 1 tablespoon sugar and seasonings. Drain the juice from the tomatoes into the pan and bring the mixture to a boil. Coarsely chop the tomatoes and add. Continue boiling vigorously, uncovered, until the sauce is thick, about 15 minutes. Stir frequently, especially as it thickens. Taste; if the eggplant seems bitter, add more sugar.

3. Meanwhile, preheat oven to 350F. Trim the ends from the zucchini, then thinly slice. The zucchini should measure about 4 cups. Cut the pepper into thin strips, about $1\frac{1}{2}$ to 2 inches long. Chop the parsley and measure out $\frac{2}{3}$ cup. When the tomato mixture is thick, remove it from the heat and stir in the zucchini, pepper, parsley and 1 cup grated cheese. Turn the mixture into the bottom of a 9x13-inch casserole dish.

4. For the topping, place the cottage cheese, eggs, flour, garlic and remaining seasonings in a blender or food processor fitted with a metal blade. Whirl, using an on-and-off motion, until the mixture is smooth. Spoon over the vegetable mixture. Sprinkle 1 cup mozzarella over top. Place the casserole dish on a large baking sheet, to catch any spills, then place it on the centre rack of the preheated oven and bake, uncovered for 25 to 30 minutes. Let stand for 5 minutes before cutting.

PER SERVING: *299 calories, 20.9 g protein, 20.7 g carbohydrates, 15.5 g fat, 289 mg calcium, 2.2 mg iron, 1.8 g fiber.*

THYME

PARTY PAELLA

Enriched with golden saffron and the blended flavors of chicken, seafood and hot sausage, paella is a gorgeous entertaining dish. Make ahead to the point of heating, if you wish, then refrigerate. Before the party, place on a burner and let it simmer away.

Preparation time: 20 minutes / Cooking time: 50 minutes
Makes: 8 servings

2 chicken breasts, skinned and boned
3 tbsp olive oil
$\frac{1}{2}$ lb (250 g) fresh or frozen shrimp
$\frac{1}{2}$ lb (250 g) spicy sausages, preferably chorizo
1 Spanish onion, finely chopped
1 large red pepper, cut into julienne strips
2 crushed garlic cloves
$1\frac{1}{2}$ cups short-grain white rice, such as Arborio
19-oz (540-mL) can whole tomatoes, including juice
2 (10-oz/284-mL) cans undiluted chicken broth
1 cup water
$\frac{1}{4}$ cup finely chopped parsley
1 tsp saffron threads
$\frac{1}{4}$ tsp freshly ground black pepper
1 lb (500 g) mussels, cleaned and scrubbed (optional)

1. Cut the chicken into 1-inch cubes. Heat 2 tablespoons oil in a large wide saucepan over medium heat. Add the chicken and sauté for 3 to 4 minutes or until cooked through. Set aside in a bowl.

2. Add the shrimp and sauté for 2 to 3 minutes or until pink. Set aside with the chicken. Cut the sausages into $\frac{1}{2}$-inch slices. Then, add 1 tablespoon oil to the saucepan. Add the sausages and sauté for 4 to 5 minutes or until cooked through. Set aside with the chicken.

3. Add the onion, red pepper and garlic to the pan and sauté for 5 minutes. Stir in the rice until coated with oil. Then, add the tomatoes along with their juice, chicken broth, water, parsley, saffron, black pepper and chicken mixture. (If making ahead, cover and refrigerate at this point.) Then, bring the mixture to a boil. Cover, reduce heat to low and simmer for 25 to 30 minutes or until the liquid is almost absorbed.

4. Just before the rice is cooked, arrange the mussels, if using, on top of the rice. Cover and continue to cook for 5 more minutes or until the mussels open. Discard any mussels that do not open. Remove from the heat and let stand for 5 minutes before serving. Serve immediately.

PER SERVING: 315 calories, 18.6 g protein, 33.3 g carbohydrates, 11.6 g fat, 55 mg calcium, 3.5 mg iron, 1.3 g fiber.

MUSSEL KNOW-HOW

Store mussels in the refrigerator, covered with a damp cloth. Just before cooking, tug off the beards and scrub the shells. Place the mussels in a steamer over rapidly boiling water or as recipe directs. Cover, reduce heat and simmer, stirring after a couple of minutes. Simmer until the mussels open, about 4 to 6 minutes. Discard any that don't open. Put the mussels in individual bowls, strain the broth, and concentrate the flavor by boiling for a few minutes. Then, smooth the broth with a little cream, if you like, and pour it over the mussels.

PAELLA

PERFECT
POT ROASTS

• Always choose a well-marbled roast. Pot roasting is one of the best ways to tenderize inexpensive cuts of meat such as shoulder or rump roast.

• Lightly coat the roast with flour. Then, evenly brown in oil. The browning produces a rich deep flavor and the flour protects the meat from drying out.

• Adding wine, apple juice or even a little vinegar helps to tenderize the meat while it simmers.

• Most pot roasts need at least 2 to 2½ hours' simmering to become fork-tender. Vegetables can be added to the broth at any point.

• Instead of thickening the broth with gravy, it can be boiled until thickened. Adding a little crushed garlic or a sprinkling of herbs near the end of simmering gives a freshness of flavor to the broth.

BEEF BRAISED IN BAROLO

A full-bodied Barolo brings the simmering beef to fork-tender goodness. We add large chunks of earthy root vegetables, instead of finely chopped bits, for a truly substantial country dinner to serve up in big earthenware bowls.

Preparation time: 10 minutes / Cooking time: 3¼ hours

Makes: 8 servings

2 tbsp vegetable or olive oil
3-lb (1.5-kg) boneless short-rib roast
1 large onion
5½-oz (156-mL) can tomato paste
2 cups beef broth or bouillon
2 cups Barolo or other dry red wine
19-oz (540-mL) can whole tomatoes, including juice
2 bay leaves
½ tsp fresh or dried rosemary leaves
¼ tsp allspice
3 cups vegetables, such as potatoes, yams, rutabagas, squash or turnips, cut into large chunks

1. Place the oil in a large saucepan that is deep enough to accommodate the roast. Set the pan over medium-high heat. Add the beef and cook, turning occasionally, until well browned on all sides, about 8 minutes. Meanwhile, chop the onion.

2. Transfer the beef to a plate. Reduce heat to medium-low and remove the pan from the heat to cool for 2 minutes. Stir in the onion and return the pan to the heat. Cook, stirring occasionally, until the onion is soft, about 5 minutes.

3. Stir in the tomato paste, followed by the broth, wine and tomatoes with their juice. Break up the tomatoes as you stir. Add the bay leaf and seasonings.

4. Return the meat and any juices that have collected on the plate to the saucepan. Cover and bring to a gentle boil. Then, reduce heat and simmer, turning occasionally, for 2 hours. Then, add the vegetables to the broth and continue simmering, covered and stirring occasionally, for another hour or until meat is fork-tender and the vegetables are done as you like.

5. Transfer the beef to a cutting board and let stand for 10 minutes before slicing. Cut, across the grain, into thick slices. Arrange on a platter or in deep soup bowls. Spoon the sauce and vegetables over top.

PER SERVING: *605 calories, 47.4 g protein, 43.1 g carbohydrates, 24.6 g fat, 190 mg calcium, 8.4 mg iron, 5.3 g fiber.*

PHOTO: *Beef Braised in Barolo, see recipe at right.*

ELEGANT SEAFOOD CHOWDER

Two things we love about chowder: you can make most of it ahead of time and you don't have to prepare a lot of other dishes to go with it. Good crusty bread and a simple salad round out the meal. Make the tomato-wine base ahead and refrigerate it; use whatever firm-fleshed fish is a good buy, and add the seafood just before serving.

Preparation time: 20 minutes / Cooking time: 1¼ hours

Makes: 8 servings

1 to 2 tbsp butter
3 onions, coarsely chopped
5 crushed garlic cloves
3 slices bacon, sliced into ½-inch pieces (optional)
2 cups each of chicken bouillon and white wine
1 cup dry sherry
2 (28-oz/796-mL) cans plum tomatoes, including juice
2 hot peppers, finely chopped (optional)
¼ cup chopped fresh basil or 1 tbsp dried basil
1 tbsp chopped fresh thyme or 1 tsp dried leaf thyme
1 tsp each of ground cumin and granulated sugar
¼ tsp dried dillweed (optional)
¼ tsp each of salt and cayenne pepper
1 bay leaf
2 small whole red snapper or trout
1½ lbs (750 g) firm-fleshed fillets
2 small zucchini (optional)
2 lbs (1 kg) mussels or clams
½ lb (250 g) fresh or frozen shrimp, thawed

1. To make the tomato-wine base, melt the butter in a large saucepan. Add the onions and garlic and bacon, if using, and cook over medium heat for 5 minutes, stirring often, until the onions are soft. Add the bouillon, wine, sherry, tomatoes along with their juice, hot peppers, if using, seasonings and the bay leaf.

2. Bring the mixture to a boil, stirring occasionally and breaking up the tomatoes with a fork. Then, place the whole snapper on top of the tomato mixture. Cover, reduce heat and simmer for 45 minutes to develop the flavors. Stir occasionally, being careful not to break up the fish.

3. Remove from the heat. Leave the whole fish in the chowder to further develop the flavors, and refrigerate. The chowder can be made ahead and refrigerated up to 24 hours. The flavor improves with a day's refrigeration.

RICHLY FLAVORED STEW

• For maximum flavor in a stew, taste the sauce as soon as it heats up. Flavors soften and blend as the stew simmers, so it should be highly seasoned from the beginning.

• Once the stew has come to a boil, reduce the heat so it barely simmers. It can also be baked, covered, in a 325F or 350F oven.

• Refrigerating cooked stew overnight always improves the flavor. The fat rises to the surface and solidifies so it can be easily removed.

• When reheating, if the sauce is too thick, add a little stock. For extra flavor stir in ¼ cup wine or sherry, a couple of tablespoons of brandy, a sprinkling of fresh herbs, or some minced garlic. Most stews can be reheated in small quantities at medium power in a microwave.

PHOTO: Elegant Seafood Chowder, see recipe at left.

4. When ready to reheat, remove the snapper and bay leaf from the chowder. Discard the bay leaf and the heads, bones and skin. Return the fish pieces to the chowder and place the chowder over medium heat. Stir frequently until the chowder is piping hot.

5. Meanwhile, cut the fillets into 1-inch pieces and cut the zucchini, if using, into bite-size pieces. Just 10 minutes before serving, stir the fillets into the hot chowder. Cover, reduce heat to medium-low and simmer for 5 minutes.

6. Meanwhile, scrub the mussels. Then, stir the shrimp into the chowder and place the mussels on top. Cover and continue simmering just until the mussels open. This should take from 4 to 6 minutes. Discard any mussels that have not opened by that time. Immediately ladle the chowder into bowls. Serve with garlic-butter toast.

PER SERVING: *392 calories, 44 g protein, 18.2 g carbohydrates, 8 g fat, 205 mg calcium, 6.8 mg iron, 2 g fiber.*

PHYLLO-TOPPED CHICKEN POT PIE

Our good friends and great cooks, Ruth and Gordie Gooder of Toronto, throw an annual pot pie party. This creamy sophisticated version with a paper-thin phyllo crust, plus a big spinach salad and lots of wine, keeps us coming back year after year.

Preparation time: 30 minutes / Baking time: 40 minutes
Cooking time: 25 minutes / Makes: 6 to 8 servings

PHYLLO
PASTRY

FILLING
8 chicken breasts, skinned and boned
1 cup (250-mL container) whipping cream
3 thin leeks
½ cup butter
2 cups carrots, thinly sliced
¼ lb (125 g) small fresh mushrooms, halved
1 celery stalk, thinly sliced
½ cup all-purpose flour
10-oz (284-mL) can undiluted chicken broth
1¼ cups water
¼ cup dry white wine
1 tbsp dried tarragon
½ tsp each of salt and freshly ground black pepper

CRUST
¼ to ⅓ cup butter
8 sheets phyllo pastry

1. To make the filling, preheat the oven to 350F. Place the chicken in 1 layer in a 9x13-inch baking dish. Pour the cream over the chicken. Cover and bake in the centre of the preheated oven for 20 to 25 minutes or until the chicken feels springy to the touch. Then, remove the chicken from the baking dish. Reserve the cream mixture. (Don't worry if it is not smooth.) Cut the chicken into bite-size pieces and set them aside in a medium-size bowl.

2. Trim the roots off the leeks and discard the tough outer leaves. Slice off and discard the dark green tops, leaving no more than 2 inches of the light green portion. Then, gently spread out the leaves and hold them, root-end up, under cold running water to remove all the grit. Then, thinly slice. They should measure about 2 cups.

3. Increase the oven temperature to 425F. In a large wide saucepan, melt 2 tablespoons butter over medium heat. Add the leeks, carrots, mushrooms and celery and sauté the vegetable mixture for 8 to 10 minutes or until the leeks are soft. Remove the vegetables with a slotted spoon and set them aside in the bowl with the chicken pieces.

4. Add remaining $\frac{1}{3}$ cup butter to the saucepan. Stir in the flour and cook, stirring constantly, for about 2 minutes. Do not let the flour brown. Gradually add the chicken broth, water and wine, stirring constantly, until thickened and smooth, about 6 to 8 minutes. Then, stir in the reserved cream mixture, tarragon, salt and pepper. Continue to cook, stirring continuously, for about 5 more minutes to develop the flavors and thicken the sauce. It must be very thick.

5. Remove the saucepan from the heat and stir in the chicken and vegetables. If baking right away, turn the hot mixture into a deep 10-inch pie plate. (If making ahead, cover and refrigerate the filling. It will keep well for a day. Reheat over low heat or in the microwave before topping with the crust.)

6. To prepare the crust, melt the butter over low heat or in the microwave. Lay the 8 sheets of phyllo pastry on the counter. Cover the entire surface of the phyllo with waxed paper and a damp kitchen cloth to prevent the dough from drying out and cracking.

7. Place 2 sheets of phyllo on the counter, 1 on top of the other. Lightly brush with melted butter. Carefully lay 2 more sheets of phyllo over top, making sure that all corners match perfectly. Lightly brush with melted butter. Repeat layering twice more with remaining phyllo.

8. Place the stacked phyllo butter-side up on top of the hot chicken mixture to form a crust. Using scissors, trim the phyllo to about 1 inch beyond the edge of the pie plate. Tuck the sides under half an inch to form a ridge and crimp the edges to the pie plate. Brush the edges with melted butter. Make 4 small slits in the centre of the phyllo. Bake in the centre of the preheated oven for 20 to 25 minutes or until the top is golden and crisp.

PER SERVING: *498 calories, 22.9 g protein, 30.2 g carbohydrates, 31.9 g fat, 78 mg calcium, 3.3 mg iron, 1.1 g fiber.*

PERFECT PHYLLO POINTERS

Phyllo, tissue-thin layers of melt-in-your-mouth pastry, is sold in most supermarkets and Middle Eastern food shops. Once unwrapped it dries out quickly.

• Keep phyllo refrigerated until ready to use. If frozen, thaw overnight in the refrigerator.

• Before unrolling, preheat oven. Have the filling ready, along with a small bowl of melted butter, a pastry brush and fine dry bread crumbs. Dampen 3 kitchen cloths.

• Smooth out 2 damp cloths on the counter. Cover 1 with waxed paper. Place the roll of phyllo on top and unfold.

• Remove 1 layer of pastry to the other damp cloth and quickly cover the rest with the third cloth. Lightly brush the layer you're working on with melted butter. Sprinkling lightly with bread crumbs at this point helps to keep the layers crisp. Top with another sheet of phyllo and repeat until you have the number of layers called for in the recipe.

• Then, proceed as your recipe directs.

CHILI CROWD PLEASER

There's nothing delicate about this two-alarm chili. Spicy sausage, red wine and Dijon mustard give it a gutsy, contemporary edge. It will go down beautifully with a jug of red wine at your next boisterous Grey Cup party.

Preparation time: 20 minutes / Cooking time: 1½ hours

Makes: 11 cups

¼ cup olive oil or vegetable oil
1 lb (500 g) round steak, about ¾ inch thick
1 lb (500 g) sweet Italian sausages or regular sausage meat
4 onions, chopped
4 large crushed garlic cloves
28-oz (796-mL) can tomatoes, including juice
7½-oz (213-mL) can tomato sauce
½ cup full-bodied dry red wine
1 tbsp Dijon mustard
3 tbsp chili powder
1 tbsp each of dried basil and dried leaf oregano
½ tsp crushed dried chilies
1 tbsp brown sugar
½ tsp salt (optional)
2 (19-oz/540-mL) cans kidney beans, drained and rinsed
1 cup (250-mL container) sour cream (optional)

1. Heat the oil in a very large heavy-bottomed saucepan. Cut the steak into ½-inch cubes. Add the steak to the oil in the pan and stir-fry over medium-high heat until the meat is no longer red, about 10 minutes. Remove the steak with a slotted spoon to a separate dish. Remove the casings from the sausages and add the meat to the fat remaining in the pan. Cook over medium-high heat, crumbling the meat with a fork until no longer pink, about 10 minutes. Reduce heat to medium and add the onions and garlic. Add more oil, if needed. Continue to cook, stirring occasionally, until the onions are soft, about 5 minutes.

2. Then, return the cooked beef to the pan along with the tomatoes and their juice, tomato sauce, wine, Dijon, seasonings and sugar. Stir together over medium heat and bring to a boil. Taste and add salt, if needed. Cover, reduce heat and simmer for 1 hour or until the beef is tender.

3. Then, stir in the kidney beans. Simmer, uncovered, for 5 more minutes, stirring occasionally, until the chili is thickened. Serve with dollops of sour cream on top, if you like.

PER CUP: *435 calories, 29.5 g protein, 29.7 g carbohydrates, 24.3 g fat, 111 mg calcium, 4.1 mg iron, 6.9 g fiber.*

CELEBRATION COUNTRY CHICKEN

Here's the answer when you feel like chicken with a little extra something. See photo opposite page 97.

Preparation time: 20 minutes / Cooking time: 50 minutes

Makes: 6 servings

1 pint (227 g) pearl onions or 2 small onions, cut into
   1-inch pieces
6 serving-size pieces of chicken
Salt and freshly ground black pepper
1 tbsp olive oil
3 fresh large tomatoes
3 crushed garlic cloves
$\frac{1}{2}$ cup red wine
$\frac{1}{4}$ cup coarsely chopped parsley
1 cup canned diced or crushed tomatoes
1 cup beef bouillon or $\frac{1}{2}$ cup canned beef broth
   and $\frac{1}{2}$ cup water
1 tsp dried tarragon
1 tsp granulated sugar
Fresh tarragon (optional)

TARRAGON

1. If using pearl onions, bring a large saucepan of water to a full rolling boil. Trim the tops from pearl onions but do not slice off the root ends, or the onions may fall apart during cooking. Plunge the pearl onions into the water and boil for 3 minutes. Drain and immerse in cold water to stop the cooking. Trim the roots, peel and pat dry.

2. Season the chicken pieces on both sides with salt and pepper. Heat the oil in a large saucepan set over medium heat. Cook the chicken, turning once, until well browned on both sides, about 10 minutes. Meanwhile, cut the fresh tomatoes into $\frac{1}{2}$-inch pieces.

3. Remove the chicken to a plate. Reduce heat to medium-low. Discard all but 1 tablespoon fat. Add the onions to the pan. Cook, stirring often, until lightly browned, about 5 minutes. Drain off any fat. Then, add the garlic. Stir for 1 minute. Stir in the wine, scraping the bottom of the saucepan. Then, add remaining ingredients, except fresh tarragon. Add the chicken to the sauce and any juice that has accumulated.

4. Cover the saucepan and simmer gently until the chicken is no longer pink, about 30 to 40 minutes. If you prefer a thicker sauce, remove the chicken and boil the sauce until reduced to desired thickness. Garnish each serving of chicken with fresh tarragon, if you wish.

PER SERVING: *457 calories, 38.6 g protein, 8 g carbohydrates, 29.2 g fat, 56 mg calcium, 2.8 mg iron, 1.1 g fiber.*

CURRIED SHRIMP

A lively curry marinade does double duty. First it permeates the tender shrimp, then it acts as a base for the vine-ripened-tomato sauce.

Preparation time: 20 minutes / Marinating time: 1 hour
Cooking time: 20 minutes / Makes: 3 to 4 servings

1 lb (500 g) large or medium shrimp, unshelled
½ tsp turmeric
2 tsp ground coriander
1 tsp ground cumin
Juice of 1 lemon
¼ cup vegetable oil
3 onions, finely chopped
3 cloves garlic, finely chopped
2 tbsp peeled, finely chopped fresh gingerroot
¼ tsp cayenne pepper or 2 green chilies, seeded
   and finely chopped
½ tsp salt
5 ripe tomatoes, peeled and coarsely chopped or 28-oz
   (796-mL) can tomatoes, drained and chopped

1. For appearance' sake, purchase unshelled shrimp. Carefully shell, leaving the last shell segment and tail attached. Devein by making a shallow incision down the back. Lift out the black or white intestinal vein with the point of a knife.

2. Measure the turmeric, coriander, cumin and lemon juice into a deep bowl. Stir until well mixed. Add the shrimp and stir until well coated. Cover and refrigerate. Let the shrimp marinate for 1 hour, stirring occasionally.

3. Heat the oil in a large wide frying pan. Add the onions, garlic, gingerroot, cayenne pepper and salt. Cook over medium heat, stirring frequently, for about 5 to 7 minutes or until the onions are soft and pale golden. Reduce the heat if any part of the mixture starts to burn.

4. Drain the marinade from the shrimp into the pan. Add the tomatoes. Then, cook, uncovered, for 15 minutes or until the mixture is thick. Stir frequently. Just before serving, stir in the shrimp and heat through. Serve over rice.

PER SERVING: 354 calories, 21.9 g protein, 24.2 g carbohydrates, 20.9 g fat, 102 mg calcium, 5.5 mg iron, 4.6 g fiber.

S H R I M P

FAMILY FAVORITES

For many of us a substantial chili, a light but nourishing ragout or country-style chicken and dumplings is the ultimate one-dish dinner. They can always be counted on to gratify the heartiest of your family's appetites. Along with a warming harvest stew, we include a satisfying chicken pot pie and a fast shepherd's pie. Today's ragouts and stews are a far cry from yesterday's gooey flour-laced brews with hunks of stringy meat and soft veggies. The stews and pot pies of the '90s have a fresh look and a new nutrient profile. Chicken and meat are cooked in light broths for maximum flavor retention. We hold off adding vegetables until close to the end of simmering time, so they maintain their pure taste and interesting textures. These slow simmers and fast takes are guaranteed to become family favorites.

MICROWAVE SWISS FONDUE

Cheese fondue, that trendy party food of the '50s, is enjoying a revival. This time we're preparing it the no-stick foolproof way — in the microwave.

Preparation time: 10 minutes / Microwave time: 10 minutes

Makes 2⅓ cups, about 6 servings

1 crushed garlic clove
2 tbsp butter
1 tbsp Dijon mustard
2 tbsp all-purpose flour
⅔ cup dry white wine
1 lb (500 g) Swiss cheese, grated

1. Measure the garlic, butter, Dijon, flour and wine into a 12-cup (3-L) microwave-safe casserole dish. Microwave, uncovered, on high for 2 minutes. Whisk twice during cooking. Then, continue cooking on high until the mixture bubbles slightly, about 30 seconds. Whisk, then stir in the cheese. Microwave, uncovered, on medium for 8 minutes. Stir every 2 minutes. Serve hot with cubes of crusty bread, pieces of apple and raw vegetable. To reheat, microwave, uncovered, on medium for about 5 minutes, stirring occasionally.

PER SERVING: *378 calories, 24.1 g protein, 5.2 g carbohydrates, 26.8 g fat, 803 mg calcium, 0.4 mg iron, 0.07 g fiber.*

FONDUE MAKES IT

• Add extra heat to a smooth-flavored fondue with the addition of white or cayenne pepper, chili flakes, dashes of Tabasco sauce or flavored mustard.

• Vary the taste by substituting beer for the wine and using a sharp, aged cheddar.

• When using Swiss cheese, a couple of tablespoons of kirsch liqueur are an elegant addition, as well as a light crumbling of Roquefort or goat cheese.

• Reheat leftover fondue in the microwave and pour over thick slices of toasted crusty bread topped with sliced ripe tomatoes.

Zucchini and Mushroom Vegetarian Lasagna

Zucchini is a flavorful and extremely low-calorie stand-in for noodles in this substantial lasagna. Although meat isn't used, the ricotta provides sufficient protein to make it a great vegetarian entrée.

Preparation time: 15 minutes / Cooking time: 20 minutes
Baking time: 30 to 40 minutes / Makes: 12 servings

4 long zucchini
1 lb (500 g) fresh mushrooms
3 tsp butter
4 crushed garlic cloves
28-oz (796-mL) can spaghetti sauce
$5\frac{1}{2}$-oz (156-mL) can tomato paste
$\frac{1}{2}$ tsp Italian seasoning
8 oz (250 g) mozzarella or Swiss cheese, grated
1 lb (500 g) ricotta, well drained
2 eggs
$\frac{1}{4}$ cup all-purpose flour

1. Preheat oven to 350F. Slice the unpeeled zucchini lengthwise into large pieces no more than $\frac{1}{4}$-inch thick. Some of these pieces will take the place of noodles in the lasagna. Take the 8 outside pieces of zucchini (the ones that are primarily peel) and finely chop. Wipe the mushrooms and slice.

2. Melt 1 teaspoon butter in a large wide saucepan. Add the garlic and chopped zucchini. Sauté over medium heat for 2 minutes. Remove and set aside on paper towels. Add remaining butter and the mushrooms to the pan and stir for 5 minutes. Drain off all the liquid.

3. Add the spaghetti sauce, tomato paste, Italian seasoning and chopped zucchini. Bring the mixture to a boil. Simmer, uncovered, stirring frequently for 10 minutes to blend the flavors. Stir in half the grated cheese. Remove the pan from the heat. Cover and set aside.

4. Place the ricotta, eggs and flour in a food processor fitted with a metal blade or in a blender. Whirl, using an on-and-off motion, until the mixture is smooth. Or place the cheese, eggs and flour in a bowl and beat until smooth.

5. Cover the bottom of a 9x13-inch baking dish with the large zucchini slices. Spread with half the cheese mixture. Top with half the tomato sauce. Add another zucchini layer, cheese layer and remaining tomato sauce. Sprinkle with remaining grated cheese.

Great Garlic

• Don't store garlic in the refrigerator. Put it in a cool, dry, well-ventilated spot, in a perforated clay pot or a small open-wire basket. It stays fresh for weeks.

• To peel, separate into cloves. Place on a cutting board and using the flat side of a knife, press down on the cloves. The skins will split, making them easy to peel.

• For large quantities, simmer unpeeled cloves in water or bouillon for a couple of minutes. Drain and press gently. The skins will slip off.

• To remove garlic's pungent smell from your hands or a cutting board, rub with half a lemon.

6. Bake in the preheated oven for 30 to 40 minutes or until hot in the centre. If making ahead, cover the uncooked lasagna and refrigerate up to 12 hours. Bring to room temperature before baking.

PER SERVING: *229 calories, 12.9 g protein, 20.8 g carbohydrates, 11.3 g fat, 261 mg calcium, 2.1 mg iron, 0.6 g fiber.*

FAST 'N' EASY
CHICKEN AND DUMPLINGS

Old-fashioned chicken stew with a no-fuss fast biscuit mix topping.

Preparation time: 10 minutes / Cooking time: 40 minutes

Makes: 4 servings

4 chicken breasts or drumsticks
3 cups chicken bouillon
2 cups milk
2 onions, thickly sliced
$\frac{1}{4}$ tsp each of ground sage and savory
1 bay leaf
Freshly ground white pepper
$\frac{1}{2}$ tsp celery seed or 1 cup chopped celery tops

DUMPLINGS

2 cups variety baking mix or biscuit mix
$\frac{2}{3}$ cup milk
$\frac{1}{2}$ cup chopped parsley (optional)

1. Place all the ingredients except the baking mix, $\frac{2}{3}$ cup milk and parsley in a large saucepan that is no more than 10 inches wide. Submerge the chicken in the bouillon. Cover and bring to a boil. Reduce heat and simmer for 20 minutes.

2. Then, prepare the dumplings according to package directions, using 2 cups mix and $\frac{2}{3}$ cup milk. Stir in the chopped parsley. Drop large spoonfuls of dumpling batter over the simmering stew. Do not submerge the batter in the sauce. Tightly cover the pan and continue simmering for 15 to 18 minutes.

Note: If you prefer small pieces of chicken instead of serving-size pieces, let the chicken simmer until it will easily come off the bone, about 40 minutes. Remove the chicken pieces from the pot. Discard the bones and skin. Cut the chicken into bite-size pieces. Return to the broth. Then, add the dumplings.

PER SERVING: *491 calories, 35 g protein, 53.3 g carbohydrates, 14.8 g fat, 237 mg calcium, 1.5 mg iron, 1.5 g fiber.*

PERFECT ROLY-POLY DUMPLINGS

The secret to superb light dumplings is to steam them on top of a simmering liquid.

• Use a large wide pan and have enough liquid in the pan so there's ample room for the dumplings to expand.

• Dip a spoon into the simmering liquid then into the batter to scoop up a rounded spoonful. Drop this batter into the liquid. Repeat until dumplings are just touching.

• Immediately cover and don't lift the lid until the recommended cooking time is up. When dumplings look fluffy, insert a wooden pick into the centre. If it comes out clean, they're done.

• Give new life to bland dumplings by stirring in chopped fresh basil, dill or tarragon, grated cheese or chopped whole green onions.

Hot 'n' Spicy Chicken Lasagna

Because one can never have too many good lasagna recipes, we've created a gutsy new version with big cubes of moist chicken, colorful salsa, hot 'n' sweet peppers and three kinds of cheese.

Preparation time: 30 minutes / Cooking time: 15 minutes
Baking time: 40 minutes / Makes: 10 servings

8 lasagna noodles
1 tbsp vegetable oil

SAUCE
1 tbsp vegetable oil
2 crushed garlic cloves
1 onion, finely chopped
1 red or green pepper, cored, seeded and finely chopped
12-oz (341-mL) jar medium salsa
12½-oz (375-mL) bottle meatless spaghetti sauce
1½ tsp ground cumin

FILLING
2 cups well-drained ricotta
2 eggs
¼ cup chopped coriander or Italian parsley
1 tbsp seeded and chopped jalapeno pepper
1½ cups grated old cheddar cheese
1½ cups grated mozzarella cheese
4 cups cooked cubed chicken

HOT
PEPPERS

1. Bring a large pot of salted water to a full rolling boil. Add the pasta and boil, uncovered, stirring occasionally, until cooked al dente, about 10 minutes. Drain well, but do not rinse. Gently toss with 1 tablespoon oil to prevent sticking. Spread out on waxed paper.

2. Meanwhile, to prepare the sauce, heat 1 tablespoon oil in a large wide frying pan over medium-low heat. Add the garlic, onion and red pepper. Sauté for about 5 minutes or until the onion is soft. Then, stir in the salsa, spaghetti sauce and cumin. Taste and add more cumin, if necessary. Bring the mixture to a boil. Then, cover, reduce heat and simmer for about 5 to 7 minutes to allow the flavors to develop. Stir. Turn the sauce into a bowl and set aside.

3. To prepare the filling, place the ricotta, eggs, coriander and jalapeno pepper in a food processor fitted with a metal blade. Whirl until the mixture is evenly blended. Scrape down the sides occasionally to ensure an even purée. Turn the filling into a bowl and set aside. Or combine the ingredients in a bowl and mash with a spoon until smooth.

4. Stir the grated cheeses together in a small bowl and set aside.

5. Preheat oven to 375F. Lightly cover bottom of a 9x13-inch baking dish with about ½ cup sauce. (It will be a very thin coating of sauce.) Completely cover the bottom of the pan with a single layer of noodles, about 4 noodles. Spread half the sauce evenly over the noodles, then dot with half the ricotta mixture, followed by half the chicken, then half the grated cheese.

6. Add another layer of noodles. Repeat layering, ending with cheese. If not baking right away, cover and refrigerate overnight, if you wish. Then, bake, uncovered, in the centre of the preheated oven for 35 to 40 minutes or until the lasagna bubbles around the sides and the top is golden. If refrigerated, the lasagna may need 45 to 50 minutes' baking. Let stand for 10 minutes before cutting.

PER SERVING: *465 calories, 36.6 g protein, 27.4 g carbohydrates, 24.3 g fat, 415 mg calcium, 3.3 mg iron, 0.3 g fiber.*

BLACK BEAN HARVEST STEW

When we think of black beans we often connect them to sauces served in Chinese restaurants. But now black beans are taking a prominent role on restaurant menus as side dishes and in stews and ragouts. They offer a firm bite and hearty texture and here they form the substantial background for a richly flavored stew.

Preparation time: 20 minutes / Soaking time: 1 hour
Cooking time: 2 ¼ to 2 ¾ hours / Makes: 6 servings

1 cup dried black beans
6 serving-size pieces of chicken (optional)
2 large onions
2 tbsp vegetable oil
2 crushed garlic cloves
28-oz (796-mL) can diced tomatoes, including juice
4 cups chicken or vegetable broth or bouillon
2 tbsp chopped canned or fresh jalapeno peppers
2 tsp ground cumin
1 tsp ground coriander
Generous pinch of salt
Freshly ground black pepper
1 large sweet potato
1½ lbs (750 g) squash, such as pepper, butternut or acorn
2 zucchini
Sprigs of fresh coriander

HOT STUFF
All hot peppers have their own distinct flavor, from tart to nutty, velvety to hot.

Anaheim
Also called California green chili, this long, green pepper can be bought fresh, canned or in jars. The Anaheim is the least fiery of peppers and adds mild heat to all types of cooking.

Fresno
Bright green or red-skinned, it's frequently labelled the "hot" chili pepper. When added to hot pickles or sauces, its fiery touch will leave you speechless!

Jalapeno
This more common thick-fleshed dark green pepper is available fresh, canned or pickled. It's moderately hot and adds an even heat to all kinds of dishes.

Serrano
Don't let this tiny, dark green pepper deceive you: it's the hottest of them all.

Yellow Wax
Also dubbed "banana pepper" because of its shape and color, it's frequently available fresh. Great in relishes and sauces or roasted and peeled.

1. To soak the beans, cover them with water and leave at room temperature for 8 hours. Or place them in a saucepan and cover with water. Set the saucepan over medium heat and slowly bring to a boil to avoid breaking the skins. Continue boiling the beans, uncovered, for 3 minutes. Then, cover and remove from the heat. Let sit at room temperature for 1 hour. When ready to use the beans, drain and discard the soaking water.

2. Chop the onions. Heat the oil in a large saucepan set over medium-low heat. Add the chicken, if using, and sauté until browned. Remove and refrigerate. Add the onions and garlic to the fat in the pan and sauté for about 5 minutes, stirring often, until the onions are soft. Stir in the tomatoes and their juice, chicken broth, jalapeno peppers and seasonings. Add the beans. Bring to a boil, then reduce heat and simmer, covered, for 1¼ hours.

3. Meanwhile, peel the potato and cut it into ¾-inch pieces. Peel the squash, remove the seeds and cut it into ¾-inch pieces. Stir the potato, squash and chicken into the stew after it has simmered for 1¼ hours. Cover and simmer for 1 to 1½ more hours, until the beans and vegetables are tender.

4. Slice the zucchini in half lengthwise. Cut crosswise into ⅓-inch slices. If serving right away, add the zucchini to the stew when the beans are tender. Continue simmering, uncovered, until the zucchini is hot, about 5 minutes. Garnish with sprigs of fresh coriander. The stew can be refrigerated for a day or frozen. If making ahead, only add the zucchini when reheating.

PER SERVING: *290 calories, 13.3 g protein, 48.3 g carbohydrates, 6.8 g fat, 147 mg calcium, 4.7 mg iron, 1.9 g fiber.*

LAMB RAGOUT PROVENÇAL

This robust stew brings to mind all the flavors of sensuous Southern French cooking — tender lamb, garlic, niçoise olives, rosemary and thyme and makes enough for a big party.

Preparation time: 30 minutes / Cooking time: 40 minutes
Baking time: 2 to 2½ hours / Makes: 16 cups

⅓ cup olive oil
1 cup all-purpose flour
4 lbs (2 kg) lean boneless lamb or beef, cut into 1-inch cubes
2 dozen small pearl onions or 8 small cooking onions
2 tbsp granulated sugar
750-mL bottle burgundy or other dry red wine
4 cups beef stock or bouillon
6 crushed garlic cloves
1½ tsp dried leaf thyme

We often give the yield for soups and stews in cups instead of suggested number of servings since we find one cup of stew may be quite satisfying for a weekday dinner accompanied by a big salad, but we can easily eat three cups of chili after a day on the slopes.

1 tsp dried rosemary, crumbled
1 tsp salt
¼ tsp freshly ground black pepper
2 bay leaves
1 cup black olives, preferably Mediterranean-style
2 lbs (1 kg) carrots
2 leeks (optional)

1. Heat the oil in a wide heavy-bottomed frying pan. Pour all the flour into a large bowl. Toss about one-quarter of the lamb pieces with the flour until coated. Add to the hot oil. Cook over medium heat until lightly browned. Transfer with a slotted spoon to a large deep ovenproof casserole that will hold at least 16 cups (4 L). Or use two 8-cup (2-L) casserole dishes that will fit into the oven at the same time. Repeat until all meat is browned. Save remaining flour.

2. Meanwhile, peel the onions. Cut a shallow "X" in the root end of each peeled pearl onion. If using cooking onions, cut them into wedges. When all the meat is browned, add more oil to pan, if needed, to measure about 3 tablespoons oil. Add the onions and sprinkle with the sugar. Stir fairly frequently over medium heat until a golden color. Remove the onions with a slotted spoon and add to the casserole.

3. Preheat oven to 350F. Stir remaining flour into the fat in the bottom of the pan. (There should be about ⅓ cup flour.) Stir over medium heat until bubbly. Gradually stir in the wine, stock, garlic and seasonings. Whisk frequently over medium heat until slightly thickened and piping hot. Pour over the lamb. Submerge the bay leaves in the sauce. Stir in the olives. Cover and bake in the centre of the preheated oven for 1 hour for lamb or 1½ hours for beef.

4. Meanwhile, clean the carrots and cut them into 2-inch bite-size pieces. Clean the leeks, if using, and slice them into ⅓-inch pieces. After the meat has cooked, stir in the carrots. Cover and continue baking for an additional 30 minutes. Stir in the leeks, if using. Continue baking for another 30 minutes or until the meat is tender and the vegetables are done as you like. Remove the bay leaves.

5. If making ahead, cook the meat in the sauce until tender, then freeze. Defrost in a microwave or in the refrigerator overnight. Stir in the carrots and bake, covered, in a preheated 350F oven for 30 minutes. Add the leeks, and continue baking until the vegetables are cooked.

PER CUP: 309 calories, 25.5 g protein, 16.4 g carbohydrates, 12.4 g fat, 48.3 mg calcium, 3 mg iron, 0.4 g fiber.

RAGOUT
PROVENÇAL

CURRIED CHICKEN POT PIE WITH BUTTERMILK-BISCUIT TOPPING

Here's a delicious way to swing into a leisurely low-gear Friday night with friends. Just add a bottle of good white wine and relax.

Preparation time: 30 minutes / Cooking time: 12 minutes
Baking time: 1 hour / Makes: 6 servings

CHICKEN

POT

PIE

FILLING
4 chicken breasts, skinned and boned
3 carrots
1 small apple
$\frac{1}{2}$ cup butter
2 onions, finely chopped
$\frac{1}{3}$ cup all-purpose flour
1 tsp curry powder
2 cups homogenized milk
$\frac{1}{2}$ tsp each of salt and dried sage
$\frac{1}{4}$ tsp freshly ground black pepper

TOPPING
1 cup all-purpose flour
1 tsp baking powder
$\frac{1}{8}$ tsp each of salt and cinnamon
$\frac{1}{4}$ cup cold shortening
$\frac{1}{2}$ cup buttermilk

1. To prepare the filling, slice the chicken into 1-inch pieces and place in a 12-cup (3-L) casserole dish. Cut the carrots into $\frac{1}{3}$-inch slices. Peel and core the apple and cut it into $\frac{1}{3}$-inch pieces. Add to the chicken along with the carrots.

2. Preheat oven to 350F. Melt 2 tablespoons butter in a saucepan set over medium heat. Add the onions and sauté until soft, about 5 minutes. Pour the onions over the chicken.

3. Melt remaining butter in the same saucepan set over medium heat. Blend in the flour and curry powder. Cook for about 2 minutes, stirring continuously. Gradually whisk in the milk and remaining seasonings. Stir until the sauce is very thick. Pour over the chicken and vegetables and stir well.

4. To make the topping, in a medium-size bowl, using a fork, stir the flour with the baking powder, salt and cinnamon. Add the shortening and blend in with a pastry blender or 2 knives until the mixture is crumbled into pea-size pieces.

5. Make a well in the centre of the mixture and pour in the buttermilk. Mix with a fork just until blended. Do not overmix.

6. Drop the batter over the filling in large spoonfuls. Bake in the centre of the preheated oven for about 1 hour, until golden.

PER SERVING: 477 calories, 22.9 g protein, 32.9 g carbohydrates, 28.4 g fat, 161 mg calcium, 2.2 mg iron, 2.7 g fiber.

BIG-BATCH BAKED CHICKEN IN CHILI SAUCE

No browning needed, just measure everything into a huge baking dish. Then pop it into the oven. An hour and a half later, you have a wholesome dinner for twelve or a terrific family supper plus two more dinners to tuck into the freezer.

Preparation time: 30 minutes / Baking time: 1½ hours

Makes: 10 servings

12 chicken pieces
2 tbsp chili powder
¼ tsp salt
2 onions
2 sweet peppers
2 (19-oz/540-mL) cans red kidney beans, drained and rinsed
2 hot banana peppers
28-oz (796-mL) can diced tomatoes, including juice
14-oz (398-mL) can tomato sauce
1 cup smoke-flavored barbecue sauce
3 crushed garlic cloves
1 tbsp each of ground cumin and ground coriander
1 tsp each of dried leaf oregano and cinnamon

1. Preheat oven to 375F. Remove the skin from the chicken pieces, then arrange the chicken in a single layer in two 9x13-inch baking pans or in a huge roasting pan. Sprinkle with the chili powder and salt.

2. Coarsely chop the onions. Dice the sweet peppers into small pieces. Scatter the onions and sweet peppers over the chicken along with the beans. Finely chop the hot peppers and place them in a large bowl. Stir in all remaining ingredients. Pour the sauce over the chicken. Cover the pans loosely with foil or leave the roasting pan lid slightly ajar.

3. Bake in the centre of the preheated oven for 1½ hours. Stir gently after 1 hour. Serve immediately, refrigerate for up to 2 days or freeze.

PER SERVING: 293 calories, 31 g protein, 33.4 g carbohydrates, 6.6 g fat, 105 mg calcium, 4.6 mg iron, 8.2 g fiber.

PEPPER SAVVY
• When shopping for fresh peppers, choose bright-colored pods with no visible signs of decay. Store in the vegetable crisper of the refrigerator for up to 5 days.

• Freezing peppers will soften the texture but not the taste.

*A shepherd's pie is
extremely easy to jazz
up. Consider these
variations.*

Creamy Chicken
Use ground chicken in
place of beef, cream of
mushroom soup and
poultry seasoning or
tarragon for
seasonings.

Sassy Italian
Remove Italian
sausage from the
casing and use instead
of beef. Chopped
sweet pepper could be
used as the vegetable.

Mexican
Stir ¼ to ½ cup hot
salsa into the cooked
beef and add ¼ to ½
teaspoon of dried
chilies.

**Mashed Potato
Stir-Ins**
For extra flavor stir
grated cheese,
chopped chives or
green onions, crushed
garlic or cayenne
pepper into the
mashed potatoes
before spreading over
the filling.

SPEEDY SHEPHERD'S PIE

We're constantly amazed at the number of fellow staffers who
come into the test kitchen in the afternoon to ask how to make
a shepherd's pie fast because they want to have it that night. Here's
what we tell them.

Preparation time: 15 minutes / Cooking time: 10 minutes
Baking time: 30 minutes / Makes: 6 servings

1 tbsp vegetable oil
1½ lbs (750 g) ground beef
1 large onion, chopped
10-oz (284-mL) can tomato soup
1 bay leaf
½ tsp dried leaf thyme
¼ tsp each of dry mustard and freshly ground back pepper
1 cup frozen peas or 12-oz (341-mL) can kernel corn
  (optional)
2½ cups dry mashed potato flakes
1¾ cups water
½ cup milk
2 tbsp butter
Pinch of salt

1. Heat the oil in a large wide frying pan. Add the meat and onion
and cook over medium-high heat, stirring often with a fork to keep meat
separated until it loses its red color. Drain off all the fat.

2. Add the undiluted soup, bay leaf and seasonings. Add the vegetables, if using, and cook, uncovered, over medium heat until heated
through, stirring occasionally. Taste and increase seasonings, if you like.
Remove the pan from the heat and stir in ½ cup potato flakes. Turn into
a deep 9-inch pie plate or square baking dish.

3. Preheat oven to 350F. Prepare the mashed potatoes following
package directions, using 2 cups mashed potato flakes along with remaining ingredients. Spread lightly over the meat mixture. Bake in the centre of the preheated oven for about 30 minutes or until potatoes are
piping hot. If not as brown as you would like, increase the oven temperature to 375F and continue baking for a few more minutes.

PER SERVING: *402 calories, 26.9 g protein, 31 g carbohydrates, 19 g fat,
46.6 mg calcium, 3.1 mg iron, 0.4 g fiber.*

BEST BREADS

When I was growing up, bread was very basic. Sliced white was the staple and whole wheat was considered venturesome. Today the word bread has taken on a whole new meaning. We can make a simple meal out of focaccia and cheese. Our no-fail pizza crust has a million uses, from Fiery Calzones to a colorful Four Seasons Pizza. The stress-relieving value of kneading fresh bread dough is surpassed only by the joy of eating it. Then there's the mystery of how a small amount of yeast can raise a mix of wholesome grains to a full country-style loaf, or the wonder of watching whole wheat pitas magically puff up in eight minutes flat. All you need is a measuring cup to perform miracles with quick breads, loaves and muffins. There's no secret to our big-batch refrigerator bran muffins, Festive Amaretto Fruit Bread or Company's Coming Corn Bread. Simply stir together and bake. Bread need never be boring again.

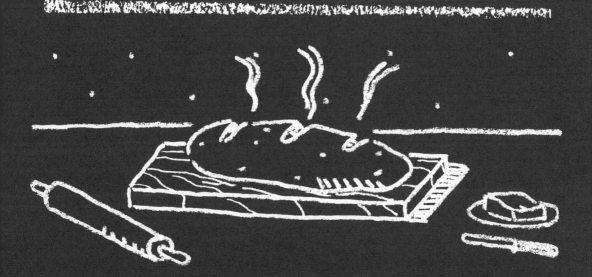

PIZZA PIZAZZ

Pizza is synonymous with relaxing. Whether we order it in, add a ton of toppings to a store-bought crust or make it completely from scratch, we associate it with easy meals. It's definitely fast food especially if you start with a prepared crust of frozen bread dough, but nothing matches a home-made, hand-formed crust laden with aromatic vegetables, hot sausage and multicolored peppers. Our pizza crust takes time, but it's well worth it.

BASIC PIZZA DOUGH

Unless your local gourmet market sells dynamite dough, make your own. It's worth the time it takes.

Preparation time: 15 minutes / Standing time: 1 hour
Makes: dough for 8 calzones or two 14-inch pizzas

1 cup lukewarm water
$\frac{1}{4}$ tsp granulated sugar
1 pkg (1 tbsp) dry yeast
4 tsp olive oil
2 cups all-purpose flour
$\frac{1}{2}$ tsp salt
1 to 2 tbsp flour

1. Pour the lukewarm (110F) water into a 2-cup (500-mL) measure or medium-size bowl. Stir in the sugar until dissolved. Sprinkle the yeast over top but do not stir. Let stand for 5 to 10 minutes, until the yeast is foamy. Add the oil and stir until evenly mixed.

2. Place 2 cups flour and salt in a food processor fitted with a metal blade. Mix, using an on-and-off motion. With the machine running, gradually pour in the yeast. Then, gradually add 1 to 2 tablespoons flour until the dough forms a ball.

3. Turn the dough out onto a lightly floured surface. Knead for about 2 minutes. Then, form into a smooth ball. Place the dough in a greased bowl and cover with greased waxed paper and a damp cloth. Let it rise in a warm spot for about 1 hour or until almost doubled in bulk. Then, punch down the dough and divide it in half.

4. If not using right away, wrap the dough well and refrigerate for up to 3 days or freeze. Use for 2 pizzas or 8 calzones. Depending on how thinly you roll the crusts, they will need from 8 to 15 minutes of baking at 475F.

FIERY CALZONES

A calzone is simply a soul-satisfying turnover made with pizza dough. We've filled it with hot 'n' spicy Italian sausage. Perfect for fireside dinners at the chalet, Grey Cup parties, cool evenings at the cottage, or your teenager's Friday night bash.

Preparation time: 20 minutes / Baking time: 12 minutes

Makes: 8 calzones

Basic Pizza Dough (see page 210)
4 hot Italian sausages
3 cups grated mozzarella cheese
$\frac{1}{2}$ cup thinly sliced stuffed green olives
2 crushed garlic cloves
$\frac{1}{4}$ to $\frac{1}{2}$ tsp cayenne pepper

1. Prepare the pizza dough. When you are ready to make the calzones, preheat oven to 500F. Lightly oil a large baking sheet.

2. Prepare the filling by sautéeing the sausages in a frying pan until they are done as you like. Slice lengthwise, then into $\frac{1}{4}$-inch-thick pieces. Place them in a medium-size bowl. Stir in the cheese, olives, garlic and cayenne pepper until the garlic is evenly distributed.

3. Place the dough on a lightly floured surface. Cut it into 8 pieces. Pat 1 piece into a flattened round. Using a lightly floured rolling pin, roll it into a 6-inch circle. Spread an eighth of the filling on the lower half of the circle, leaving a 1-inch border of plain dough. Brush the dough edges with cold water. Fold the top half of the circle over the filling. Then, firmly press the edges of the dough together to seal. Crimp the edges with a fork. Place on the baking sheet. Repeat with remaining dough and filling.

4. Then, lightly brush the calzones with oil. Place the pan on the bottom rack of the preheated oven and bake for 10 to 12 minutes, until puffed and golden. Serve immediately.

PER CALZONE: *271 calories, 15.3 g protein, 24.8 g carbohydrates, 12.3 g fat, 288 mg calcium, 1.8 mg iron, 1.3 g fiber.*

PRONTO PIZZA TOPPERS

Spanish Olive
Seed and chop 4 tomatoes. Spread over a crust with $\frac{1}{2}$ cup sliced green olives. Drizzle with 2 teaspoons olive oil. Sprinkle with 1 cup grated mozzarella cheese.

Cheddar and Tomato
Sprinkle a crust with 1 cup grated cheddar cheese. Add 4 strips cooked bacon, coarsely chopped, and 2 seeded and chopped tomatoes. Top with another cup of grated cheddar.

Herbed Cheese
Spread a 4-oz (125-g) package of creamy herb cheese over a crust. Sprinkle with 1 to 2 seeded and chopped tomatoes and $\frac{1}{2}$ cup freshly grated Parmesan cheese.

Hot Mexican
Stir 2 tablespoons hot taco sauce with 1 cup tomato sauce, 1 teaspoon ground cumin and $\frac{1}{2}$ cup chopped, canned jalapeno peppers. Spread over a crust. Sprinkle with 2 cups grated Monterey Jack or farmer's cheese.

FOUR SEASONS PIZZA

An upscale pizza to whip up when you've invited friends over for an evening of gossip. Serve with white wine or a designer beer.

Preparation time: 25 minutes / Baking time: 15 minutes

Makes: 4 servings

1 lb (500 g) pizza dough
Olive oil
1 tomato, seeded and diced
¼ tsp Italian seasoning
1 tbsp pesto
6 sweet pepper rings, preferably red and green
6 black olives, whole or sliced
2 tbsp tomato or pizza sauce
3 oz (85 g) pepperoni, thinly sliced
1 whole green onion, thinly sliced
2 tbsp ricotta or feta cheese
½ cup broccoli flowerets, raw or cooked
Thinly sliced red onion rings, cut in half
1 cup grated mozzarella cheese, about 4 oz (125 g)

PIZZA

1. Preheat oven to 425F. Break off 2 small pieces of pizza dough, each about the size of a 2-inch ball and set aside.

2. Lightly grease a 12- or 14-inch pizza pan. Roll out remaining dough on a lightly floured surface. Place it in the pan and shape the dough over the bottom and up the sides of the pan to form a ½-inch rim.

3. Using the palms of your hands, roll 1 of the reserved pieces of dough into a ⅓-inch-thick rope 12 inches long. Place the rope across the centre of the pizza, anchoring it to the sides of the pan. Form the second rope and place it across the pizza dough, perpendicular to the first rope, dividing pizza into quarters. Brush dough with olive oil, making sure the rim and dividing ropes are well coated so they don't dry out.

4. Fill the first pizza quarter with the diced tomato and sprinkle with the Italian seasoning. Spread the pesto on the second quarter. Add the sweet pepper rings and whole or sliced olives. Spread the tomato sauce over the third pizza quarter. Top with the pepperoni slices and sprinkle with the sliced green onion. For the final quarter, spread the ricotta cheese over the dough. Add the broccoli and top with the red onion rings.

5. Sprinkle cheese over all, leaving ropes exposed. Bake on the bottom rack of preheated oven for 15 to 20 minutes or until crust is golden.

PER SERVING: *631 calories, 21.7 g protein, 62 g carbohydrates, 33.2 g fat, 270 mg calcium, 4.1 mg iron, 1.2 g fiber.*

WONDROUS YEAST BREADS

A basketful of breads worth baking — including whole-some whole wheat pitas, herbed golden focaccia and high-ly textured, multigrain country loaves.

UNBEATABLE FOCACCIA

This cross between a crusty pizza and Italian flat bread with its chewy texture and sprinkling of herbs has already become the darling of the decade. Our rosemary version is terrific with squash soup or roasted chicken. It also makes a great appetizer spread with pesto, sprinkled with goat cheese or topped with chopped sun-dried tomatoes and fresh basil. Make several at a time and store them in the freezer after they've cooled.

Preparation time: 25 minutes / Standing time: 1½ hours
Baking time: 30 minutes / Makes: 12 servings

1 cup lukewarm water
1 tsp granulated sugar
1 pkg (1 tbsp) dry yeast
2½ to 3 cups all-purpose flour
1 tsp salt
¼ cup olive oil
½ tsp coarse salt
2 tsp dried rosemary, crumbled

1. Pour the lukewarm (110F) water into a medium-size bowl. Add the sugar and stir until dissolved. Sprinkle the yeast over top. Do not stir. Let stand for 10 minutes.

2. Meanwhile, in a large mixing bowl, stir 2 cups flour with salt. Once the yeast is foamy, stir it vigorously with a fork. Pour the yeast and 2 tablespoons olive oil into the centre of the flour mixture. Stir with a wooden spoon.

3. Using your hands, blend in ½ cup more flour. When the dough becomes stiff, turn it onto a lightly floured surface. Knead the dough, working in more flour as it becomes sticky, until the dough can be formed into a smooth satiny ball, about 10 minutes. Shape the dough into a ball and place it in a large greased bowl. Cover with a piece of

FRESH FLOURS
Store a bay leaf in your all-purpose flour to keep it insect-free. Keep large quantities in the freezer. Whole-grain flours must be stored in the refrigerator or freezer, as they go rancid quickly at room temperature.

greased waxed paper and a damp cloth. Let the dough rise in a warm place until almost doubled in bulk, about $1\frac{1}{4}$ hours.

4. Then, punch down the dough. Shape it into a ball, cover with a cloth and let stand for 15 minutes. Preheat oven to 400F. On a floured surface, roll the dough into a 12-inch circle. Place it on an ungreased baking pan. Using your fingertips, make light indentations every 3 inches. Sprinkle with the coarse salt. Drizzle with remaining oil. Sprinkle with the rosemary.

5. Bake on the bottom rack of the preheated oven for 25 to 30 minutes or until golden. Remove from the oven and let cool on a wire rack. To store, seal in clear wrap. Keeps well at room temperature for 1 to 2 days. Or wrap tightly and freeze.

PER SERVING: *131 calories, 2.7 g protein, 19 g carbohydrates, 4.8 g fat, 9.1 mg calcium, 1.3 mg iron, 0.8 g fiber.*

NIPPY CHEDDAR CHEESE BREAD

The swirls of cheddar cheese in this free-form loaf make it a marvelous bread for toasting or sandwich making. We can never resist cutting it while warm — that's when it's best with Caesar salad. Do use an orange-colored cheddar for a marbled effect.

Preparation time: 25 minutes / Standing time: $1\frac{3}{4}$ hours
Baking time: 40 to 50 minutes / Makes: 2 loaves, 9 slices per loaf

$\frac{1}{2}$ lb (250 g) orange-colored old cheddar cheese
$\frac{1}{2}$ cup lukewarm water
1 tbsp granulated sugar
1 pkg (1 tbsp) dry yeast
2 cups milk
2 tbsp butter, melted and cooled
2 eggs
1 tsp salt
6 to $6\frac{1}{2}$ cups all-purpose flour, preferably unbleached

1. Grate the cheddar. It should measure about $2\frac{1}{2}$ cups. Place the cheese in a plastic bag and freeze until ready to work into the dough. Pour the lukewarm (110F) water into a large bowl. Stir in the sugar until dissolved. Sprinkle the yeast over top but do not stir. Let stand for 10 minutes, until the yeast is foamy. Then, stir it vigorously with a fork.

2. In a medium-size bowl, whisk the milk with the butter, eggs and salt. Then, stir into the yeast mixture. Using a wooden spoon, beat 6 cups flour into the yeast mixture until well mixed. When the dough becomes stiff, turn it onto a lightly floured surface. Knead for about 10 minutes, working in remaining $\frac{1}{2}$ cup flour if necessary. When the dough is smooth and satiny, form it into a ball.

MEDITERRANEAN OLIVE SPREAD

For a superb olive spread for cheese bread or focaccia, place $\frac{1}{2}$ cup each of stuffed green and black pitted olives, 2 tablespoons drained capers and 2 chopped garlic cloves in a food processor. Whirl and slowly pour $\frac{1}{4}$ cup olive oil through the feed tube. Continue whirling until coarsely ground. Keep in a sealed jar in the refrigerator. Spread on bread or pizzas, or toss in tomato salads. It's wonderful thickly spread on Nippy Cheddar Cheese Bread. Makes 1 cup.

3. Rotate the ball in a large greased bowl until it's lightly coated with grease. Cover the bowl with greased waxed paper and a damp cloth. Let the dough rise in a warm place until almost doubled in bulk, about 1 hour.

4. Punch down the dough. Then, evenly knead in the chilled grated cheddar. Shape into 2 loaves about 6x4½ inches each. Place on a large lightly greased baking sheet. Cover with greased waxed paper and a damp cloth. Let rise until almost doubled in bulk, about 45 minutes.

5. Preheat oven to 375F. Bake the loaves in the centre of the preheated oven for about 40 to 50 minutes or until golden brown. Cool on a rack. Serve warm. Bread freezes well.

PER SLICE: *131 calories, 5.2 g protein, 17.8 g carbohydrates, 4.1 g fat, 80.5 mg calcium, 1.1 mg iron, 0.7 g fiber.*

WHOLESOME WHOLE WHEAT PITAS

As these pitas bake they magically form their own pockets. There's certainly no comparison between a freshly baked pita and the plastic-wrapped, store-bought variety.

Preparation time: 40 minutes / Standing time: 2 hours
Baking time: 8 minutes / Makes: 12 pitas

2 cups lukewarm water
1 tbsp granulated sugar
1 pkg (1 tbsp) dry yeast
3½ to 4 cups all-purpose flour
2 cups whole wheat flour
1 tsp salt
¼ cup cornmeal

1. Pour the lukewarm water (110F) into a medium-size bowl. Add the sugar and stir until dissolved. Sprinkle the yeast over top but do not stir. Let stand for 10 minutes, until the yeast is foamy.

2. Meanwhile, measure 2½ cups all-purpose flour, 2 cups whole wheat flour and 1 teaspoon salt into a large bowl. Stir with a fork until well blended. Once the yeast is foamy, stir it vigorously with a fork. Then, pour the yeast into the centre of the flour mixture and stir until mixed.

3. Then, using your hands, blend in 1 to 1½ cups more flour. When dough becomes stiff, turn onto a lightly floured surface. Knead, working in more flour as it becomes sticky, until dough can be formed into a satiny ball, about 10 minutes. Shape into a ball and place in a large greased bowl. Cover with a piece of greased waxed paper and a damp cloth. Let rise in a warm place until almost doubled in bulk, about 1 hour.

4. Then, punch down the dough and divide it into 12 sections. Shape each section into a small smooth ball. Cover with greased waxed paper and

CURRIED CHUTNEY SPREAD

For a superb spread for wholegrain bread or whole wheat pitas, stir 4 oz (125 g) whipped cream cheese with 2 tablespoons mango chutney and ¼ teaspoon curry powder. Spread in pitas, then fill the pitas with sliced chicken or shrimp, or spread on top of pumpernickel rounds and top with a large shrimp. Makes ½ cup.

a damp cloth and let stand for 5 minutes. Meanwhile, lightly grease a large baking sheet. Sprinkle with about 1 tablespoon cornmeal. Set aside.

5. On a lightly floured surface, shape each ball of dough into a 6-inch flat-topped round, making sure it is of even thickness. Set aside on a floured surface. Cover the dough with greased waxed paper and a damp cloth. Let it rise in a warm place until increased by half its size, about 50 to 60 minutes.

6. Preheat oven to 500F. Place the rounds 2 inches apart on the prepared baking sheet. Bake on the bottom rack of the preheated oven for 6 to 8 minutes or until puffed and a pale golden color. Pitas are baked when they sound hollow when lightly tapped. Cool completely on a wire rack. Repeat with remaining rounds of dough, sprinkling the baking sheet with 1 tablespoon cornmeal before each batch.

7. To store the pitas, seal tightly in clear wrap. They will keep well at room temperature for 1 to 2 days. Or seal tightly in clear wrap and freeze.

PER PITA: 206 calories, 6.7 g protein, 43.6 g carbohydrates, 0.7 g fat, 14.2 mg calcium, 2.5 mg iron, 3.8 g fiber.

HEARTY MULTIGRAIN BREAD

Our favorite healthy loaf with a good mix of natural bran, rolled oats, whole wheat flour and just a hint of molasses.

Preparation time: 20 minutes / Standing time: 2¼ hours
Baking time: 1 hour / Makes: 1 loaf, 20 slices

MULTIGRAIN

BREAD

1 cup milk
½ cup natural bran
½ cup regular rolled oats
2 tbsp each of shortening, molasses and brown sugar
2 tsp salt
1 cup lukewarm water
1 tsp granulated sugar
1 pkg (1 tbsp) dry yeast
1½ cups whole wheat flour
2 to 2½ cups all-purpose flour

1. Heat the milk almost to boiling. Meanwhile, measure the bran, rolled oats, shortening, molasses, brown sugar and salt into a large mixing bowl. Add the hot milk and stir until the shortening is dissolved. Set the oat mixture aside to cool to room temperature.

2. Meanwhile, pour 1 cup lukewarm (110F) water into a small bowl. Stir in 1 teaspoon granulated sugar until dissolved. Sprinkle the yeast over top but do not stir. Let stand for 10 minutes, until the yeast is foamy. Then, stir it vigorously with a fork. Stir into the oat mixture.

3. Using a wooden spoon, beat in the whole wheat flour until well mixed. Start working in the all-purpose flour. When the dough becomes stiff, turn it out onto a floured surface. Knead for about 10 minutes, working in more flour as the dough becomes sticky. When the dough is smooth and satiny, form it into a ball.

4. Rotate the dough in a large greased bowl until it's lightly coated with grease. Cover with greased waxed paper and a damp cloth. Let dough rise in a warm place until almost doubled in bulk, about 1¼ hours.

5. Punch down the dough. Shape it into a large oval or round loaf no more than 2 inches high and place it on a greased baking sheet. Cover the dough with greased waxed paper and a damp cloth. Let it rise until almost doubled in bulk, about 1 hour.

6. Preheat oven to 375F. Bake in the centre of the preheated oven at 375F for 15 minutes. Reduce the oven temperature to 350F and continue baking for 45 more minutes or until the bread sounds hollow when lightly tapped. Cool on a rack. The bread will keep well in the refrigerator for 2 to 3 days and also freezes well.

PER SLICE: 138 calories, 4.5 g protein, 26.7 g carbohydrates, 2.5 g fat, 35.4 mg calcium, 1.7 mg iron, 2.6 g fiber.

STICKY PECAN-CINNAMON BUNS

Sticky, gooey and irresistible! Make these buns the night before to the point of second rising, then refrigerate. Take them out as soon as you get up in the morning so they'll rise before baking. For a festive touch, soak raisins in rum or brandy before adding.

Preparation time: 30 minutes / Standing time: 1¾ hours

Baking time: 40 minutes / Makes: 12 buns

½ cup milk
¼ cup granulated sugar
½ tsp salt
⅓ cup unsalted butter, at room temperature
½ cup lukewarm water
1 tsp granulated sugar
1 pkg (1 tbsp) dry yeast
1 egg
2¾ to 3 cups all-purpose flour
⅓ cup unsalted butter, melted
⅔ cup light brown sugar
1 tsp cinnamon
½ cup finely chopped pecans or almonds
¼ cup raisins
½ cup chopped mixed candied fruit

1. Heat the milk in a saucepan until bubbles appear around the edges of the pan. Remove the milk from the heat and stir in $\frac{1}{4}$ cup sugar, salt and $\frac{1}{3}$ cup butter. Stir until the butter melts. Set aside and cool until lukewarm.

2. Then, pour the lukewarm (110F) water into a bowl. Stir in 1 teaspoon sugar until dissolved. Sprinkle the yeast over top but do not stir. Let stand for 10 minutes or until the yeast is foamy. Then, stir it vigorously with a fork and add to the lukewarm milk along with the egg. Beat by hand or with an electric mixer until blended.

3. Then, gradually beat in 2 cups flour. Using a wooden spoon, gradually stir in an additional $\frac{3}{4}$ cup flour. As soon as the dough is stiff, turn it out onto a floured surface. Knead for 8 to 10 minutes, working in more flour as the dough becomes sticky, until it feels smooth and satiny. Shape the dough into a smooth ball and place it in a large greased bowl. Cover with greased waxed paper and a damp cloth. Let the dough rise in a warm place until almost doubled in bulk, about 1 hour.

4. Then, punch down the dough and roll it into an 18x10-inch rectangle on a floured surface. Brush with 2 tablespoons melted butter. Stir in $\frac{1}{3}$ cup brown sugar with the cinnamon and $\frac{1}{4}$ cup finely chopped nuts. Evenly sprinkle over the dough. Starting at the 18-inch side of the dough, roll up tightly in a jelly-roll fashion. Cut the dough crosswise, into 12 slices.

5. Stir remaining $\frac{1}{4}$ cup melted butter with $\frac{1}{3}$ cup brown sugar. Evenly spread over the bottom of a deep 9-inch cake pan or springform pan. Scatter remaining $\frac{1}{4}$ cup chopped nuts over top with the raisins and chopped mixed candied fruit. Place the dough slices cut-side down in the pan. Gently press down. Cover the pan with greased waxed paper and a damp cloth. Let the dough sit at room temperature for about 45 minutes or until almost doubled in bulk.

6. Preheat oven to 375F. Bake the buns in the centre of the preheated oven for 35 to 40 minutes, until the buns are golden on top and the bread sounds hollow when lightly tapped. Immediately run a knife around the edge of the pan and invert the buns onto a large serving plate. Cool before serving.

PER BUN: *238 calories, 3.9 g protein, 33.3 g carbohydrates, 10.5 g fat, 38.3 mg calcium, 1.6 mg iron, 1.2 g fiber.*

SPEEDY SOFT BUTTER

When a recipe calls for room-temperature or softened butter, remove foil wrapping and place the cold butter in a microwave-safe dish. For every $\frac{1}{2}$ cup butter, microwave on defrost for 45 seconds to 1 minute.

STICKY BUN

Fast Breads, Biscuits, Big-Batch Muffins

If you have a measuring cup, you can make perfect quick breads and muffins. They couldn't be more straightforward: Mix the dry ingredients — flour, sugar, spices — in one bowl, and combine the liquid ingredients — milk and eggs — in another. And since the secret is to not overmix, stir together just until blended. Our fast homebakes include Old-Fashioned Tangy Lemon Loaf, 12-Minute Yogurt Biscuits and Bake-Anytime Refrigerator Bran Muffins.

12-Minute Yogurt Biscuits

We used to make these easy biscuits with heavy cream. To our delight we found that yogurt gives a refreshing tang and lighter texture without losing the appealing creaminess.

Preparation time: 10 minutes / Baking time: 15 minutes

Makes: 16 to 20 biscuits

$2\frac{1}{4}$ cups all-purpose flour
$\frac{1}{2}$ tsp salt
2 tsp baking powder
$\frac{1}{2}$ tsp baking soda
$\frac{1}{4}$ cup shortening
$1\frac{1}{4}$ cups Balkan-style yogurt

1. Preheat oven to 425F. Measure the dry ingredients into a large bowl. Stir with a fork until blended. Add the shortening and cut it in with 2 knives or a pastry blender until crumbly. Stir in the yogurt until the dough can be gathered into a ball.

2. Place the dough on a lightly floured surface. Knead gently 8 times. Pat to $\frac{1}{2}$-inch thickness. Cut out biscuits with a 2-inch floured cookie cutter and place them on an ungreased baking sheet. Bake in the centre of the preheated oven for 12 to 15 minutes.

Per biscuit: 78 calories, 1.8 g protein, 10.6 g carbohydrates, 3.2 g fat, 25.2 mg calcium, 0.6 mg iron, 0.4 g fiber.

Rising to the Occasion

If baking powder picks up moisture from the air, it loses leavening power. To test before using, mix 1 teaspoon in $\frac{1}{2}$ cup water. If it bubbles furiously, the baking powder is still active and will make your loaves rise.

OLD-FASHIONED TANGY LEMON LOAF

We make this new version of our favorite quick bread with cake and pastry flour for extra lightness. In the summer we love it chilled and thinly sliced with tea.

Preparation time: 20 minutes / Baking time: 60 minutes
Makes: 1 loaf, 16 slices

1¾ cups cake and pastry flour*
1 tsp baking powder
½ tsp salt
½ tsp ground cardamom (optional)
1 large lemon
¼ cup granulated sugar
½ cup unsalted butter, at room temperature
1 cup granulated sugar
2 eggs
⅔ cup milk
½ tsp vanilla

1. Preheat oven to 350F. Thoroughly grease a 9x5x3-inch loaf pan or two 7x4x2-inch pans. Fit a piece of waxed paper into the bottom and grease. Measure the flour, baking powder, salt and cardamom, if using, into a medium-size bowl. Stir together with a fork until well blended. Finely grate the peel from the lemon and stir it into the flour mixture. Set aside. Squeeze out 3 tablespoons lemon juice and stir with ¼ cup sugar. Set aside to use as a glaze.

2. Place the butter and 1 cup sugar in a medium-size mixing bowl. Beat with an electric mixer at medium speed until creamy. Beat in the eggs. Then, gradually beat in one-third of the flour mixture, followed by ⅓ cup milk. Repeat additions, ending with remaining third of flour mixture. Beat in the vanilla. Pour into the prepared loaf pan. Bake in the centre of the preheated oven for 55 to 60 minutes or until a cake tester inserted in the centre of the loaf to the bottom of pan comes out clean.

3. Remove the loaf from the oven, leave it in the pan and place the pan on a rack. Immediately drizzle half of the lemon mixture over the top of the hot loaf. Let sit 10 minutes, then drizzle with remaining lemon mixture. Let sit another 10 minutes, then turn the loaf out of the pan and finish cooling it on the rack. If not serving right away, wrap in heavy foil and freeze. It will keep well for at least 5 to 6 months.

*You can also use 1⅔ cups all-purpose flour in place of the cake and pastry flour but the loaf won't be as light.

PER SLICE: 169 calories, 2.2 g protein, 25.2 g carbohydrates, 6.9 g fat, 23.4 mg calcium, 1 mg iron, 0.3 g fiber.

THE RIGHT MIX FOR FAST BREADS

Measure the dry ingredients into a large bowl. Loaf recipes used to call for sifting the dry ingredients, but we've eliminated that step and simply stir the ingredients with a fork until the flour and baking powder are well blended. A few minutes is enough.

Measure the liquid ingredients into another bowl and whisk or beat them with a fork until mixed. Pour them into the dry ingredients and immediately add the nuts and fruit called for. Stir only until all the dry ingredients are moistened. (A spatula works well.) Immediately pour the batter into the greased pan. If the top of the batter is lumpy, gently smooth it with a spatula.

COMPANY'S COMING CORN BREAD

Corn bread is making a comeback. Many of us grew up calling it Johnnycake, eating it drizzled with maple syrup. Today, it's a more interesting alternative to dinner rolls and a sturdy companion to chili, stews and soups. We've also included buttermilk, hot chili and cheddar, and jalapeno pepper versions.

Preparation time: 10 minutes / Baking time: 40 minutes

Makes: Sixteen 2-inch squares

$\frac{1}{2}$ cup butter, at room temperature
$\frac{1}{4}$ cup granulated sugar
1 egg
$1\frac{1}{2}$ cups milk
1 cup all-purpose flour
1 cup cornmeal
$2\frac{1}{2}$ tsp baking powder
$\frac{1}{2}$ tsp salt

1. Preheat oven to 350F. Grease an 8-inch square or round pan. Beat or stir the butter with the sugar and egg until creamy. Gradually stir in the milk. In a large bowl, use a fork to blend the flour with the cornmeal, baking powder and salt until well mixed.

2. Make a well in the centre of the dry ingredients. Add the liquid ingredients and stir just until mixed. Turn the batter into the greased pan. Bake in the centre of the preheated oven for 35 to 40 minutes, until the bread springs back when lightly touched in the centre.

VARIATIONS

Buttermilk
Use buttermilk in place of milk. Reduce the baking powder to 1 teaspoon and add 1 teaspoon baking soda to dry ingredients.

Hot Chili
Stir $\frac{1}{2}$ teaspoon crushed dried chilies and $\frac{1}{2}$ cup grated old cheddar cheese into the flour mixture. Stir until well mixed.

Jalapeno Plus
Stir 1 tablespoon finely chopped canned jalapeno peppers into the flour mixture.

PER SQUARE: *136 calories, 2.7 g protein, 16.5 g carbohydrates, 6.7 g fat, 42.1 mg calcium, 0.8 mg iron, 0.6 g fiber.*

BAKING FAST BREADS

Bake in the centre of a preheated 350F oven for 1 to $1\frac{1}{4}$ hours or until the crust is golden, a large crack has opened down the centre and a thin knife inserted to the bottom of the loaf comes out clean.

Remove the pan from the oven, and place it on a rack to cool for about 5 minutes. Then, run a knife around the inside edges of the pan to loosen loaf and turn the pan upside down on a flat surface. Quickly turn the loaf right-side up again on the rack. Don't cover or cut until it's cool, about 2 hours.

Light 'n' Lemony Zucchini Bread

Flecks of zucchini moisten this afternoon tea bread and lemon adds zest.

Preparation time: 15 minutes / Baking time: 60 minutes
Makes: 1 loaf, 16 slices

2 medium-size zucchini
1 lemon
1 cup whole wheat flour
1 cup all-purpose flour
2 tsp baking powder
$\frac{1}{2}$ tsp baking soda
$\frac{1}{2}$ tsp salt
$\frac{1}{4}$ tsp cinnamon
Pinch of allspice
$\frac{3}{4}$ cup brown sugar
1 egg
$\frac{1}{2}$ cup milk
$\frac{1}{2}$ cup vegetable oil
$\frac{1}{2}$ cup chopped nuts

1. Preheat oven to 350F. Grease a 9x5x3-inch loaf pan. Grate the unpeeled zucchini on a medium grater or in a food processor. Place the zucchini in a kitchen cloth and wring out all the moisture. Dry the zucchini on paper towels and measure out 1½ cups. Finely grate the lemon peel and squeeze out the juice from the lemon.

2. Measure all the dry ingredients into a large bowl. Stir with a fork until well blended. Beat the egg with the milk, oil and 2 tablespoons lemon juice. Pour into the centre of the flour mixture. Immediately add the zucchini, lemon peel and nuts and stir with a fork only until the dry ingredients are moistened. The batter will be very thick. Turn it into the prepared pan. Smooth the top and bake in the centre of the preheated oven for 55 to 60 minutes.

3. Remove the pan from the oven and set it on a rack to cool for 5 to 10 minutes. Then, run the edge of a knife around the inside edges of the pan to loosen the bread. Turn the bread out of the pan and place it on the rack to cool completely before slicing.

4. Once cooled, seal the loaf in clear wrap or foil and refrigerate. The flavor is actually better after a day's refrigeration.

PER SLICE: *187 calories, 3.2 g protein, 23 g carbohydrates, 9.8 g fat, 38.5 mg calcium, 1.2 mg iron, 1.6 g fiber.*

SPEEDY SOFT BROWN SUGAR

If your brown sugar has hardened, place about 1 cup brown sugar in a microwave-safe dish along with a slice of fresh bread. Microwave, uncovered, on high for 20 to 40 seconds.

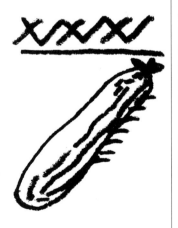

ZUCCHINI

BAKE-ANYTIME REFRIGERATOR BRAN MUFFINS

This is an amazing recipe. Make up this big batch, store the batter in the fridge for up to six weeks, then bake whenever you crave hot muffins. We've cut the sugar considerably since the first time we made them in the early '80s, but we continue to marvel at how good and moist they are. Just before baking, we sometimes add chunks of chocolate, tart cranberries, cubes of apple, orange zest, rum-soaked candied fruit or slivers of crystallized ginger to the batter.

Preparation time: 10 minutes / Baking time: 20 minutes

Makes: 3 dozen muffins

5 cups whole wheat or all-purpose flour
2 tbsp baking soda
1 tbsp salt
1 tsp cinnamon
1 tsp mace (optional)
1¾ cups brown sugar
3 cups natural bran
3 cups all-bran cereal
2 cups raisins or a mix of chopped dates, dried apricots
    and nuts
3 eggs
1 cup vegetable oil
¼ cup molasses
4 cups (1L) buttermilk
1½ cups water

1. Measure the flour, soda, salt, cinnamon, mace, brown sugar, bran, bran cereal and raisins into a very large bowl. Stir together with a fork until well blended.

2. In a medium-size bowl, whisk the eggs with the oil and molasses. Beat in the buttermilk and water. Pour the egg mixture into the dry ingredients and stir just until blended. Bake right away or cover tightly and keep refrigerated for up to 6 weeks.

3. To bake, preheat oven to 400F. Grease muffin tins or use paper liners. Since these muffins rise very little, fill the tins almost to the top with the cold or room-temperature batter. Bake in the preheated 400F oven for 20 minutes.

PER MUFFIN: *220 calories, 5.3 g protein, 39.5 g carbohydrates, 7.3 g fat, 51.9 mg calcium, 3 mg iron, 5.3 g fiber.*

EASY WHOLE WHEAT LOAF

Measure 1½ cups each of all-purpose and whole wheat flour into a large bowl. Add ⅓ cup brown sugar, 2½ teaspoons baking powder and ½ teaspoon each of baking soda and salt. Stir with a fork until blended. Then, whisk 1⅔ cups milk with ¼ cup melted butter and 1 egg. Pour into the flour mixture and stir until blended. Pour into a greased 9x5x3-inch pan. Bake at 350F for 60 to 65 minutes.

FESTIVE AMARETTO FRUIT BREAD

An impressive loaf studded with jewel-like candied cherries, glistening pineapple and spiked with amaretto. It's a glorious holiday alternative to heavy fruitcake and a fraction of the work.

Preparation time: 20 minutes / Baking time: 1¼ hours

Makes: 1 loaf, 16 slices

1¾ cups all-purpose flour
1 tbsp baking powder
½ tsp salt
⅔ cup granulated sugar
1 egg
¼ cup vegetable oil
1 cup milk
3 tbsp amaretto liqueur or milk
1 tsp almond flavoring
½ cup coarsely chopped candied cherries
½ cup coarsely chopped glazed pineapple
½ cup chopped mixed peel
½ cup toasted slivered almonds

1. Preheat oven to 350F. Grease a 9x5x3-inch loaf pan. Measure all the dry ingredients into a large bowl. Stir with a fork until well blended.

2. Beat the liquid ingredients together, then pour them into the centre of the flour mixture. Immediately add the fruits, mixed peel and nuts and stir only until all the dry ingredients are moistened. The batter will be lumpy. Turn it into the prepared pan.

3. Bake in the preheated oven for 1 hour and 5 minutes to 1¼ hours, or until a thin knife inserted in the centre of the bread to the bottom of the pan comes out clean, except for a bit of fruit on it.

PER SLICE: 195 calories, 3 g protein, 31.6 g carbohydrates, 6 g fat, 42.8 mg calcium, 0.8 mg iron, 0.8 g fiber.

SAVE-AND-STORE PEELS

Save orange, lemon or lime peels to use in baking. Grate peel finely and place ¼ cup of it in a small microwave-safe dish. Spread the peel out evenly. Microwave on high 15 to 30 seconds, stirring once. Store the dried peel in an airtight container in the refrigerator or freezer.

PHOTO: Festive Amaretto Fruit Bread, see recipe at right. Overleaf: Unbelievably Decadent Chocolate Cake, see recipe on page 237.

FESTIVE

PERFECT ENDINGS

For many of us a meal isn't quite complete without a little taste of something sweet. Be it as refreshing and light as a mélange of brightly colored fresh berries cascading from crisp white meringue, as rich and seductive as a chocolate cake brimming with toasted hazelnuts, or as comforting and old-fashioned as Grandma's fresh peaches 'n' cream pie — for everyone there's a just dessert. Of course, we've included lots of easy yet elegant ideas — from a no-cook Italian party trifle to a no-fuss Chocolate Pound Cake, a gingery apple flan and Swirled Cheesecake Brownies, as well as the country's best recipes for butter tarts and Nanaimo bars. What would a Canadian cookbook be without them?

PERFECT ENDINGS · TRIPLE TESTED

COMFORTING CLASSICS

In the '80s we had our fill of fancy restaurant creations that looked far better than they tasted. Now the natural swing of the pendulum turns our attention back to simpler homey desserts — fresh fruit pies, peach upside-down cakes and old-fashioned pudding cakes — the treats our mothers used to make. When we work with these recipes in the test kitchen today, we start by cutting the sugar and trimming back the butter and cream. We've definitely slashed the calories, but all the satisfying taste is still there.

PRIME-TIME PEACHES

Brandied Peaches

Peel, halve and remove the stones from 2 peaches. Place the peaches hollow-side up in an ovenproof dish. Sprinkle with 2 teaspoons brown sugar and 4 teaspoons brandy. Broil until hot, about 3 minutes. Dollop with sour cream. Serves 2 to 4.

Easy Flambé

Sauté 2 peeled sliced peaches in 1 tablespoon butter in a small frying pan over medium heat for 3 minutes. Sprinkle with 1 teaspoon brown sugar and a pinch of allspice. Add 3 tablespoons rum. Flambé. Spoon over ice cream. Serves 4.

FRESH PEACHES 'N' CREAM PIE

There's nothing better than a country-fresh peach pie. A touch of cream and lemon zest heighten its naturally good taste.

Preparation time: 25 minutes / Baking time: 1 hour
Makes: 10 to 12 servings

$^3/_4$ cup sour cream
$^1/_4$ cup all-purpose flour
$^1/_2$ cup granulated sugar
1 tsp finely grated lemon peel
1 cup all-purpose flour
$^1/_2$ cup light brown sugar
$^1/_3$ cup butter
6 medium-size peaches
9-inch unbaked pie shell

1. Preheat oven to 350F. Prepare the filling by beating together the sour cream, $^1/_4$ cup flour, granulated sugar and lemon peel until smooth. Prepare the topping by blending 1 cup flour with the brown sugar. Cut in the butter with 2 knives or a fork until crumbly. Set aside.

2. Peel the peaches. Cut them into eighths and arrange them in the bottom of the pastry. Stir the filling and pour it over the peaches. Sprinkle the topping evenly over the filling. Place the pie on a baking sheet, to catch any spills, and bake on the bottom rack of the preheated oven for 1 hour or until the peaches are fork-tender. Let the pie cool for at least 15 minutes before cutting.

PER SERVING: 333 calories, 3.6 g protein, 45.6 g carbohydrates, 15.7 g fat, 36.3 mg calcium, 1.6 mg iron, 1.5 g fiber.

CHOCOLATE POUND CAKE

This is the best pound cake we've ever created — absolutely irresistible with a mix of ripe berries and Amazing Whipped Cream.

Preparation time: 20 minutes / Baking time: 50 minutes

Makes: 9 slices

3 (1-oz/28-g) squares bittersweet or semisweet chocolate
1½ cups all-purpose flour
2 tbsp cocoa
½ tsp baking powder
¼ tsp salt
1 cup butter, at room temperature
1 cup granulated sugar
3 eggs
1 tsp vanilla

1. Preheat oven to 325F. Grease a 9x5x3-inch loaf pan. Melt the chocolate in the top of a double boiler or in the microwave (see page 234). Measure the flour, cocoa, baking powder and salt into a small bowl. Stir well with a fork until all the ingredients are evenly distributed.

2. In a large mixing bowl, beat the butter until creamy. Add the sugar and beat until light and fluffy. Beat in the eggs, 1 at a time, beating well after each addition. Beat in the vanilla, then the melted chocolate. Scrape down the sides of the bowl occasionally. Stir in the flour mixture all at once, beating just until moistened.

3. Pour the batter into the prepared pan. Smooth the top and bake in the centre of the preheated oven until a cake tester inserted in centre of the cake comes out clean, about 50 minutes. Cool the cake in the pan set on a rack for 10 minutes. Then invert it onto the rack and cool completely.

PER SERVING: *400 calories, 4.9 g protein, 40.1 g carbohydrates, 25.9 g fat, 37.2 mg calcium, 1.5 mg iron, 0.4 g fiber.*

AMAZING WHIPPED CREAM

Whipped cream was never lighter or more flavorful than this easy version. Use to dress up any combination of fresh fruits or spoon over warm fruit crisps.

In a small bowl, whip 1 cup whipping cream with ¼ cup sugar until it will hold peaks when the beaters are lifted. Fold in ⅔ cup 2% yogurt and 1 teaspoon vanilla or 2 tablespoons coffee or orange liqueur, rum or cognac. Wonderful with chocolate cake too!

AMAZING
WHIPPED
CREAM

BROWNIE

SWIRLED CHEESECAKE BROWNIES

Creamy cheesecake swirls its way through moist, dark brownies. For more glamour, add candied cherries soaked in dark rum or brandy, or a teaspoon or two of orange zest and some toasted chopped almonds.

Preparation time: 20 minutes / Baking time: 40 minutes

Makes: 25 squares

¾ cup all-purpose flour
¼ tsp salt
1 cup granulated sugar
3 (1-oz/28-g) squares unsweetened chocolate
¼ cup shortening
¼ cup butter, at room temperature
2 eggs
1 tsp vanilla
4-oz (125-g) pkg cream cheese
1 egg
½ cup granulated sugar
2 tbsp all-purpose flour
½ cup drained maraschino or candied cherries,
    chopped (optional)

1. Preheat oven to 325F. Lightly grease an 8-inch square baking pan. Measure ¾ cup flour, the salt and 1 cup sugar into a large bowl. Stir with a fork until blended.

2. Melt the chocolate in a microwave or place it in the top of a double boiler over simmering water and heat until melted (see page 234). Meanwhile, measure the shortening, butter, 2 eggs and vanilla into a mixing bowl. Beat with an electric mixer until smooth. Then, beat in the melted chocolate. Stir in the flour mixture until well mixed. Pour two-thirds of the batter into the prepared pan. Set aside.

3. Then, place the cream cheese and 1 egg in a small mixing bowl. Beat together with an electric mixer until light and fluffy. Blend ½ cup sugar and 2 tablespoons flour together and gradually blend into the cream cheese mixture. Fold in the cherries, if using. Pour the mixture over the chocolate base. Gently spoon remaining chocolate batter on top to completely cover the cheese mixture. Draw a spatula or knife back and forth through the layers to give a marbled effect.

4. Place the pan in the preheated oven and bake for 35 to 40 minutes. Cool in the pan on a rack. Cut into 25 squares and refrigerate.

PER SERVING: *136 calories, 1.9 g protein, 15.9 g carbohydrates, 8.1 g fat, 11.1 mg calcium, 0.6 mg iron, 0.1 g fiber.*

COUNTRY PEACH UPSIDE-DOWN CAKE

Fresh slices of sweet peaches form a glazed pinwheel atop a simple old-fashioned butter cake. Serve warm with vanilla ice cream.

Preparation time: 25 minutes / Baking time: 40 minutes

Makes: 10 to 12 servings

2 tbsp butter
3 tbsp granulated sugar
3 to 4 ripe peaches
1 cup all-purpose flour
1½ tsp baking powder
¼ tsp cinnamon
¼ tsp salt
⅓ cup butter
½ cup granulated sugar
1 egg
⅛ tsp almond extract
⅛ tsp vanilla
¼ cup milk

1. Preheat oven to 350F. Place 2 tablespoons butter in a deep 9-inch round cake pan. Then place the pan in the warm oven just until the butter is melted. Brush the sides of the pan with this butter. Stir 3 tablespoons sugar into remaining butter in the bottom of the pan until the sugar is dissolved. Move the pan until the bottom is evenly covered.

2. Peel the peaches and thinly slice. Arrange them in a circular pattern in the butter-sugar mixture.

3. Prepare the batter by first combining the flour, baking powder, cinnamon and salt together. Stir with a fork until blended. Set aside.

4. In a large mixing bowl, beat ⅓ cup butter until creamy. Gradually beat in ½ cup sugar until the mixture is light and fluffy. Beat in the egg, then the flavorings. Gradually beat in one-third of the flour mixture, then half the milk. Repeat additions, ending with remaining flour mixture. Spoon evenly over the peaches. Then, smooth the top.

5. Bake in the centre of the preheated oven for 35 to 40 minutes or until the cake springs back when lightly touched. Remove from the oven and let stand in the pan for just 5 minutes. Then, invert the cake onto a large cake plate. This cake is excellent served warm.

PER SERVING: 156 calories, 1.9 g protein, 21.2 g carbohydrates, 7.6 g fat, 20.9 mg calcium, 0.5 mg iron, 0.5 g fiber.

AN APPLE A DAY

Hot, wholesome ways with that recommended apple a day.

Nutty Baked Apples
Stir ¼ cup raisins with 2 tablespoons each of chopped nuts and butter and a dash of vanilla. Stuff into 2 cored apples. Bake, uncovered, at 350F for 30 minutes, or microwave, covered, on high for 6 minutes.

Old-Fashioned Sauce
Peel, core and thinly slice 6 apples. Combine in a saucepan with ¼ cup each of water and brown sugar. Cook over medium heat, stirring often until tender. Add ½ teaspoon vanilla and purée. Makes 3 cups.

Terrific Turnovers
Toss 2 peeled, cored and finely diced apples with 2 teaspoons freshly squeezed lemon juice and 1 teaspoon brown sugar. Use as a filling for 1 package of refrigerator crescent dinner rolls. Fold into a turnover shape. Seal the edge. Bake according to package directions. Makes 8.

CHOCOLATE-ZUCCHINI CAKE

We always test our *Chatelaine* recipes at least three times! One of our test kitchen assistants found this cake so irresistible she couldn't confine herself to tiny taste bites and wound up gaining seven pounds during the two weeks we perfected this recipe.

Preparation time: 30 minutes / Baking time: 45 minutes

Makes: 20 servings

3 medium-size zucchini
$\frac{1}{2}$ cup raisins
$\frac{1}{2}$ cup chopped nuts
$2\frac{1}{2}$ cups all-purpose flour
$1\frac{1}{2}$ tsp baking powder
1 tsp baking soda
1 tsp each of cinnamon and salt
$\frac{1}{4}$ tsp ground nutmeg
4 (1-oz/28-g) squares semisweet chocolate
1 cup granulated sugar
4 eggs
$\frac{1}{2}$ cup vegetable oil
$1\frac{1}{2}$ tsp vanilla
1 cup milk
1 tbsp vinegar or freshly squeezed lemon juice

1. Preheat oven to 350F. Grease a 9x13-inch baking dish. Grate the unpeeled zucchini, using a food processor fitted with a grating attachment or the medium side of a grater. Measure out $2\frac{1}{2}$ cups grated zucchini and place it in a kitchen cloth. Gently wring out as much moisture as possible, then place the grated zucchini in a bowl. Stir the raisins and chopped nuts with the grated zucchini, then set the mixture aside while preparing the flour mixture.

2. Measure the flour, baking powder, baking soda, cinnamon, salt and nutmeg into a small bowl. Stir the mixture with a fork until blended. Set the mixture aside. Melt the chocolate in the top of a double boiler over simmering water, or in a microwave (see page 234).

3. Place the sugar, eggs and oil in a large mixing bowl. Beat with an electric mixer at medium speed for about 2 minutes, until slightly frothy. Reduce speed to low and gradually beat in the melted chocolate, then the vanilla. Pour milk into a measuring cup, then stir the vinegar into the milk.

4. Beat one-third of the dry ingredients into the egg mixture, followed by half of the milk-and-vinegar mixture. Repeat the process, beating the mixture briefly after each addition, ending with the flour mixture. The

NO-FLOP CAKE FIXES

• If a cake won't turn out after you've run a knife around the edges of the pan, return it to a warm oven for 1 to 2 minutes. Then, turn it out immediately.

• If a cake sinks in the centre, fill it with fresh fruit and frost the sides, or patch the centre with frosting or whipped cream.

• If a cake bulges too much in the centre, just slice off the top and frost.

• If the cake is dry, slice it in half horizontally and brush with a liqueur or concentrated orange juice. It can also be cut into pieces and used to make trifle or bread pudding.

batter is very thick, so you should stir in the last part of the dry ingredients with a wooden spoon. Stir the mixture just until no streaks of flour remain. Add the zucchini mixture and stir until well distributed.

5. Pour the chocolate-zucchini mixture into the prepared baking dish. Bake in the centre of the preheated oven until the cake springs back when lightly touched in the centre, about 40 to 45 minutes. Leave the cake in the pan and place it on a rack to cool. The cake is very moist and keeps well when stored in the refrigerator. It may also be frozen.

PER SERVING: 221 calories, 4.3 g protein, 29 g carbohydrates, 10.8 g fat, 38.4 mg calcium, 1.3 mg iron, 1.0 g fiber.

GIANT OATMEAL COOKIES

Dad's favorite cookie. Our version is so easy, it's a great way to introduce kids to baking. Forget the electric mixer, it makes the batter tough — just stick to the old-fashioned wooden spoon.

Preparation time: 20 minutes / Baking time: 15 minutes

Makes: 13 cookies

1 cup all-purpose or whole wheat flour
½ tsp each of baking soda and salt
¼ tsp cinnamon
¾ cup unsalted butter, at room temperature
½ cup brown sugar
½ cup granulated sugar
1 egg
2 tbsp milk or water
1 tsp vanilla
2 cups quick-cooking oatmeal (not instant)
½ cup raisins, chocolate chips or chopped nuts (optional)

1. Preheat oven to 325F. Grease 2 cookie sheets and set aside. Prepare the dry ingredients by measuring first the flour, then the baking soda, salt and cinnamon into a large bowl. Stir together with a fork until well blended.

2. Then, place the butter in a large bowl. Stir, preferably with a wooden spoon, until creamy. Gradually stir in the sugars. Then, add the egg, milk and vanilla. Stir vigorously until well mixed. Gradually stir in the flour mixture until combined. Stir in the oatmeal, then raisins, chocolate chips or nuts, if using.

3. Form giant cookies by placing ¼ cup dough on the cookie sheet. Wet your hands and press the dough into a 4- or 5-inch round, ¼ to ⅓ inch thick. Place the next mound of dough at least 4 inches from this one and repeat.

OATMEAL COOKIES

4. Bake in the centre of the preheated oven for 12 to 15 minutes, until the edges are a light golden color but the centre is still soft. Remove to a rack to cool.

PER SERVING: 241 calories, 3.6 g protein, 30.9 g carbohydrates, 11.9 g fat, 24 mg calcium, 1.3 mg iron, 0.8 g fiber.

A TRIO OF SHORTBREADS

I never understood why people loved shortbread so much until I bit into the buttery, melt-in-your-mouth wedges made by my neighbor Alasdair's Scottish mother. Here's the closest we can come to Mrs. Hogg's basic recipe, plus a trio of stir-ins.

Preparation time: 20 minutes / Refrigeration time: 1 hour
Baking time: 20 minutes / Makes: 4 dozen cookies

BASIC RECIPE
$1\frac{1}{2}$ cups unsalted butter, at room temperature
3 cups cake and pastry flour
$\frac{1}{2}$ cup rice flour
$\frac{1}{2}$ cup fruit or powdered sugar

VARIATIONS
1 tsp finely grated orange peel
Whole unblanched almonds
1 tsp finely grated lemon peel
$\frac{1}{2}$ tsp ground cardamom
$\frac{1}{2}$ cup toasted desiccated coconut

1. Prepare the basic dough by placing the butter in a mixing bowl. Beat with a wooden spoon until very creamy. Measure the flours and sugar into a separate bowl. Stir together with a fork until well mixed. Very gradually beat the flour mixture into the butter mixture until thoroughly combined.

2. Add the variations at this point, if you wish, following the directions below, or roll the dough into a ball, cover and refrigerate until firm enough to roll out easily, about 1 hour. Then, preheat oven to 300F. Roll the dough to a $\frac{1}{4}$-inch thickness and cut into desired shapes.

3. Bake the cookies on an ungreased baking sheet in the centre of the preheated oven for 18 to 20 minutes, depending on the size of the cookies, until they are a pale beige color. Leave on the sheets for 5 minutes before removing and cooling. Store in a tightly covered container in a cool place or in the refrigerator.

RICE FLOUR
Rice flour is a fine, powdery flour made from regular white rice. It gives the characteristic texture to shortbread cookies.

POWDERED SUGAR
Powdered or confectioners' sugar is granulated sugar crushed into a fine powder with a small amount of cornstarch added to prevent clumping.

VARIATIONS

To make the variations, divide the dough into thirds and place each portion in a separate bowl. Stir in the additions that follow.

Almond and Orange

Stir 1 teaspoon grated orange peel into one-third of the dough. Cover and refrigerate for 1 hour. Then, roll into small 1-inch balls. Place on an ungreased baking sheet. Flatten slightly with a fork and press a whole unblanched almond into each centre. Bake according to directions in step 3 above.

Cardamom and Lemon

Stir 1 teaspoon grated lemon peel and ½ teaspoon ground cardamom into one-third of the dough. Cover and refrigerate for 1 hour. Place the dough on a lightly floured board. Using a lightly floured rolling pin, roll the dough out to a ¼-inch thickness. Cut shapes with a floured cookie cutter or round metal rings, or use a sharp knife for free-form shapes. Place the cookies on an ungreased baking sheet and bake according to directions in step 3 above.

Coconut

Stir ½ cup toasted desiccated coconut into one-third of the dough. Cover and refrigerate for 1 hour. Then, roll out and bake according to directions for the Cardamom and Lemon variation above.

PER SERVING: *85 calories, 0.7 g protein, 7.7 g carbohydrates, 5.8 g fat, 2.8 mg calcium, 0.5 mg iron, 0.2 g fiber.*

THE COOKIE JAR

Store crisp cookies in a separate container from soft cookies to maintain the different textures. Crisp cookies should be stored in a container with a loose cover in a cool, dry place. To recrisp, put in a warm oven for about 5 minutes. Store soft cookies in an airtight container with a piece of apple or bread.

SHORTBREAD

SAUCY WAYS WITH RHUBARB

Savor the tangy taste of rhubarb year-round — fresh from the garden or frozen.

Rhubarb Applesauce

Heat 3 cups peeled sliced apples, ⅓ cup granulated sugar and 1 cup chopped rhubarb over medium heat until the apples are soft, about 15 minutes. Stir often. Makes 1½ cups.

Raspberry-Rhubarb Compote

Heat 2 cups sliced rhubarb with ⅓ cup granulated sugar over medium heat for 5 minutes. Stir often. Then, stir in an 11-oz (340-g) package of unsweetened frozen raspberries and a dash of vanilla. Heat through. Makes 2 cups.

Tangy Rhubarb Crisp

Stir 2 cups sliced rhubarb into your favorite apple crisp filling.

Easy Rhubarb Fool

Whip ½ cup whipping cream. Fold in 2 cups cold stewed rhubarb. Makes 2 cups.

Stewed Rhubarb

Heat 4 cups sliced rhubarb with ⅔ cup granulated sugar over medium heat until tender, about 15 minutes. Stir often. Makes 2 cups.

Ruby Rhubarb Cherry Pie

Stir 1 cup coarsely chopped rhubarb into a 19-oz (540-mL) can of cherry pie filling. Bake as you would a regular cherry pie. Serves 10.

DECADENT NANAIMO BARS

There are few things as Canadian or as addictive as Nanaimo bars. For a festive flair, add candied fruit and rum-soaked ginger.

Preparation time: 20 minutes / Cooking time: 2 minutes
Freezing time: 15 minutes / Refrigeration time: 1 hour
Makes: 45 small bars

THE BIG MELT

• Chocolate should be melted in the top of a double boiler over gently simmering water, never over direct heat. Stir occasionally. Chocolate scorches easily, so watch it carefully.

Or chocolate may be melted in the microwave. If chocolate is microwaved on high, it may burn. For best results, break the chocolate into small pieces and melt, uncovered, on medium. Stir occasionally and at least every minute near the end of heating. Remove from the oven before it looks completely melted, then stir gently until smooth.

• If chocolate comes into contact with water or steam while it's melting, it will seize, become lumpy and clump together. If this happens, stir in shortening, unsalted clarified butter or vegetable oil, 1 teaspoon at a time, until the chocolate is smooth again.

¾ cup butter
¼ cup granulated sugar
⅓ cup cocoa
1 egg, slightly beaten
1 tsp vanilla
1½ cups graham cracker crumbs
1 cup finely shredded coconut
½ cup finely chopped walnuts
½ cup mix of finely chopped red and green candied cherries (optional)
2 tbsp finely chopped crystallized ginger (optional)
¼ cup butter, at room temperature
3 tbsp milk
2 tbsp vanilla custard powder
2½ cups sifted icing sugar
4 (1-oz/28-g) squares semisweet chocolate

1. Lightly grease a 9-inch square pan and set aside. Melt ¾ cup butter in a heavy-bottomed saucepan. Turn into a bowl. Stir in the sugar and cocoa until blended. Cool to room temperature. Then, whisk in the egg and vanilla until smooth. Then, stir in graham cracker crumbs, coconut, walnuts, cherries and ginger, if using. Press into the bottom of the prepared pan in an even layer.

2. Combine ¼ cup butter, milk, custard powder and 2 cups icing sugar in a small bowl. Stir until creamy. Spread over the cracker crumb base. Place the mixture in the freezer to set slightly, about 15 minutes.

3. Meanwhile, melt the chocolate in the top of a double boiler set over simmering water or in a microwave (see left). Spread the chocolate in a thin even layer over the cooled custard layer. Refrigerate until the chocolate is firm, about 1 hour.

4. Prepare a glaze by stirring together ½ cup sifted icing sugar with 2 teaspoons water. Drizzle over the chilled mixture. Cut into 45 bars and store in a tightly covered container in the refrigerator.

PER SERVING: *106 calories, 1 g protein, 11.3 g carbohydrates, 6.6 g fat, 15.2 mg calcium, 0.4 mg iron, 0.3 g fiber.*

Gooey Butter-Tart Squares

It's hard to beat a good butter tart, but these squares have all the gooey greatness and you don't have to fiddle with pastry. Just pat the shortbread crust in a pan and spoon the filling over top. What could be easier?

Preparation time: 5 minutes / Baking time: 35 minutes

Makes: 32 squares

2 cups all-purpose flour
½ cup brown sugar
½ cup butter, at room temperature
4 eggs
2 tsp vanilla
Generous pinch of salt
⅔ cup granulated sugar
⅔ cup corn syrup
2 cups raisins

1. Preheat oven to 350F. Lightly grease two 8-inch square pans or one 9x13-inch pan. Measure 1½ cups flour into a small bowl along with the brown sugar and butter. Stir together until well blended.

2. Firmly press the mixture into the bottom of the prepared pans. Bake in the centre of the preheated oven until light brown and set, about 12 to 14 minutes. Remove the pans to a rack while preparing the filling. Leave the oven temperature at 350F.

3. To make the filling, whisk the eggs with the vanilla and salt until foamy. Beat in the granulated sugar. Gradually beat in remaining flour. Stir in the corn syrup, then raisins. Pour the filling over the partially cooked base.

4. Immediately return the pans to the oven and continue baking until the squares are well browned and the edges start to pull away from the sides of the pan, about 20 to 23 more minutes. Remove the pan to a rack to cool. The squares will sink slightly and the filling will set as they cool.

5. Cut into 32 squares. Serve at room temperature. Store, covered, in the refrigerator for up to 4 days, or freeze for up to 6 months.

PER SERVING: *139 calories, 1.8 g protein, 25 g carbohydrates, 3.9 g fat, 15.4 mg calcium, 1 mg iron, 0.7 g fiber.*

Rum 'n' Raisins

If your recipe calls for raisins or currants, improve texture and flavor by plumping them first. In a small bowl, stir 1 tablespoon rum, brandy, juice or liqueur with 1 cup fruit. Microwave, covered, on high, for 20 to 30 seconds. Stir once during heating.

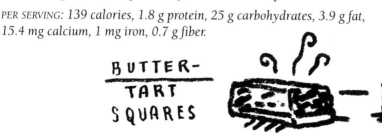

INCREDIBLE CHOCOLATE PUDDING CAKE

Magically, during the baking time, this butter cake forms its own rich chocolate sauce. Spoon the hot cake into big soup bowls and ladle the comforting sauce over top.

Preparation time: 20 minutes / Baking time: 30 minutes

Makes: 8 servings

PUDDING
1 cup all-purpose flour
$\frac{1}{2}$ cup granulated sugar
$2\frac{1}{2}$ tsp baking powder
$\frac{1}{4}$ tsp salt
$\frac{1}{2}$ cup milk
1 tsp vanilla
3 tbsp cocoa
3 tbsp butter, melted
$\frac{1}{3}$ cup coarsely chopped bittersweet chocolate, about 3 oz (85 g)

SAUCE
$\frac{1}{3}$ cup granulated sugar
$\frac{1}{4}$ cup brown sugar
2 tbsp cocoa
1 cup cold water

1. Preheat oven to 350F. Lightly grease an 8-cup (2-L) casserole dish, preferably with a rounded bottom. Place flour, $\frac{1}{2}$ cup sugar, baking powder and salt in a large bowl. Stir with a fork until well blended. Then, beat in the milk and vanilla until you form a thick, fairly smooth batter.

2. Stir 3 tablespoons cocoa into the melted butter until evenly mixed. Then, stir the butter-cocoa mixture into the batter. Add the chocolate and stir just until evenly distributed. Turn into the prepared dish and smooth the top.

3. Prepare the sauce immediately. Stir remaining sugars with 2 tablespoons cocoa in a small bowl. Sprinkle the mixture over the batter. Gradually pour the cold water evenly over the top of batter. Do not stir the water into batter.

4. Bake in the centre of the preheated oven for 25 to 30 minutes, until the cake appears slightly glazed on top and the sauce is bubbling around the sides of the dish. Spoon into dessert dishes and serve hot with vanilla ice cream.

PER SERVING: 270 calories, 3.6 g protein, 46.7 g carbohydrates, 9.1 g fat, 88.1 mg calcium, 1.7 mg iron, 0.4 g fiber.

GRAND FINALES

A decadent dense cake made with nearly a pound of top quality chocolate, a spectacularly colored warm crisp brimming with six different kinds of fruit or a perfect hazelnut truffle — these impressive grand finales will end any dinner party on the sweetest of notes.

UNBELIEVABLY DECADENT CHOCOLATE CAKE

This is the test kitchen staff's favorite dessert. As if it isn't already rich enough, sometimes we add toasted almonds or hazelnuts. Serve thin wedges on large plates with chocolate sauce and fresh berries, or slices of mango and a little crème fraîche. See photo opposite page 225.

Preparation time: 20 minutes / Baking time: 55 minutes

Makes: 16 slices

12-oz (375-g) bar bittersweet chocolate, coarsely chopped
2 cups all-purpose flour
$\frac{1}{4}$ tsp salt
$1\frac{1}{2}$ cups unsalted butter, at room temperature
$\frac{3}{4}$ cup granulated sugar
4 eggs, at room temperature
1 tbsp vanilla
$\frac{1}{4}$ cup dark rum
$\frac{1}{2}$ cup coarsely chopped toasted almonds or hazelnuts (optional)

1. Preheat oven to 325F. Lightly grease the bottom and sides of a 9-inch springform or cake pan. Line the bottom with waxed paper.

2. Melt chocolate in top of a double boiler set over simmering water, stirring often, until smooth. Or place in a 4-cup (1-L) microwave-safe measuring cup. Microwave, uncovered, on medium for about 3 minutes. Stir after each minute. Remove from the microwave before the chocolate looks completely melted. Then, stir until smooth. Set aside.

3. Blend flour and salt together in a bowl. In a large mixing bowl, beat butter with sugar, using an electric mixer, until fluffy. Add eggs, all at once, and beat just until combined. Gradually beat in melted chocolate, vanilla and 2 tablespoons rum. Then, gradually beat in flour mixture, just until an even color is reached. Do not overmix. Stir in nuts.

THE ICING ON THE CAKE

A dusting of icing sugar over chocolate cake can be very impressive. Put a tablespoon of icing sugar, no more, in a sieve. Carefully lift the sieve over the cake and gently shake. To make a design, place a paper doily star or other cutout over the cake before sifting. Or cut out letters to spell a name or a message.

4. Turn into the prepared pan. Bake in the centre of the preheated oven for 55 minutes or until a cake tester inserted in the centre of the cake comes out almost clean. Do not overbake. The centre should still be slightly moist since the cake firms up as it cools.

5. Leave the cake in the pan and place it on a rack. Brush some rum over the hot cake and let it sit for 30 minutes. Then, run a knife around the inside edge of the pan. Remove the sides and bottom of the spring-form pan. Brush the top and sides of the cake with remaining rum.

6. Refrigerate, if not serving right away, but bring to room temperature before serving.

PER SLICE: 598 calories, 7.7 g protein, 54.7 g carbohydrates, 40.7 g fat, 37.2 mg calcium, 2.7 mg iron, 1 g fiber.

BABY BUTTER-PECAN TARTS

We scaled these favorites down to a two-bite size so you can indulge without a sweet overload.

Preparation time: 15 minutes / Baking time: 15 to 25 minutes

Makes: 12 tarts

BUTTER-PECAN
TARTS

12 mini tart shells, frozen or homemade
¼ cup butter, melted and cooled
½ cup brown sugar
1 cup corn syrup
2 eggs, lightly beaten
1 tsp vanilla
2 tsp freshly squeezed lemon juice
36 pecan halves, about ½ cup

1. Preheat oven to 375F. Place the tart shells on a baking sheet. Or line miniature tart pans with the homemade pastry. Do not prick.

2. In a large measuring cup or medium-size bowl, stir the butter with the brown sugar. Then stir in the corn syrup, eggs, vanilla and lemon juice until blended.

3. Pour or spoon the mixture into the tart shells, filling each about two-thirds full. Place 3 pecan halves on top of each tart. Bake on the bottom rack of the preheated oven for 12 to 15 minutes if using frozen tart shells, 20 to 25 minutes for homemade pastry or until the pastry is golden brown. Set on a wire rack to cool. Serve warm or store in a tightly sealed container in the refrigerator. They also freeze well.

PER SERVING: 284 calories, 2.7 g protein, 39 g carbohydrates, 13.4 g fat, 28.8 mg calcium, 2.2 mg iron, 0.6 g fiber.

GLORIOUS CHRISTMAS EVE CRISP

This ruby-red mélange of warm, tart berries and fruit under a buttery crunch topping is Canadian fashion designer Shelley Walsh's traditional Christmas Eve make-ahead dessert. Come summer, use fresh fruits in season.

Preparation time: 15 minutes / Baking time: 1 hour
Makes: 10 to 12 servings

3 cups fresh or frozen sliced rhubarb
3 tbsp all-purpose flour
10-oz (300-g) pkg frozen blueberries, about 2 cups
7½-oz (225-g) pkg frozen raspberries, about 2 cups
½ cup golden raisins
1 cup green seedless grapes
4 cups sliced peeled apples
½ cup chopped walnuts (optional)
14-oz (398-mL) can peaches, drained and chopped
1½ cups brown sugar
1 tsp cinnamon
⅔ cup butter, at room temperature
1¼ cups all-purpose flour

1. Preheat oven to 350F. Lightly butter the sides of a 9x13-inch baking dish. If using frozen rhubarb, place it in a sieve and run under cold water until the pieces are separated and the ice crystals have melted. Drain well and pat dry.

2. Spread the rhubarb over the bottom of dish. Sprinkle with 1 tablespoon flour. Scatter the blueberries over top. Sprinkle with another tablespoon flour. Spoon the raspberries over top. Sprinkle with remaining tablespoon of flour. Then, scatter the raisins and grapes over the berries.

3. Cover with the sliced apples. Scatter the nuts over top, then the cubed peaches. Stir ½ cup brown sugar with ½ teaspoon cinnamon. Sprinkle over the peaches. Then, stir the butter with the remaining cup of brown sugar until creamy. Gradually stir in 1¼ cups flour and remaining ½ teaspoon cinnamon, working with a fork or your fingers until the mixture is crumbly. Evenly sprinkle over the fruit.

4. If making ahead, refrigerate. We often put the crisp in the oven just before sitting down to a dinner party.

5. Bake in the centre of the preheated oven for 55 to 60 minutes, until the apples seem tender when pierced with a fork. Remove from the oven and let sit for 10 minutes before serving.

PER SERVING: *360 calories, 3 g protein, 67.2 g carbohydrates, 10.9 g fat, 74.6 mg calcium, 2.1 mg iron, 4.4 g fiber.*

STORING NUTS

Store nuts in the refrigerator or freezer. They have a high fat content that quickly goes rancid at room temperature. Always taste before buying, if possible, and definitely before using; some nuts, particularly walnuts, go rancid very quickly. There's no need to defrost; use straight from the freezer.

IMPRESSIVE FRESH FRUIT MERINGUES

Luscious ripe berries and a swirl of light cream overflow from cloudlike meringues. A feast for the eye, not for the waistline.

Preparation time: 15 minutes / Baking time: 1 to 1¼ hours
Standing time: 1 hour / Makes: 4 servings

4 egg whites, at room temperature
¼ tsp salt
¼ tsp cream of tartar
½ cup granulated or fruit sugar
½ tsp vanilla
2 cups fresh berries, such as sliced strawberries, blueberries
   and raspberries
2 tbsp rum or Grand Marnier liqueur
1 cup (250-mL container) light sour cream

1. Preheat oven to 225F. Lightly butter a sheet of waxed paper and dust lightly with cornstarch, shaking off the excess. Place it on a baking sheet.

2. Prepare the meringues by placing the room-temperature egg whites in a large mixing bowl. Add the salt and cream of tartar. Beat with an electric mixer at high speed until the whites will just hold soft moist peaks when the beaters are lifted.

3. Very gradually beat in the sugar, 1 tablespoon at a time, at medium speed. Continue to beat until stiff shiny peaks will form. Beat in the vanilla.

4. Immediately spoon about one-eighth of the meringue onto the prepared waxed paper. Using the back of a spoon, form the meringue into a 3-inch circle, about ⅓ inch thick. Repeat until 4 circles are formed. Either use remaining meringue to build 1-inch-high borders or to pipe 1-inch-high rosettes, using a piping bag, around the edges.

5. Bake in the centre of the preheated oven for 1 to 1¼ hours. Turn off the oven but leave the meringues in the oven for at least 1 more hour, preferably overnight. Then, slide the waxed paper holding the meringues onto a rack. Cool the meringues completely. To remove the meringues from the waxed paper, gently slide a sharp knife between the paper and the meringues. Then, peel them off carefully.

6. When ready to serve, stir the fruit and rum together. Add a little sugar, if needed. Place the meringues on large dessert plates. Spoon a little sour cream into each shell, then add the fruit, letting it tumble down over the plate.

PER SERVING: *232 calories, 8.2 g protein, 38.3 g carbohydrates, 4.5 g fat, 81 mg calcium, 0.3 mg iron, 1.9 g fiber.*

VOLUMINOUS EGG WHITES

Beat room-temperature egg whites in a copper, metal or ceramic bowl. Be sure that no spots of yolk are in with the whites: even a speck of fat will prevent the whites from beating up into soft peaks. Beat to a foamy stage then add ⅛ teaspoon cream of tartar, or ½ teaspoon vinegar or lemon juice, for every 3 egg whites.

ELEGANT ITALIAN TRIFLE

This Italian translation of English trifle layers rich, creamy mascarpone cheese with brandy and espresso-soaked ladyfingers for a classic ending to an Italian dinner party. The Pusateris, purveyors of fine foods in North Toronto, kindly shared their family recipe with us.

Preparation time: 30 minutes / Refrigeration time: overnight
Makes: 8 to 10 servings

ESPRESSO

4 eggs
¼ cup Tia Maria liqueur or brandy
1 lb (500 g) mascarpone cheese*
½ cup granulated sugar
6½-oz (200-g) pkg crisp or toasted ladyfingers
½ cup strong espresso coffee
2 (1-oz/28-g) squares semisweet chocolate

1. Prepare the filling by separating the eggs. Place the whites in a large mixing bowl and set aside the yolks in another large bowl.

2. Add the liqueur to the egg yolks and whisk or stir until blended. Then, add the cheese. Stir until evenly blended.

3. Using the high speed of an electric mixer, beat the egg whites until soft peaks will form when the beaters are lifted. Then, continue to beat and gradually add the sugar, a tablespoon at a time, until all the sugar is added and the egg whites will hold stiff peaks when the beaters are lifted.

4. Add about one-quarter of the egg whites to the cheese mixture. Stir together until mixed. Then, add remaining egg-white mixture and gently fold together just until the whites are incorporated. Set aside.

5. Immediately brush both sides of the ladyfingers with the espresso coffee. Place enough ladyfingers, flat-side down, to cover the entire bottom of an oval (9x12-inch) gratin dish or shallow round dish. Add half the cheese mixture and smooth the top. Grate half the chocolate over top, generously covering the entire surface. Then, add another layer of espresso-coated ladyfingers. Top with remaining cheese mixture and smooth the top. Generously cover with remaining grated chocolate. Refrigerate, covered, overnight.

* Mascarpone cheese, a soft creamy cheese, is available at Italian grocery stores, specialty cheese shops and some supermarkets.

PER SERVING: 368 calories, 6.4 g protein, 29.1 g carbohydrates, 24.6 g fat, 20 mg calcium, 0.8 mg iron, 0 g fiber.

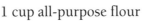

PARISIENNE CITRON TART

This is the impressive party tart you may have thought only a French pastry chef could make. The food processor does all the mixing and there's no rolling. Just pat the dough right into the baking pan. Atop your perfect shortbread crust is a tangy lemon cream garnished with fresh berries and sprigs of mint. Voilà.

Preparation time: 15 minutes / Refrigeration time: 30 minutes
Baking time: 25 minutes / Makes: 12 servings

CITRON
TART

1 cup all-purpose flour
3 tbsp granulated sugar
Pinch of salt
½ cup cold unsalted butter
1 tbsp white vinegar or lemon juice
2 tbsp apricot jam
5 eggs
1 cup granulated sugar
½ cup freshly squeezed lemon juice
½ cup whipping cream
Toasted sliced almonds (optional)

1. Preheat oven to 400F. Measure the flour, 3 tablespoons sugar and pinch of salt into a food processor fitted with a metal blade. Whirl, using an on-and-off motion, just until blended. Cut the cold butter into 6 cubes and add. Whirl, using an on-and-off motion, until coarsely ground. Add the vinegar and continue to whirl until the mixture just begins to form a ball. Remove the dough and gather it into a ball.

2. Place the dough in the centre of a 10-inch-wide tart pan with a removable bottom. Using the palm of your hand, press the dough from the middle of the pan to the outside edges. Then, using your fingertips, press the dough up the edges of the pan until the dough is even with the rim. Refrigerate for at least 30 minutes to firm dough a little.

3. Then, preheat oven to 400F. Spread the bottom of the crust with the jam. Prepare the filling by measuring the eggs, 1 cup sugar and ½ cup lemon juice into a bowl. Whisk together until the mixture is evenly blended. Add the cream and whisk just until blended. Place the tart pan on a baking sheet. Pour the filling into the pastry crust.

4. Bake on the bottom rack of the preheated oven for 20 to 25 minutes or until the crust is golden. The filling should seem set in the centre when the pan is jiggled. Cool completely before serving. Keep refrigerated. Sprinkle with toasted sliced almonds just before serving.

PER SERVING: *282 calories, 4.4 g protein, 33.9 g carbohydrates, 15.2 g fat, 24.8 mg calcium, 0.9 mg iron, 0.4 g fiber.*

JEWELLED CHOCOLATE FRUITCAKE

The only thing we really like about fruitcake is the boozy candied fruit, so we tried combining it with our favorite dense chocolate cake. The result is the best of both worlds — an incredibly moist liqueur-laced cake studded with jewels of candied fruit.

Preparation time: 20 minutes / Marinating time: 30 minutes
Cooking time: 5 minutes / Baking time: 50 minutes
Makes: 36 pieces

1 cup candied red cherries
1 cup candied green cherries
1 cup dark or golden raisins
$\frac{1}{2}$ cup cut mixed peel
$\frac{3}{4}$ cup dark rum or brandy
1 cup coarsely chopped walnuts or blanched almonds
2 cups all-purpose flour
$\frac{1}{2}$ tsp baking powder
$\frac{1}{2}$ tsp salt
6 (1-oz/28-g) squares unsweetened chocolate
$\frac{3}{4}$ cup unsalted butter
$1\frac{1}{3}$ cups granulated sugar
4 eggs
$\frac{1}{2}$ cup milk
$1\frac{1}{2}$ tsp vanilla
Dark rum (optional)

1. Grease or butter a 9x13-inch baking dish and set aside. Cut the cherries in half. Place them in a bowl along with the raisins and mixed peel. Stir in $\frac{3}{4}$ cup rum. Cover and marinate at room temperature for at least 30 minutes. Measure out the nuts. Set aside.

2. Just before baking, preheat oven to 325F. Using a fork, stir the flour, baking powder and salt together until evenly blended. Set aside. Melt the chocolate in the top of a double boiler over simmering water or in a microwave (see page 234).

3. In a large mixing bowl, beat the butter and sugar together until creamy. Add the eggs, 1 at a time, beating constantly. Then, beat in the milk, vanilla and then the melted chocolate. Drain any rum that has not been absorbed by the fruit and beat it into the mixture.

4. Gradually beat in the dry ingredients. Then, stir in the marinated fruits and the nuts. Turn into the prepared pan and smooth the top. Bang the pan on the counter several times to get rid of any air bubbles.

5. Bake in the centre of the preheated oven for 45 to 50 minutes

SPIRITED DESSERTS
Add a splash for a truly festive finale.

Cranberries Jubilee
Simmer 2 cups cranberries with $\frac{2}{3}$ cup granulated sugar, $\frac{1}{3}$ cup water, $\frac{1}{8}$ teaspoon each of cinnamon and ground nutmeg and a pinch of allspice. Bring to a boil and simmer, covered, for 20 minutes. Add $\frac{1}{4}$ cup brandy and flambé at the table for extra drama. Serve over ice cream. Makes 2 cups.

Chocolate Mandarins
Combine 4 (1-oz/28-g) squares semisweet chocolate with $\frac{1}{4}$ cup table cream in a small pan. Stir over low heat just until melted. Stir in 1 to 2 tablespoons orange liqueur and serve with mandarin orange sections for dipping. Makes about $\frac{1}{2}$ cup.

Maple Walnuts
Gently warm $\frac{1}{4}$ cup maple syrup with 1 tablespoon brandy or maple liqueur. Stir in $\frac{1}{4}$ cup walnut or pecan halves. Spoon over vanilla ice cream. Makes about $\frac{1}{2}$ cup.

or until a cake tester inserted into the centre of the cake comes out almost clean. Cool in the pan on a rack. If desired, brush with additional rum. Then, wrap in foil and keep refrigerated or freeze.

PER PIECE: *197 calories, 2.7 g protein, 26.4 g carbohydrates, 9.1 g fat, 18.9 mg calcium, 0.9 mg iron, 0.6 g fiber.*

TRIPLE-LAYER CARROT AND PECAN CAKE

When Maureen Lollar was assistant food editor of *Chatelaine*, she developed this mile-high pecan-rich party cake. Maureen comes from a family of good cooks on Wolfe Island, just off the shore from Kingston, Ontario, where homemade cakes and pies are the star feature at neighborhood get-togethers.

Preparation time: 20 minutes / Baking time: 25 minutes

Makes: 12 servings

CAKE
8 medium-size carrots
Finely grated peel of 1 orange
1 cup coarsely chopped pecans
1 cup golden raisins
1½ cups brown sugar
1 cup vegetable oil
4 eggs
1 tsp vanilla
2 cups all-purpose flour
1½ tsp each of baking powder and baking soda
1 tsp each of cinnamon, ground nutmeg and salt
½ tsp allspice

FROSTING
4-oz (125-g) pkg cream cheese
¼ cup unsalted butter
1½ cups sifted icing sugar
1 tsp vanilla
Pecan halves

1. Preheat oven to 350F. Grease three 9-inch round cake pans. Line the bottom of the pans with a circle of waxed paper. Grease again.

2. Peel the carrots. Grate, using the medium grating disc of a food processor or a hand grater. (They should measure about 4 cups.)

3. Stir the carrots, orange peel, pecans and raisins together in a medium-size bowl.

4. Measure the sugar, oil, eggs and vanilla into a large mixing bowl. Beat the mixture with an electric mixer just until blended.

5. Measure remaining dry ingredients into a large bowl. Stir with a fork until blended. Make a well in centre of dry ingredients. Pour in the egg mixture. Stir just until moist. Then, fold in the carrot mixture.

6. Immediately pour the batter into the prepared pans and smooth the tops. Bake in the centre of the preheated oven for 20 to 25 minutes or until the cake bounces back when touched lightly in the centre. Remove the pans from the oven and place them on a rack to cool for 10 minutes. Then, remove the cakes from the pans.

7. To make the frosting, place the cream cheese and butter in a large mixing bowl. Beat until creamy. Gradually beat in the sifted icing sugar. Stir in the vanilla. Spread the frosting on top of the cooled cakes. Stack cakes to form a triple-layer cake. Garnish with pecans.

PER SERVING: *613 calories, 6.6 g protein, 70.4 g carbohydrates, 35.9 g fat, 77 mg calcium, 3 mg iron, 3.1 g fiber.*

CHOCOLATE HAZELNUT TRUFFLES

When chocolate cravings overtake us at the end of a dinner party, we don't want peppermint patties, thank you. No, it's a chocolate truffle so rich that a single one satisfies. Buy the best chocolate available — one huge bar will do it. And be sure to toast the nuts, that's what makes this recipe so special.

Preparation time: 30 minutes / Cooking time: 5 minutes
Refrigeration time: 2 hours / Makes: 42 truffles

1 cup hazelnuts or whole blanched almonds
8-oz (224-g) bar bittersweet chocolate
$\frac{1}{3}$ cup each of unsalted butter and icing sugar
$\frac{1}{4}$ cup rum, almond or orange liqueur
$\frac{1}{4}$ tsp vanilla
Icing sugar

1. Preheat broiler. Whirl the nuts in food processor fitted with a metal blade until finely chopped but not ground. Spread out on a baking sheet. Place the baking sheet 6 inches from the preheated broiler. Broil 2 to 3 minutes until lightly toasted, shaking the pan often to avoid burning. Turn into a large bowl.

2. Break the chocolate into small pieces. Place it in a small saucepan along with the butter. Stir over medium-low heat until melted. Or melt in the microwave on medium (see page 234). Stir in $\frac{1}{3}$ cup icing sugar, the rum and vanilla. Stir in the nuts. Refrigerate the mixture until just firm enough to roll, about 2 hours. Form into balls, about $\frac{3}{4}$ to 1 inch wide. Roll the balls in icing sugar. Store, covered, in the refrigerator.

PER SERVING: *64 calories, 0.9 g protein, 5.4 g carbohydrates, 4.6 g fat, 9.8 mg calcium, 0.3 mg iron, 0.3 g fiber.*

DRESS-UP CHOCOLATE SHELLS
Keep a package of chocolate shells on hand and you have the ready-made beginnings for a glamorous dessert.

Festive Raspberry
Scoop a 1-pint (500-mL) tub of raspberry sherbet into 6 shells. Drizzle each with 1 teaspoon orange or raspberry liqueur and garnish with chocolate curls.

Double-Chocolate Orange
Stir the finely grated peel of $\frac{1}{2}$ an orange into a 1-pint (500-mL) tub of slightly softened chocolate ice cream. Scoop the ice cream into 6 shells. Drizzle with a little orange liqueur and sprinkle with finely chopped candied orange peel.

Italian Almond
Scoop a 1-pint (500-mL) tub of spumoni ice cream into 6 shells. Drizzle each with 1 teaspoon dark rum. Sprinkle with toasted, chopped unblanched almonds.

Phyllo Tarts with Fresh Berries and Crème Fraîche

Fresh berries and crème fraîche spill from a golden cornucopia of delicate phyllo surrounded by a brilliant red raspberry coulis. This impressive creation is from Joanne Yolles, a chef at Toronto's Scaramouche Restaurant.

Preparation time: 15 minutes / Standing time: 24 hours
Refrigeration time: 2 hours / Baking time: 10 minutes
Makes: 12 tarts

Crème Fraîche
1½ cups whipping cream
⅓ cup granulated sugar
⅓ cup yogurt
2 tbsp freshly squeezed lemon juice

Phyllo Tarts
⅓ cup unsalted butter
4 sheets phyllo pastry
2 tbsp granulated sugar

Filling
½ cup whipping cream
2 tbsp granulated sugar
1 tsp vanilla

Raspberry Coulis
7½-oz (225-g) pkg frozen raspberries
2 tbsp freshly squeezed lemon juice
Granulated sugar (optional)

Garnish
3 cups mixed berries, such as raspberries, sliced strawberries, blackberries and blueberries
2 tbsp icing sugar
12 sprigs mint (optional)

1. To make the crème fraîche, in a small bowl, stir 1½ cups whipping cream with ⅓ cup granulated sugar, yogurt and lemon juice until blended and most of the sugar is dissolved. Cover loosely with cheesecloth or a kitchen cloth. Let stand at room temperature until thickened, about 24 hours.

2. Then, line a sieve with a double layer of cheesecloth or a thin kitchen cloth. Place the sieve over a bowl and pour the thickened crème fraîche into the sieve. Refrigerate the bowl with the sieve until the liquid

Chocolate Grand Marnier Ice Cream

Melt 3 (1-oz/28-g) squares semisweet chocolate with ¼ cup strong espresso coffee. Set aside. Then combine ¼ cup Grand Marnier liqueur, ½ cup granulated sugar, 6 egg yolks, 1 tablespoon lemon juice and the peel of 2 oranges in the top of a double boiler. Place over boiling water and beat until light, about 2 minutes. Gradually stir in 2½ cups of whipping cream. Stir until thick enough to coat a metal spoon. Stir in chocolate mixture. Refrigerate until cool, then freeze in ice-cream maker according to manufacturer's directions. Makes 8 servings.

is drained off and the crème fraîche is as thick as ricotta cheese, about 2 hours. Discard the drained liquid. Remove the thickened crème fraîche from the cheesecloth and place it in a bowl. Refrigerate in the bowl until ready to use.

3. Preheat oven to 350F. To prepare the phyllo tarts, melt the butter over low heat. Lay the 4 sheets phyllo on the counter. Cover the entire surface of the phyllo sheets with waxed paper and a damp kitchen cloth to prevent them from drying out and cracking.

4. Place 1 sheet of phyllo on the counter and brush it with melted butter. Carefully lay a second sheet of phyllo over the first so that all the corners match perfectly. Brush with more butter. Sprinkle 2 tablespoons granulated sugar over the phyllo. Cover with remaining 2 sheets of phyllo, brushing each with melted butter.

5. Cut the phyllo into twelve 4x3-inch rectangles. Lightly butter 12 large muffin or tart tins, approximately 3 inches wide. Carefully place the phyllo rectangles into the muffin cups, pressing them into the bottom to form a tart shell. Keep the edges of the phyllo upright. Do not fold them over. Prick the bottom of the shells with a fork.

6. Bake for 8 to 10 minutes or until the edges are crisp and brown. Immediately remove the phyllo shells from the muffin tins and cool them on a rack. The shells can be made up to a day before serving. Store them in an airtight container at room temperature. Do not refrigerate.

7. To prepare the filling, in a small mixing bowl, using an electric mixer, beat ½ cup whipping cream with 2 tablespoons granulated sugar and vanilla until soft peaks form when the beaters are lifted. Fold into the crème fraîche just until blended. Refrigerate until ready to use.

8. Place the raspberries and lemon juice in a blender or food processor fitted with a metal blade. Whirl, using an on-and-off motion, until smooth. Strain to remove the seeds. (Taste and add sugar, if needed.) Refrigerate if not using right away.

9. Just before serving, spoon about 2 heaping tablespoons of the crème fraîche filling into each phyllo shell. Arrange a mixture of berries on top. Sprinkle with icing sugar. Spoon about 3 tablespoons raspberry coulis onto each dessert plate. Place the filled phyllo tarts in the centre of each plate. Garnish with a sprig of mint, if you wish. Serve immediately.

PER SERVING: *280 calories, 2.5 g protein, 24.7 g carbohydrates, 20.2 g fat, 54.7 mg calcium, 0.6 mg iron, 3.1 g fiber.*

PLUM

FAST PLUM GRATIN
Halve plums and remove the pits. Cut the pieces in half again. Place cut-side up on a buttered baking sheet. Sprinkle with 1 tablespoon brown sugar for 2 plums. Bake at 375F until the sugar melts and the plums soften a little. Serve with vanilla ice cream.

CREAMY APPLE-GINGER FLAN

A black-tie approach to good ol' apple pie and a glamorous ending to a regal roast of pork. This is a creation of Trudy Patterson, our test kitchen assistant, who comes from a long line of outstanding Prairie bakers in Vantage, Saskatchewan.

Preparation time: 30 minutes / Baking time: 1 hour

Makes: 10 servings

Pastry for a single-crust 10-inch pie
1 cup light brown sugar
⅓ cup all-purpose flour
¼ cup finely chopped crystallized ginger
Freshly grated nutmeg
¼ tsp salt
10 medium-size apples
½ cup whipping cream

1. Preheat oven to 400F. Place the oven rack in its bottom position. Roll out the pastry and line a 10-inch pie plate or flan pan. Trim and flute the edges but do not prick the crust. Bake on the bottom rack until golden, about 10 minutes. Then, reduce the oven temperature to 350F.

2. Measure out 1 cup of brown sugar, then take out 2 tablespoons and save for the topping. Mix remaining sugar in a large bowl with the flour, ginger, nutmeg and salt. Stir with a fork until blended. Set aside.

3. Peel and core the apples. Slice them into wedges approximately ½-inch thick. (They should measure about 10 cups.) Add the apples to the sugar-and-spice mixture. Stir until all the wedges are coated. Immediately turn the apples into the baked shell. Pour the cream over top. Gently press down the apples until most are covered with cream. Sprinkle remaining 2 tablespoons of sugar over the apples.

4. Place the pie on a baking sheet, to catch any spills. Bake at 350F on the bottom rack of the oven for 45 to 55 minutes to thoroughly cook the apples. If the apples become brown on the top before the baking time is up, gently lay a piece of foil, shiny-side up, over top of the pie. Cool on a rack for 30 minutes before cutting.

PER SERVING: 358 calories, 2.7 g protein, 53 g carbohydrates, 16.2 g fat, 43.3 mg calcium, 1.8 mg iron, 3.2 g fiber.

INDEX

S

Saffron, about, 28
Saffron risotto with shrimp, 27
Sage stuffing with variations, 115
Salad dressing *see* Dressing;
    Vinaigrette
Salads:
    asparagus, Mediterranean, 65
    apple-Roquefort, 178
    bean toss, 47
    bouillabaisse, 28-29
    Caesar, 39
        chicken, 34-35
    coleslaw:
        with apples and pears, 40-41
        hot, 40
    couscous with snow peas, 86
    Greek, 36-37
    hazelnut-chèvre, 30
    Moroccan, 44
    mozzarella, 178
    mushroom and spinach, 29
    pear and Gorgonzola, 38
    pizza summer toss, 33
    salmon, 178
    sprinklers for, 33
    sun-dried tomatoes and Asiago
        salad, 34
    three-bean, 92
    tomato and bocconcini, 43
Salmon:
    canned:
        and heart disease, 174
        hot southern, 145
        patties, 145
        salad, 178
        salsa, 145
        smoked salmon pâté, 10
    duxelle in puff pastry, 146
    grilled with smoked salmon
        crème fraîche, 147
    sauces, 158
    smoked, 187
        canapés, 17
        crème fraîche, 147
        and Dijon pasta, 164
        dip, 11
        with fresh dill lasagna,
            182-183
        pâté, 10
        phyllo rolls, 13
        tortilla pinwheels, 13
    steak:
        barbecued spicy Cajun, 148
        with capers and white wine,
            148
        Dijon cream, 148
        en papillote, 148
        with lemon, 146
        lemon and fresh herbs, 148
        Oriental, 148
        with tarragon and Dijon, 144
    whole baked, 157
    whole barbecued, 158
Salmon with dilled sour cream, 148

Salmon teriyaki, 145
Salsa, 12, 176-177
    dip, 11, 15
    and grilled lamb chops, 120-121
    southwest chicken, 94
    tomato, 41
Salt, how to remove from soup, 19
Sandwiches, pesto, 166
Sauce(s):
    for artichokes, 55
    basil and tomato, 160
    cheese, 176
    dilled white wine and shallot, 157
    low-cal pasta, 173
    Roquefort for steak, 124
    tomato and fresh basil, 62
    salmon, 158
    for spaghetti, 128, 175
    Texas rib, 129
Sausage:
    paella, 191
    suppers, 140
    see also Italian sausage
Scalloped potatoes *see* Potatoes,
    scalloped
Scallops, bouillabaisse salad, 28-29
Seafood bisque, 154
Seafood leek soup, 22
Semolina *see* Couscous
Serrano peppers, about, 203
Sesame stir-fry, sizzling, 125
Shepherd's pie, 208
Shortbread, 232-233
Shrimp:
    bouillabaisse pasta, 161
    bouillabaisse salad, 28-29
    ciopinno soup, 22-23
    curried, 198
    dip, 11
    paella, 191
    and pesto, 29
    saffron risotto, 27
    seafood chowder, 193-194
    tortilla pinwheels, 13
Skillet ratatouille, 57
Smoked salmon, incredibly easy
    pâté, 10
Smoked salmon canapés, 17
Smoked salmon and Dijon pasta,
    164
Smoked salmon and dill, quiche
    filling, 17
Smoked salmon pinwheels, 11
Smoked salmon strata, 187-188
Snow peas and couscous salad, 86
Sole, Stroganoff, 155
Sole amandine, 156
Soups, 18-25, 204
    broccoli, 53
    cheddar-tomato, 178
    cioppino, 22
    cold Borscht with dill, 19
    cream of mango, 20-21
    double cheddar, 22
    green pea, 21, 22
    honey-dew lime, 20

imperial curried fruit, 18
jalapeno chicken, 21
leek with dill, 24-25
lentil, 21
Mexican tomato, 23-24
potato Parmesan, 22
quick protein, 92
seafood leek, 22
squash, 21
tomato-basil, 21
Southern coffee heaven, 244
Southern shrimp dip, 11
Southwest chicken, 94
Spaghetti:
    bacon and eggs, 162
    pecan and hot chili, 165
Spaghetti alla carbonara, 162
Spaghetti sauce, 128, 172, 175
Spaghetti squash, herbed toss, 60
Spaghettini, with caviar, 30
Spanish couscous, 85
Spanish olive pizza topping, 211
Speedy Italian sausage lasagna,
    172
Speedy shepherd's pie, 208
Spiced carrots, 66
Spices, how to buy, 196
Spinach, 59
    and bacon salad, 59
    and cream, 59
    Florentine supper, 180
    and mushroom salad, 29
    and rice, 84
Spread(s):
    crab, 11
    curried chutney, 215
    hummus, 92
    Mediterranean olive, 214
    mustard for steaks, 124
Spring lamb stuffed with lemon
    rice and spinach, 118-119
Squares, butter-tart, 235
Squash:
    black bean harvest stew, 203-204
    curried bisque, 60
    herbed sautéed, 60
    soup, 21
    see also Acorn squash; Spaghetti
        squash
Steak side dish, 178
Steamed rice, unbeatable, 79
Stew(s), 193, 204
    beef, 186-187
    black bean, 203-204
    chicken, 201
        coq au vin, 184
    fish, 152
        bouillabaisse, 28-29
    how to cook, 186
    lamb, 204-205
Sticky pecan-cinnamon buns,
    217-218
Stilton berry tarts, 10
Stilton cheese, 10
Stir-fried Oriental pasta, 178
Stir-fry: